INMILLENNIALISM

Redefining the Last Days

"I've always had the conviction that Christians should be "people of the Book." Theological creeds and confessions can be helpful, but in one sense, they can at times be detrimental. If a Christian trusts more in what others say about the Bible than investigating for himself the language, context, and theme of the biblical text, then that Christian misses out on thinking for himself. Apocalyptic literature in Scripture is an example. Denominational creeds or confessions typically lock the Bible student into a particular interpretation, ignoring potential life-transforming truth because "it isn't taught like that in the creeds." Mike Rogers' book *Inmillennialism* is a great way to begin understanding the Book trumps any creed or confession. Mike doesn't demand conformity of the reader, nor does he denigrate past confessions or creeds. What Mike does is expertly call Christians to let the Scriptures speak for themselves. I came away from reading *Inmillennialism* with a fresh sense of God's providence, the power of God's grace in the Person and work of Jesus Christ, and a deeper understanding that this world is headed toward that time when the Prince of Peace reigns in the hearts of all men and rules over all the nations."

Wade Burleson. Pastor, Historian, Writer. Author, *Happiness Doesn't Just Happen*

"*Inmillennialism: Redefining the Last Days* by Michael A. Rogers belongs on the shelf of every pastor and student of eschatology. As a graduate of a Southern Baptist seminary and a minister with many years of experience it is hard to admit that I have always found eschatology to be frustratingly ambiguous. All of the conventional Evangelical eschatological systems seem to leave some major questions unanswered. This book helps answer some of the most difficult of those eschatological questions. I am a wary person and am especially cautious about claims of new or unique doctrines, so I kept looking for the flaw in Rogers' system. But, instead of finding errors, I found myself intrigued by his clear biblical exposition. I believe this tome has the potential to challenge and strengthen the biblical eschatology of everyone who reads it. I highly recommend this book for the minister or student who is studying eschatology. It's worth the read for the scholarship and exposition alone."

Woodie Turner, M.Div. Minister to Families, First Baptist Church, Gadsden, AL

"Mike Rogers makes things clear enough to finally and actually have a non-agnostic approach to eschatology. Inmillennialism is superior to the existing prophetic systems because it rests on simple contextual analyses and is more complete. I am thankful for his excellent work!"

Doug Albertson. Executive Director, African Canadian Continuing Education Society

"With the precision of an engineer, the heart of a pastor, and the diligence of a scholar, Mike Rogers systematically examines the Bible's teaching on prophecy. Like many students of scripture, I have found the existing prophetic models unsatisfactory. Even the best of them are unable to incorporate key passages of scripture without forced interpretive methods. The worst lead to theological absurdities and lack a coherent vision for God's kingdom in the present age. Inmillennialism is an eschatological tour de force. Mike takes seriously the abundant New Testament teaching about the nearness of Christ's coming and the inauguration of the Kingdom of God, consistently compares scripture with scripture, and gives no quarter to the hermeneutical gymnastics employed to defend the existing systems. He expounds a paradigm for interpreting last days prophecy that is faithful to scripture, intellectually satisfying, and provides an inspiring and practical vision of the kingdom of God for Christians today. Every serious student of prophecy should read this book and reckon with its arguments."

Andy White. Pastor, Southampton Primitive Baptist Church, Southampton, PA

"In my years growing up in church and in ministry I've seen that discussions of eschatology are too often more heat than light. What the Spirit gave us to bolster our hope in trials and difficulties has devolved into intramural debate and even sinful divisions. I've often longed to see a development of "Mere Eschatology" that could bypass the unhelpful skirmishes so that saints can receive much needed future hope today. My friend Michael Rogers has taken a step toward this very thing. His book is well researched, thorough, exegetical, and helpful. I am still mulling over the entirety of his argument, and I'm sure I will be for years. However, the most important factor that Mike has brought to this discussion is humility. He is humble not only in the content and tone of his writing, but also in the way he handles himself in real life."

Mat Alexander, MDiv. Pastor, First Baptist Church, Gadsden, AL

"Michael Rogers' faith journey first touched my life some five decades ago. Life took us in different directions, but every time our paths crossed again, I have always been reassured of his faithful pursuit of God's truth. It is without reservation that I commend his integrity, his love for God, his wisdom, and his scholarship as he mines the gold of God's Word in his desire to learn more, teach more, and challenge believers to be open to new insights into the Scriptures. Those traits manifest themselves in his book, *Inmillennialism: Redefining the Last Days*. I highly recommend it to students of prophecy for serious consideration."

Randall Murphree. Editor, AFA Journal, American Family Association

About the Logo

The logo depicts the transition from one age to another. The lower, incoming arrow is the preparatory Mosaic age. The upper, outgoing arrow depicts the superior messianic age. The circle stands for the generation during which the change occurred. It began with the coming of Christ, his ministry, death, and resurrection. The cross within the circle symbolizes these (and other) works of salvation at the start of the transition generation. The destruction of the temple in AD 70 closed both the transition generation and the Mosaic age with its rituals and sacrifices. During the interval between the cross and AD 70, the apostles of Christ built up the church, gave her the New Testament Scriptures, and prepared her for life in the new age

INMILLENNIALISM
Redefining the Last Days

Michael A. Rogers

Foreword by Dr. Tom J. Nettles

Inmillennialism: Redefining the Last Days
Copyright © 2020 by Michael A. Rogers

All rights reserved. No part of this publication may be reproduced, stored in a retrieval system, or transmitted in any form or by any means—electronic, mechanical, photocopy, recording, or any other—except for brief quotations in printed reviews, without the prior permission of the publisher.

Unless otherwise indicated, Scripture quotations are from the Authorized (King James) Version. All emphases in the quoted verses are the author's, except as noted in the appendices.

Scripture taken from the New King James Version®. Copyright © 1982 by Thomas Nelson. Used by permission. All rights reserved.

Scripture quotations marked ESV are from The ESV® Bible (The Holy Bible, English Standard Version®), copyright © 2001 by Crossway, a publishing ministry of Good News Publishers. Used by permission. All rights reserved.

Scripture quotations marked HCSB are taken from the Holman Christian Standard Bible®, Used by Permission HCSB ©1999,2000,2002,2003,2009 Holman Bible Publishers. Holman Christian Standard Bible®, Holman CSB®, and HCSB® are federally registered trademarks of Holman Bible Publishers.

Scripture quotations marked RSV are from Revised Standard Version of the Bible, copyright © 1946, 1952, and 1971 National Council of the Churches of Christ in the United States of America. Used by permission. All rights reserved worldwide.

Scripture quotations marked NIV are taken from the Holy Bible, New International Version®, NIV®. Copyright © 1973, 1978, 1984, 2011 by Biblica, Inc.™ Used by permission of Zondervan. All rights reserved worldwide. www.zondervan.com. The "NIV" and "New International Version" are trademarks registered in the United States Patent and Trademark Office by Biblica, Inc.™

Scripture quotations taken from the New American Standard Bible® NASB, Copyright © 1960, 1962, 1963, 1968, 1971, 1972, 1973, 1975, 1977, 1995 by The Lockman Foundation. Used by permission. www.Lockman.org

MCGAHAN PUBLISHING HOUSE
Lynchburg, Tennessee 37352, U.S.A.
www.mphbooks.com
Requests for information should be sent to:
info@mphbooks.com

Diagram designs by Drew Sanders of DSDSGN (www.dsdsgn.com)

ISBN 978-1-951252-02-1

LIBRARY OF CONGRESS CONTROL NUMBER: 2020942340

I dedicate this book to **Betty Jenkins Rogers**, my precious wife of forty-one years. Her courage first blessed me on July 14, 1978 when she obeyed her pastor's sermon on Christian hospitality: she saluted a Rufus from Alabama even after saying she would not (cf. Romans 16:13). Eight days later, she had the courage and presence of mind to read Spurgeon's devotion aloud at a picnic even when she saw the words of his title: "I am married unto you" (Jeremiah 3:14). She has been a source of strength and blessing to me ever since.

List of Figures & Tables

Figures

Figure 1. Ptolemy's Model of the Solar System	2
Figure 2. Copernicus' Model of the Solar System	3
Figure 1-1. Amillennialism	13
Figure 1-2. Postmillennialism (Literal 1,000 Years)	15
Figure 1-3. Postmillennialism (Symbolic 1,000 Years)	16
Figure 1-4. Historic Premillennialism	18
Figure 1-5. Dispensational Premillennialism	20
Figure 4-1. The Subject of the Olivet Discourse	57
Figure 6-1. The Sign Question – Matthew vs. Mark and Luke	64
Figure 6-2. Inmillennialism through the End of the Mosaic Age	70
Figure 7-1. The Relationship between Parousia and Erchomai	79
Figure 7-2. Inmillennialism through the Sign Question	87
Figure 8-1. Inmillennialism through the Preliminary Signs	108
Figure 9-1. Israel's Latter Days as the End of the Mosaic Age	120
Figure 9-2. Israel's Latter Days as the Beginning of the Messianic Age	123
Figure 9-3. Israel's Latter Days and the Two Ages	124
Figure 9-4. Inmillennialism through the Later Sign	133
Figure 10-1. Interconnections of the Immediate Signs	178
Figure 10-2. The Immediate Signs	179
Figure 10-3. Inmillennialism through the Sign Answer	180
Figure 11-1. The Olivet Discourse Cannot be Divided	198
Figure 11-2. Inmillennialism through the Sign and When Answers	200
Figure 12-1. Five Exhortations in the Olivet Discourse	233
Figure 12-2. Inmillennialism through the Olivet Discourse	234
Figure 13-1. Paul's Reasoning in 1 Corinthians 15	262
Figure 13-2. Inmillennialism through 1 Corinthians 15	263
Figure 14-1. Exodus Types	271
Figure 14-2. Exodus Types and Antitypes	274
Figure 14-3. Exodus Types, Antitypes, and the Inmillennial Model	275
Figure 15-1. Inmillennialism: a Framework for Prophecy	285

Tables

Table 1-1. Summary of Existing Prophetic Models	21
Table 10-1. The Sign of the Coming of the Son of Man	163
Table 15-1. Summary of Prophetic Models (including Inmillennialism)	285

Contents

Acknowledgments	xi
Foreword	xiii
Preface	xix
Introduction	1
CHAPTER 1: Existing Prophetic Models	9
CHAPTER 2: Benefits of a Better Model	25
CHAPTER 3: Discovering a Better Model	45
CHAPTER 4: The Prophecy	53
CHAPTER 5: The Two Questions: Similarities	59
CHAPTER 6: The Sign Question in Matthew: End of the Age	63
CHAPTER 7: The Sign Question in Matthew: Coming of Christ	73
CHAPTER 8: Response: Preliminary Signs	91
CHAPTER 9: Response: Later Sign	111
CHAPTER 10: Response: Immediate Signs	137
CHAPTER 11: Response: Time	185
CHAPTER 12: Exhortations	203
CHAPTER 13: Two Details from 1 Corinthians 15	237
CHAPTER 14: Confirmation through Typology	265
CHAPTER 15: A Better Model	281
APPENDIX A: List of Key Points	289
APPENDIX B: The Olivet Discourse – Matthew	293
APPENDIX C: The Olivet Discourse – Mark	299
APPENDIX D: The Olivet Discourse – Luke	303
APPENDIX E: The Song of Moses	307
APPENDIX F: 1 Corinthians 15	319
Bibliography	323

Acknowledgments

I WILL EXPRESS my thanks for help with this book in overlapping categories without suggesting any of the following persons accept my views of prophecy in their totality. My prayer and conversation partners include our children and their families—Elisabeth LaByer (Luke and Peter), Benjamin (Mary), Stephen (Abby), John, and Caleb Rogers—Luke Crocker, Jackie Duncan, Bart Watts, Lyn Caudle, Anthony Copeland, Greg Duran, Jarrett Atkinson, Tony Martin, Matt Carpenter, R. Howard Locke, Andy White, John Formsma, Jay Chambers, Alex Smith, and many others.

For editorial help and advice, I thank Betty Rogers, Abby Rogers, Elisabeth LaByer, Bernice Jenkins, Susan Huffstutler, and Randall Murphree.

For help without which, humanly speaking, this book would not exist, I thank Charleen Sirmon for starting the challenging process that led me to write it; Kip Jacobs for technical help, personal encouragement, theological challenges, and advice over several years; Jessica Spradlin Harbin for early help with blogging; and Caleb Poston of McGahan Publishing House for his willingness to make this book one of their first projects.

I am indebted to a host of writers who have proposed prophetic views similar to my own. The most notable include: Gary DeMar, Kenneth Gentry Jr., Douglas Wilson, R. C. Sproul, John Bray, David Chilton, Philip Mauro, N. T. Wright, James M. Campbell, Ezra P. Gould, Samuel Lee, Milton Terry, and Israel P. Warren. I have also profited from several writers who hold unorthodox positions, but who, I believe, desire(d) to remain faithful to the Word of God. Among these are James Stuart Russell, Ed Stevens, Don K. Preston, and Max King. I regret that these men deny what King calls a "future resurrection from biological death," but their observations have challenged me to find a better way to explain Biblical prophecy.

I thank Dr. Tom Nettles for inspiring classroom instruction and for writing the foreword. I am also thankful for Pastors Mat Alexander and Woodie Turner at The First Baptist Church of Gadsden, AL for their support and encouragement in the study of prophecy.

I am responsible for the contents of this book. May the Lord our God forgive mistakes in it and use the truth it contains to his glory.

Foreword
Tom J. Nettles

"BEHOLD THE JUDGE is standing at the door" (James 5:9). I read these verses today and considered seriously the possibility that James, the pastor of Christians in Jerusalem, was reminding his hearers of the presence of Christ to judge the unbelieving Jews and bring the Mosaic Age to an end. Soon, Jesus, by the hand of the Romans would destroy the temple and bring great tribulation on those who had rejected his Messiahship even in the presence of his having fulfilled the prophetic word. They were to realize it was very near, for Jesus had said that these things would happen within this generation. Certainly, extended implications for every age reside within that sobering reminder of James, but perhaps he had in mind the final gasps of the Mosaic Age and the fruition of the Messianic Age in that dramatic display of the reigning presence of Jesus. I deduce that such would be the interpretive gravity of an "inmillennial" view of those words.

The basic outline of the inmillennial viewpoint is clear and simple to state. Michael Rogers focuses principally on what he calls the Mosaic Age and the Messianic Age. He uses Matthew 24 and 25 along with 1 Corinthians 15 to fill in the details of his alternative reading of the tribulation, the millennium, the Parousia, resurrection, and judgment. The Mosaic Age was established by the giving of the Law of God at Mount Sinai; the Messianic Age was established by the perfect fulfillment of the Law by Jesus Christ in his death burial and resurrection. We are presently in the millennium, a symbolic term for an indefinite time until the general judgment at the resurrection. It will be characterized by the presence and reign of Jesus in which through the preaching of the gospel he gradually subdues all nations and human organizational structures to himself. This will continue, perhaps exponentially increasing, until the last enemy, death, is destroyed in the general resurrection at which time we see the gathering of all nations in the sheep and goats judgment. The Great Tribulation preceding this millennial reign of Christ through his presence was the siege of Jerusalem for more than three years culminating in the destruction of the Temple in 70 AD. When it burned, 6000 people seeking refuge in it were burned. All of Jesus' giving of signs in both those Chapters until Matthew 25:31 relate to that event. This horrific and intensely brutal ravaging of the Jews ended the Mosaic Age and ushered in the Messianic Age. Perhaps Paul refers to this in anticipation, knowing the certainty of Jesus' prophetic utterance, when he wrote the Thessalonians concerning the Jews' persecution of Christians, "But wrath has come upon them to the uttermost" (1 Thessalonians 2:16). The parousia of Jesus is not a visible coming, but an abiding presence of the Messianic Age promised in the Great Commission and effected by Jesus' being seated at the right hand of power and his sending of the Holy Spirit at Pentecost.

In order to keep the progress of his argument clear throughout this book, Rogers has 30 diagrams that illustrate the viewpoint. Some of these add details to the existing paradigm as the argument advances and some of them compare his viewpoint to other options. These are clear and helpful, not at all intimidating. Visual aids are added gradually as needed. Rogers constructs them like a good engineer would do when designing a machine—every part necessary, none left over. Also, at the end of sections in which crucial material is added, Rogers summarized the argument into a key point, finally having 14 of these which are conveniently included in an appendix. Throughout the book, they grow gradually into a full expression of his model of eschatology.

This is not a quick devotional read giving a small dose of spiritual encouragement for the morning. Not that it is void of spiritual benefit; it has plenty of that. But Rogers has constructed a carefully connected detailed argument that requires disciplined power of attention and concentration. You must get your soul and mind ready for some expanded cogency in reasoning. This need for concentrated attention is not because the basic thesis is obtuse and complicated. Rather, the need for discipline resides first with Rogers' challenge to some of the prevailing views of Matthew 24 and 25 and the eschatological systems surrounding those interpretations. Second, the exegetical evidence is so vigorously pursued that it involves punctilious attention to argument and a careful reframing of relevant elements of New Testament language and context. For example, he makes clear distinctions between "presence" (parousia) and "coming" (erchomai) showing how this distinction gives a fundamental framework to the relationship between the Mosaic Age and the Messianic Age.

The key to investigating the biblical soundness and theological coherence of this viewpoint is found in the details of Rogers' hermeneutics. He gives much attention to the way in which certain themes, phrases, and images are developed throughout the canon of Scripture as an aid to interpreting phrases in the Olivet Discourse of Matthew 24, 25. He refers to Psalm 110 frequently and shows its importance in the New Testament as a testimony to the present reign of Christ and his gradual overcoming of all enemies throughout the millennium. His recurring discussion of the "Song of Moses" in Deuteronomy has key elements in his understanding of how the end of the Mosaic Age would come about. Jesus' discussion of the "Great Tribulation" (Matthew 24:21) uses language of extremities (Rogers calls it hyperbole) that had been established in the Old Testament as an accepted figure of speech to indicate outstanding significance and consummate intensity. His demonstration of the canonical legitimacy of his interpretive framework establishes the credibility of his overall argument.

Along this line is the author's study of "cosmic collapse imagery"—sun darkened, moon not giving light, and the stars falling from heaven, etc. Again, he shows that this kind of language does not really mean that the physical world ceases to function in its established order, but that the language of physical calamity carries a meaning of social and ideological overthrow. The collapse of the latter is a more devastating reality than that of the former, but not as sensibly obvious. Images, therefore, from the physical and natural realm are used to give sensible impressions of the complete collapse of the social/ideological. This collapse and devastation often is manifest in the physical destruction of a society (Egypt, Judah, Babylon, the Temple) as if to say, "Your ideas cannot sustain you; they are evil and idolatrous; you are weighed in the balances and found wanting." The physical destruction at the first level indicates the elimination of the physical presence of a society sustained by falsehood. At a more important level, it shows that eternal judgment awaits the devotees and purveyors of lawless, godless, idolatrous, and rebellious ideas. The loss of a soul is more horrific in its consequences than the loss of sun, moon, and stars. "What will it profit a man if he gains the whole world but loses his soul?"

One effect of the concept of inmillennialism is an intensification of the covenantal theology of the New Testament, the warnings concerning persecution and apostasy, and the Jews' resistance to the readiness and exuberance of the Gentile reception of the Jewish Messiah. Paul's assertion that the gospel has come "in all the world" (Colossians 1:6), his confidence that he would go to Spain (Romans 15:28), that he escaped the mouth of the lion "that by me the preaching might be fully known, and that all the Gentiles might hear" (2 Timothy 4:17) is related to the intensity of concentration for evangelism before the fall of Jerusalem: "And this gospel of the kingdom shall be preached in all the world for a witness unto all nations; and then shall the end [the end of the Mosaic Age] come" (Matthew 24:14).

Rogers also employs carefully and artfully (often commenting on the beauty of this scriptural device) the chiastic form of pivotal passages of Scripture. His careful analysis of the formal relations of the chiasm have interpretive power as well as mnemonic value. He introduces each chiasm with clear justification and then summarizes the content it adds to the model he is developing.

The idea of optimistic gradualism is important for affirming the present reign of Christ "until ..." and the place of 1 Corinthians 15 at that point is instructive. Also this idea feeds off the implications of many biblical phrases such as Isaiah 9:7, "Of the increase of his government there shall be no end," and Daniel 2:35 where the stone that smote the image "became a great mountain and filled the whole earth." He also makes short suggestions concerning the impact of this understanding of the Olivet Discourse for interpretation of Revelation. He intends to expand this investigation to other texts throughout the biblical corpus. This naturally invites serious engagement for discussion, an invitation Rogers issues heartily. I think the discussion would be spiritually intriguing and edifying for evangelicals.

Rogers also has unwavering critiques of some of the unwarranted interpretive jumps made in other systems to accommodate faulty assumptions. Though he does not claim to be another Copernicus, he uses that heliocentric discovery to demonstrate how a changed perspective can clarify many mysteries and do away with puzzling exegetical gymnastics. He speaks of one exegetical move as an "outrageous price to pay for faulty beginning assumptions." When words are translated or ideas promulgated without canonical precedence and sometimes in opposition to the most credible etymological studies, he commented that interpreters would not resort to "unregulated corrective devices like this if their faulty assumptions did not require them to do so." Rogers applies Occam's razor to the text arguing that the simplest explanation is the most credible.

He consults a massive amount of literature, includes a large bibliography, and includes helpful appendices. This book must take an important place in the literature concerning the kingdom of God, the manner of Christ's coming at the "end of the age," and the nature of the blessed hope.

Read well. Read seriously. Read with an intention to engage and advance the possibility of achieving greater agreement on this important element of biblical revelation.

Tom J. Nettles, PhD. Former Professor of Historical Theology, The Southern Baptist Theological Seminary; Author, *Baptists and the Bible*, *By His Grace and For His Glory*, and more.

Preface

IN COMMON with many students, my college experience forced me to face a sobering fact—I had accepted Christianity with little critical thought regarding its truthfulness. Most of my professors taught from a secular worldview based on the theory of evolution. They presented explanations of reality and meaning that challenged the foundation upon which my view of the world rested.

This experience created a crisis: was my faith in Christ legitimate? To resolve it, I began a serious study of the Bible's truth claims. Is it God's revelation to mankind? Is it infallible? Does it answer life's ultimate questions? Over time, I became convinced the Bible is what it declares itself to be—the Word of God.

I graduated from college in 1974 with an engineering degree. During the next few years, God provided many proofs of his grace and mercy. He gave me the most beautiful and Spirit-filled woman I could imagine as my wife. He placed us in a wonderful church. I sometimes preached the gospel there and in other churches.

My interest in the study of Scripture deepened: the elders in our church taught me Greek, systematic theology, and other subjects. I also took seminary classes and studied independently. These pursuits gave me an acceptable knowledge of the Bible's major teachings with one very prominent exception—prophecy. Regarding this subject, I remained in a state of bewildered uncertainty. I was a classic "pan-millennialist."[1]

This lack of prophetic clarity had not improved by the time a small church in rural Arkansas asked me to be their pastor. I accepted their call, and our home church arranged for my ordination as a gospel minister. I am thankful the ordination presbytery did not ask me to explain my views on prophecy.

This fresh ministry opportunity furnished me with great joy and excitement. I relished the study required to preach expository messages from the Bible. I sometimes experienced a measure of discomfort, however, when I encountered a prophetic passage in these expositions. These texts reminded me of my lack of insight in this area. I tried to hide my uncertainty from the congregation and hurried on to the next section of Scripture, a cover-up that lasted about seven years.

My second "crisis" of faith began on October 12, 1997. My wife Betty and I were now the parents of five lovely (and lively) children. I was the bi-vocational pastor of a congregation of God's precious children. My professional career at a great company was challenging and rewarding. The outlook for the future appeared grand until a young mother in our congregation did something disruptive: she gave me a book—on prophecy.

This sister longed to understand biblical prophecy. She had ordered a book "at a venture," like the Syrian soldier who shot an arrow (1 Kgs 22:34). When the book arrived, its contents overwhelmed her. She asked me to read it and give my opinion of its contents. Her request surprised me, but I rejoiced that she had come to her pastor for advice. Neither of us knew the unintended consequences of her actions.

I knew nothing about *The Parousia* by James Stuart Russell,[2] but it gripped my attention as I read it. The section titles in the table of contents intrigued me: "The *Parousia* in the Gospels," "The *Parousia* in the Acts and the Epistles," and "The *Parousia* in the Apocalypse." This systematic approach appealed to my engineering thought patterns.

The major thrust of Russell's view of prophecy was new to me. He emphasized that Christ and his apostles taught that the *parousia*—a Greek term I equated to the Lord's *return*—would occur in the first century. I later learned scholars call this interpretive approach *preterism*, a term "based on the Latin word *praeteritus*, which means 'gone by.'"[3]

Many New Testament prophetic passages support this view, and Russell was taking those Scriptures at face value. When Jesus said certain things would happen within a "generation," Russell said he meant it. Paul was serious when he said, "The ends of the world [or ages] are come." I liked this because I had learned years earlier to trust the written Word, even if it challenged my previous beliefs.

My panic began slowly. I had accepted Russell's explanation of the timing of key prophetic passages, but his view raised questions I could not answer. Some of his conclusions scared me. He believed God had fulfilled *all* prophecies in Jesus' generation, including the resurrection.[4] I later learned Russell taught an unorthodox form of preterism that some commentators call *hyper*-preterism.[5]

I recognized the dilemma I faced. If Jesus returned when the Romans destroyed the temple in AD 70, then the resurrection—or, at least, the rapture—must have occurred then, too. I had always thought Jesus would return on a cloud, visible to every eye on Earth, and accompanied by the sound of a loud trumpet. He would, I believed, remain suspended in the clouds at least twenty-four hours to allow all the nations to view him. I was sure none of this had happened in the first century.

My discomfort increased by the day. The more I read Russell's book, the more it impressed me. His position accounted for New Testament prophecies within an AD 70 time frame. Yet I knew the resurrection—as I had understood it—did not happen then. The theological conflict brewing in my soul was sickening.

This problem created a turmoil in my mind. I suspected Jesus and the apostles had erred in things they taught. As Russell showed, they said Jesus would return in their generation. But the things they linked to his return—the resurrection, for example—had not happened. If they had erred on this subject, how could I trust them on any other?

My heart sank at the thought. How could I, as a Christian pastor, husband, and father, accept such ideas? But what was I to do? I saw no way to refute Russell's expositions. Would I continue to believe the Bible, even though I knew it contained errors? Would I need to resign the pastorate, change our family's life trajectory, and confess to my Christian wife that I no longer believed the Bible to be true?

I took several steps to resolve my dilemma. I prayed! Many prayers for enlightenment, wisdom, and discernment regarding prophecy went up to heaven from the cotton fields of northeast Arkansas. Many a day I shed tears on my commute to and from work, pleading with God to show me the way out of this dilemma.

I asked trusted fellow-pastors to show me the error of Russell's ways. I studied the Bible with an urgency I had not known.

Reading prophetic literature became my passion. Through this passion I learned that most Christians answer their prophetic questions by adopting one of four major "systems":[6] amillennialism, postmillennialism, premillennialism, or dispensationalism.

My experience with Russell showed my need for a thorough explanation of prophecy. But which system should I choose? As an engineering-minded person, I wanted to see how theologians had developed these systems from the beginning. Swapping to a more humanitarian metaphor, I needed to watch a theological artist begin with a blank canvas and then paint a full portrait of the prophetic landscape. I needed to understand the first strokes, all the intermediate steps, and the last touches needed to make the complete picture.

To my surprise, I could not find such an explanation for any of the existing prophetic systems. There was no engineering-like system development documentation. No artistic how-to video showed how to create the painting from scratch.

I also discovered none of these systems resolved the timing issues Russell raised. Discussions about the pros and cons of each approach filled the literature, but none of them supplied the answers I sought.

This book is my attempt to resolve my personal dilemma regarding what I found. I have used a simple approach. My goal has been to be as consistent as Russell was in his book on *The Parousia*. My conclusion is that Russell was right about the timing of the *parousia*, but wrong about its nature and the resurrection. This book develops a complete prophetic system that shows the reasoning used to reach that conclusion.

So, I am thankful—at long last—to provide a full answer to the delightfully curious sister who instigated my quest.

May the Lord use this work for his glory and the good of his people.

Notes

1 See below for a brief definition of this lighthearted view of prophecy.

2 J. Stuart Russell, *The Parousia: The New Testament Doctrine of Our Lord's Second Coming* (1887; repr., Grand Rapids: Baker, 1999).

3 Kenneth L. Gentry, Jr., *The Book of Revelation Made Easy*, 2nd ed. (Powder Springs, GA: American Vision, 2010), 21. Another writer says: "*Preterism* comes from the Latin word meaning 'past,' and so a preterist believes that some of the passages referring to the return of Christ have been fulfilled in the past." [John M. Frame, *Salvation Belongs to the LORD: An Introduction to Systematic Theology* (Phillipsburg, NJ: P&R, 2006), 302.]

4 See the explanation of 1 Cor 15:22–28 at Russell, *The Parousia*, 199–208.

5 "J. Stuart Russell ... was unquestionably an extreme or radical preterist who believed that the general resurrection of the dead spoken of in the NT occurred before A.D. 70." [Richard L. Mayhue, "Jesus: A Preterist or a Futurist?," *TMSJ* 14/1 (Spring 2003): 10.]

6 I will define these shortly.

"Almost every significant breakthrough in the field of scientific endeavor is first a break with tradition, with old ways of thinking, with old paradigms."
— Steven R. Covey
Seven Habits of Highly Effective People: Restoring the Character Ethic

Introduction

An Astronomical Analogy

THIS BOOK proposes a significant change in the way you understand biblical prophecy; an astronomical analogy will encourage you to consider it. Today's prophecy students resemble astronomers in the early sixteenth century as they sought to understand planetary movements. Those scientists wanted to explain the bewildering behavior they observed: planets sometimes reversed course and went backward! These observations caused the astronomers to use the word *planet* (Gk. *planētēs*,[1] "wanderer") to describe these heavenly bodies. This word described what the astronomers saw … or thought they saw.

Earlier observers had attempted to explain the mysterious "wandering" in creative ways. Claudius Ptolemy (AD 90–c. 168), for example, produced a model of the solar system that showed planets moving in two orbits at the same time. One—the *epicycle*—was a small circular orbit whose center moved around the circumference of a larger circular orbit—the *deferent*. Ptolemy needed additional counterintuitive devices to explain planetary motion. He also used concepts like *eccentric* and *equant* points to make his system viable. The creative use of these complex devices produced results that met most of the demands of the day, so this model dominated all others for more than a millennium.

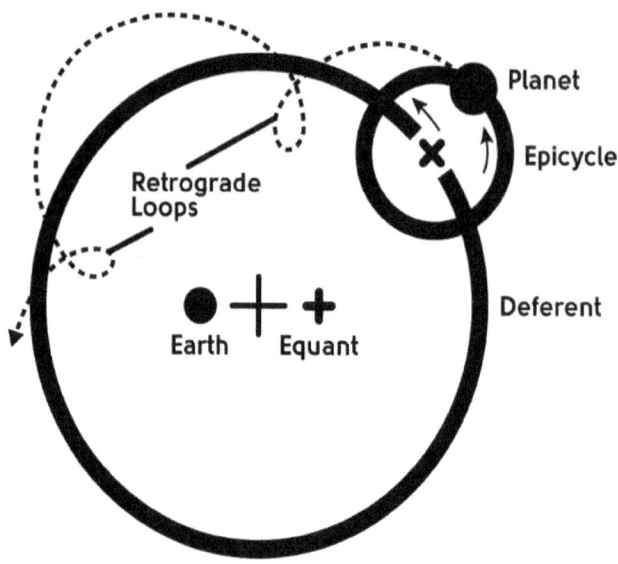

Figure 1. Ptolemy's Model of the Solar System

Even with these corrective devices, however, inherent errors in the model caused problems. Stephen Hawking provides an example:

> Ptolemy's model provided a reasonably accurate system for predicting the positions of heavenly bodies in the sky. But in order to predict these positions correctly, Ptolemy had to make an assumption that the moon followed a path that sometimes brought it twice as close to the earth as at other times. And that meant that the moon ought to sometimes appear twice as big as at other times! Ptolemy recognized this flaw, but nevertheless his model was generally, although not universally, accepted.[2]

Such flaws sprang from a bad assumption at the heart of the system. Ptolemy and other astronomers *thought* they saw the planets undergo "retrograde motion" because they *assumed* the earth was the center of the solar system. The solution for these flaws was not to invent other corrective devices or improve those already in use: someone needed to fix the central erroneous assumption.

In 1543 a Polish astronomer, Nicolaus Copernicus, challenged Ptolemy's assumption in his book *De revolutionibus orbium coelestium* (i.e., *On the Revolutions of the Celestial Spheres*). Copernicus was not interested in better epicycles, improved deferents, or more accurate eccentric and equant points. Instead, he made one simple move: he defined the sun as the center of his model instead of the earth. This change produced a simple, accurate, and elegant planetary model that led to the elimination of the corrective devices. In the Copernican model, the planets no longer "wander" across the sky, but they have never been able to shed their earlier name.

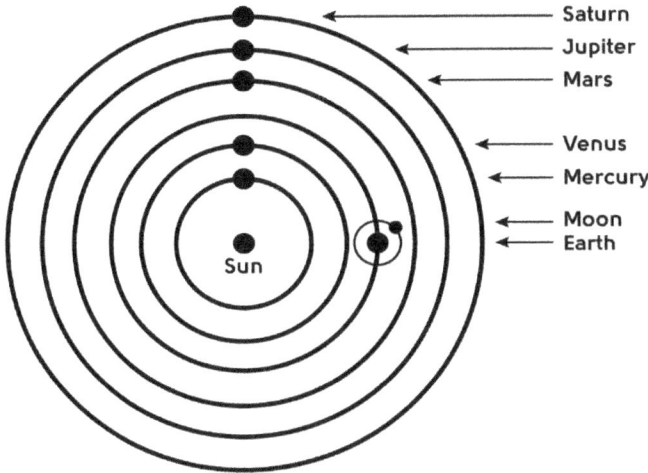

Figure 2. Copernicus' Model of the Solar System

There is a lesson here for students of biblical prophecy. As I mentioned in the preface, four prophetic models currently prevail in Christian circles, each trying to explain the "movements" of prophetic passages in the Bible. None of them accounts for all biblical prophecies. Some prophetic passages still appear to "wander" across the theological heavens. Proponents of each system use corrective devices—like "elastic time," "dual fulfillment," and "prophetic perspective"—to make the models work.

This book follows Copernicus' example. It suggests the problems with these prophetic systems arise from an erroneous assumption at their core. That assumption concerns the concept of the "last days." All the existing models define the "last days" from the perspective of the church age. This book will show this is a fundamental mistake. Redefining the "last days" as the end of the *Mosaic* age, and then recognizing the implications of doing so, produces a beautiful and simple prophetic model that eliminates the need for corrective devices.

Copernicus was not the first to suggest the sun, not the earth, is at the center of our solar system. Some of his predecessors had made this proposal over a thousand years earlier. But Ptolemy's system had triumphed because men could relate to it. They did not perceive themselves to be moving while standing on the earth. The sun, moon, and planets appeared to move across the heavens, making Ptolemy's argument for an earth-centered model seem more reasonable. For this reason, the sun-centered models almost disappeared until Copernicus published his masterpiece.

Similarly, this book will use interpretive elements once endorsed by recognized, sound, and orthodox writers. These ideas will be unfamiliar to many modern readers because they have lain dormant for a long time. They fell by the wayside, not because they were wrong, but because most scholars interpreted biblical prophecies based on what they *thought* they saw—or were *taught* to see.

My goal is to provide a better model with which to interpret biblical prophecy. The solution I propose, like that of Copernicus, may seem revolutionary to my peers. But, like him, I am championing almost-forgotten ideas that will produce better results than the existing options.

Reading this Book

The pioneering astronomer knew his proposal would bring reproach: "In the preface to his book, Copernicus expressed his reluctance to publish, saying he feared he would be 'hissed off the stage' and 'The scorn that I had to fear on account of the newness and absurdity of my opinion almost drove me to abandon a work already undertaken."³

The book you are now reading will be controversial too. Here are some thoughts to encourage your reading of it.

Why should you read this potentially controversial book? The scientific community needed Copernicus' book to document a better framework for understanding planetary motion. Today, Christians need a prophetic model that better explains God's message to them in the Bible. I will devote an entire Chapter to further explaining the benefits of a better model.

How should you read this book? Consider Mortimer Adler's observations about how to interact with *any* book:

> Reading a book is a kind of conversation.... There is an *intellectual* etiquette to be observed.... A good book deserves an active reading. The activity of reading does not stop with the work of understanding what a book says. *It must be completed by the work of criticism, the work of judging.* The undemanding reader fails to satisfy this requirement, probably even more than he fails to analyze and interpret. He not only makes no effort to understand; he also dismisses a book simply by putting it aside and forgetting it. Worse than finally praising it, he damns it by giving it no critical consideration whatever.⁴

Criticism of any book is not the fruit of arrogance. The opposite is true: "The most teachable reader is ... the most critical."⁵

Honest reading for information requires either agreement or disagreement with the author's work. But, "To agree without understanding is inane. To disagree without understanding is impudent."⁶ Intellectual etiquette requires much of readers: "Not simply by following an author's arguments, but only by meeting them as well, can the reader ultimately reach significant agreement or disagreement with his author."⁷

Adler provides four rules to guide disagreement:

> [They] can be briefly summarized by conceiving the reader as conversing with the author, as talking back after he has said, "I understand but I disagree," he can make the following remarks to the author: (1) "You are uninformed"; (2) "You are misinformed"; (3) "You are illogical—your reasoning is not cogent"; (4) "Your analysis is incomplete."[8]

Adler shows how to implement the above four remarks:

> Since you have said you understand, your failure to support any of [the first] three remarks obligates you to agree with the author as far as he has gone. You have no freedom of will about this. It is not your sacred[9] privilege to decide whether you're going to agree or disagree.[10]

Adler's advice can help you glean information from this book, but it is not sufficient. Paul says, "The things of the Spirit of God ... are spiritually discerned" (1 Cor 2:14). No set of rules can eliminate your need for the Holy Spirit to open your mind to truth and protect you from error (cp. Acts 16:14). I have prayed that the Father would grant you this blessing.

Now for two of my own suggestions for how to read this book. First, recognize the incremental process it follows. Each Chapter builds on previous Chapters: their concepts are cumulative. The ultimate model contains elements impossible to understand apart from the previous explanations. So read the Chapters in consecutive order.

Second, realize that this book is not an end in itself. Copernicus' model of the solar system was elegant, but its importance did not spring from its simplicity and accuracy. The true value of Copernicus' work lay in the vision it inspired: "His audacity to introduce the heliocentric cosmology into Western culture, essentially [triggered] the Scientific Revolution."[11]

In like manner, this book's importance lies not in its more accurate prophetic model. Its weightier matters involve how the prophecies it explains affect your actions: how you understand the kingdom of God, love and serve its King, function in one of his local churches, pursue holiness, and spread the gospel of Christ's kingdom. This book aims to encourage these things, not to win a theological battle with proponents of other prophetic models. I invite you to decide if I am uninformed, misinformed, illogical, or incomplete as far as I have gone. If none of these apply, may this book give you a deeper understanding of what God did in the "last days" of the Mosaic age, and may that knowledge enrich your life and your spiritual fellowship with Christ.

Notes

1 I will show Greek words as italicized transliterations of their *lexical* forms.
2 Stephen Hawking, *A Brief History of Time/The Universe in a Nutshell: Two Books in One* (New York: Bantam, 2007), 1:5.
3 Owen Gingerich, *The Book Nobody Read: Chasing the Revolutions of Nicolaus Copernicus* (New York: Walker & Company, 2004), 16n.
4 Mortimer J. Adler and Charles Van Doren, *How to Read a Book: The Classic Guide to Intelligent Reading*, rev. ed. (n.p.: Touchstone, 1972), 137–39 (emphasis in original).
5 Adler and Doren, *How to Read a Book*, 140 (emphasis removed).
6 Adler and Doren, *How to Read a Book*, 143.
7 Adler and Doren, *How to Read a Book*, 153 (emphasis removed).
8 Adler and Doren, *How to Read a Book*, 156 (emphasis removed).
9 This word probably means "inviolable" in this context.
10 Adler and Doren, *How to Read a Book*, 160.
11 Gingerich, *The Book Nobody Read*, 53.

CHAPTER ONE

Existing Prophetic Models

COPERNICUS BELIEVED his model provided a better way of interpreting the solar system, so he wrote a large book—longer than this one!—to explain it. To begin my emulation of his example, I will provide a brief description of the four primary models available to the church for interpreting biblical prophecies. "[These] approaches have developed and taken turns in the limelight throughout church history: historic premillennialism, amillennialism, postmillennialism, and dispensational premillennialism."[1] Each of these, like the Ptolemaic model in astronomy, provides enough value to ensure its survival, but none is persuasive enough to dislodge the others. Knowing the major teachings of each model will help us compare and contrast them to the framework this book discovers.

The name of each model contains the word *millennial* because, in Revelation 20, John says the saints will reign with Christ for "a thousand years."[2] The word *post*millennialism means the second coming of Christ will occur *after* the millennium. *Pre*millennialism—a name that occurs in the name of two models—means Christ will return *before* his kingdom reign begins. The name *a*millennialism emphasizes the non-literal nature of the term "a thousand years."

Each of these models, except for dispensationalism, has produced influential writers and respected Christian leaders from the earliest days of Christianity.³ None of them has enjoyed universal acceptance among Christ's churches. In recent years, some preterists have attempted to build a consistent prophetic model by defining the millennium as the forty years between Jesus' crucifixion and the temple's fall.⁴ James Stuart Russell knew of this interpretation and said, "This method of interpretation appears to us so violent and unnatural that we cannot hesitate to reject it."⁵ The prophetic model in this book will justify Russell's opinion on this issue,⁶ so I will not analyze this model here.

Four simple concepts differentiate between the long-standing prophetic models. Your belief about them will determine the model you accept:

1. *Israel after the flesh.*⁷ Does the nation of Israel—defined as the natural descendants of Abraham—have a unique covenant relationship with God in the present age?
2. *The thousand years.* Does the term "a thousand years" in Revelation 20 designate a literal number of years, or is it a figurative term that means a long period or age?
3. *Pre* or *post*? Does the second coming of Christ occur before or after the millennium?
4. *Optimistic or pessimistic*? Will the kingdom of God be triumphant *in history* or will it diminish in influence among the nations during the church age in which we now live?

The following survey will allow proponents of each of the existing models to state their beliefs regarding these concepts.

Amillennialism

Amillennialism was "first given systematic expression by St. Augustine in his famous City of God"⁸ (AD 413). Of all prophetic systems, this view has enjoyed the widest acceptance for the longest period. Modern proponents of amillennialism include J. I. Packer, Anthony Hoekema, and R. C. Sproul.

Kim Riddlebarger, after abandoning dispensationalism and embracing amillennialism, described his new belief:

> Amillennialists hold that the promises made to Israel, David, and Abraham in the Old Testament are fulfilled by Jesus Christ and his church during this present age. The millennium is the period of time between the two advents of our Lord with the thousand years of Revelation 20 being symbolic of the entire inter-adventual age. At the first advent of Jesus Christ, Satan was bound by Christ's victory over him at Calvary and the empty tomb. The effects of this victory continued because of the presence of the kingdom of God via the preaching of the gospel and as evidenced by Jesus' miracles. Through the spread of the gospel, Satan is no longer free to deceive the nations. Christ is presently reigning in heaven during the entire period between Christ's first and second coming. At the end of the millennial age, Satan is released, a great apostasy breaks out, the general resurrection occurs, Jesus Christ returns in final judgment for all people, and he establishes a new heaven and earth.[9]

This account allows us to begin our evaluation of amillennialism using the four concepts above.

Israel After the Flesh. Amillennialists teach "Israel after the flesh" (1 Cor 10:18) no longer holds a special covenant position with God. God fulfilled his earthly promises to that nation during the Mosaic (or, Jewish) age. The ministry of Christ and the coming of the Holy Spirit on Pentecost ended that age and started the church age. The promises God made to Abraham and his descendants now apply to the church, defined as those having faith in Christ.

The Thousand Years. Amillennialists use several terms to identify the present age: the church age, the kingdom age, the gospel age, the New Testament age, etc. They equate this age with the thousand-year reign of

Christ in Revelation 20. The term "a thousand years" is not precise, they say, but is a figurative way to show a long period of undetermined length. Amillennialists often explain their belief by appealing to God's claim to own "the cattle upon a thousand hills" (Ps 50:10). The Lord does not mean to limit his ownership to a literal number of hills; he wants us to infer he owns the cattle on *all* hills. Amillennialists interpret the "thousand years" in Revelation 20 similarly: this term refers to *all* the years of the kingdom age.

The name of this system sometimes causes confusion because *amillennial* "literally means 'no millennium.'"[10] This is misleading since proponents of this system believe in a millennial reign of Christ; they just deny it will last a thousand literal years.

Pre or Post? Amillennialism teaches that Christ will return *after* the millennium or church age. In this, it agrees with postmillennialism and differs from both forms of premillennialism (i.e., historic and dispensational).

Optimistic or Pessimistic? Amillennialists do not expect the victory of Christ's kingdom over the forces of evil *in history*. According to this system, the outlook for the church in relation to its kingdom-mission is bleak:

> Though God presently reigns in the hearts of his people (spiritual Israel), the church was forewarned by her Lord that she would face tribulation so long as she remains on the earth. This tribulation will grow progressively worse until it finally culminates in the appearance of the antichrist.[11]

> The forces of evil will grow worse and worse in the world, as Satan in his madness uses every power at his command to overthrow the church of Christ.... We have no hope or expectation that the whole world will grow better and better until it is all converted to Christianity.... We by no means expect that the whole of so-

ciety will be Christianized. In fact, we expect the forces of evil to grow more and more violent in their opposition to Christianity and Christians.[12]

Although we believe the kingdom of God began as a small mustard seed and grows steadily larger, we also believe that evil grows proportionately faster.[13]

Amillennialism teaches that Satan's briars will flourish more in the kingdom age than God's mustard seed. This historical pessimism is one of its leading characteristics.

Conclusion. The following diagram[14] depicts the general contours of amillennialism:

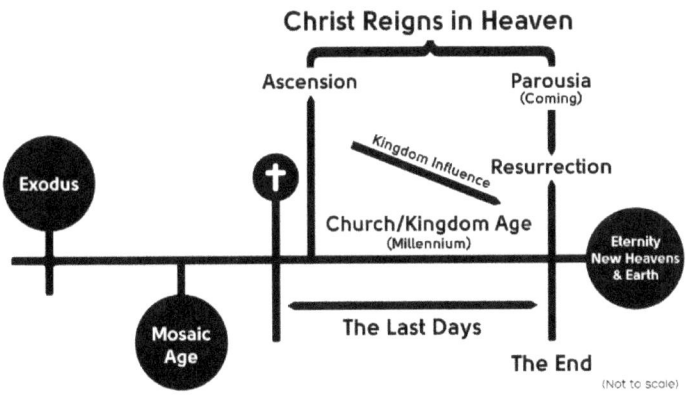

Figure 1-1. Amillennialism

Postmillennialism

Several sixteenth-century Reformers taught postmillennialism, as did many Puritans in the seventeenth and eighteenth centuries. In the nineteenth century, the Princeton theologians—including Charles Hodge, A. A. Hodge, and B. B. Warfield—held a postmillennial view. This prophetic model provided a strong impetus for powerful modern mission movements.[15] Keith Mathison provides a summary of postmillennialism that identifies its distinguishing characteristics:

> Like amillennialism, postmillennialism teaches that the thousand years of Revelation 20 occur prior to the Second Coming. Some postmillennialists teach that the millennial age is the entire period between Christ's first and second advents, while others teach that it is the last one thousand years of the present age. According to postmillennialism, in the present age the Holy Spirit will draw unprecedented multitudes to Christ through the faithful preaching of the gospel. Among the multitudes who will be converted are the Israelites who have thus far rejected the Messiah. At the end of the present age, Christ will return, there will be a general resurrection of the just and the unjust, and the final judgment will take place.[16]

This statement shows postmillennialism's view of our four evaluation concepts.

Israel After the Flesh. Postmillennialism teaches the Jewish race will enjoy kingdom blessings en masse during the last part of the millennium. But they will do so on an equal footing with all other nations. The descendants of Abraham, Isaac, and Jacob do not retain a special covenant relationship with God because of their physical birth.

The Thousand Years. Mathison identifies two kinds of postmillennialism. One form agrees with premillennialism in teaching the "thousand years" of Revelation 20 is a literal number of years. It says the kingdom of God will increase in influence during the church age and culminate in a distinct "golden age"—the millennium—that will last one thousand years.[17] The other form of postmillennialism says the "thousand years" is a symbolic representation of the entire church age that says nothing about the duration of that age. This form also teaches that the church will succeed in its mission to make disciples of all nations. **Pre or Post?** Postmillennialists believe the second coming of Christ will occur *after* his successful millennial (church-age) reign. This is true for both forms of postmillennialism and, as I noted above, accounts for the name *post*millennialism.

Optimistic or Pessimistic? Erroll Hulse inserted a bit of humor when he began his conference presentation on postmillennialism. He said, "By way of introduction I must say that I am fully aware of four great advantages as I present the case for postmillennialism. The first is that every believer hopes that the position I will expound is correct and that the sooner it comes to pass the better."[18] He said this because postmillennialism stands alone among the current prophetic models in believing that the gospel of the kingdom of God will convert the nations during the church age. It is, therefore, an optimistic prophetic model.

Conclusion. Figure 1-2 depicts the form of postmillennialism that includes a literal one-thousand-year golden age:

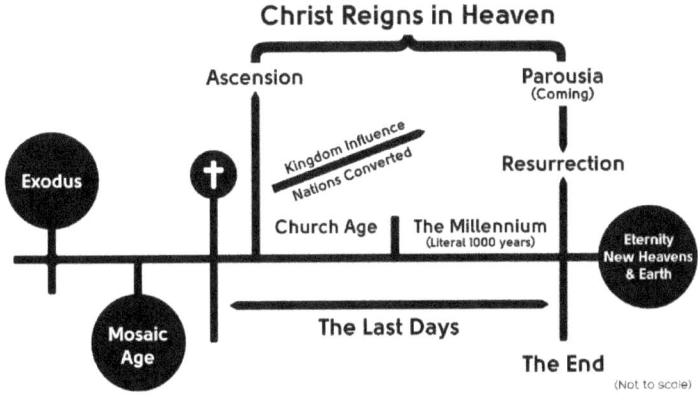

Figure 1-2. Postmillennialism (literal 1,000 years)

Figure 1-3 depicts the form of postmillennialism that equates "a thousand years" in Revelation 20 to the entire church age:

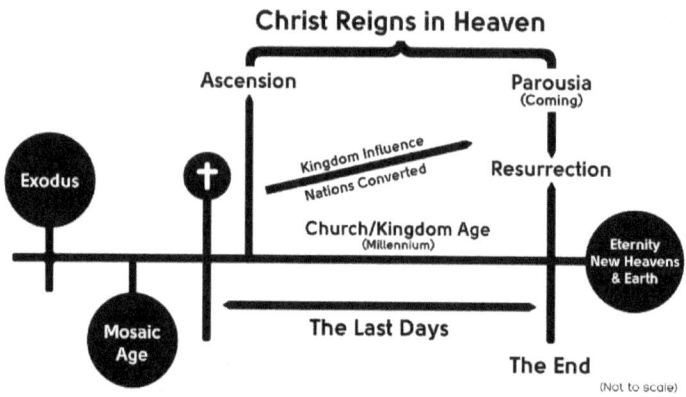

Figure 1-3. Postmillennialism (symbolic 1,000 years)

Historic Premillennialism

Two major premillennial models exist. I will examine the older version here and its younger "cousin" in the next section.

Historic premillennialism, in various forms, enjoyed widespread influence in the early church up to the time of Augustine (AD 354–430). The church fathers Polycarp, Justin Martyr, and Papias taught this view of prophecy, but its influence waned in the following centuries. A few writers—the Greek scholar Henry Alford (1810–71), for example—continued to advocate this prophetic view until a group of scholars—including John Warwick Montgomery, George Eldon Ladd, and J. Barton Payne—revived it in the twentieth century.

The following definition of historic premillennialism provides the starting point for our evaluation of it using our four key concepts:

> In its simplest form, premillennialism refers to the conviction that Christ will return at the end of human history as we know it, *prior* to a long period of time, depicted in Revelation 20:1–7 as a thousand years, in

which he reigns on earth, creating a golden era of peace and happiness for all believers alive at the time of his return, along with all believers of past eras who are resurrected and glorified at this time.[19]

Israel After the Flesh. Historic premillennialism moves one step away from amillennialism's view that the church now occupies the covenant position once held by natural Israel. "Historic premillennialists do not completely merge Israel and the church. In contrast to the tendency among classic amillennialists to discount any future role for the nation in God's program, they note that Paul clearly expected a future for racial Israel (Rom 9–11)."[20]

On the other hand, historic premillennialists distinguish themselves from dispensational premillennialists by saying, "Israel's salvation must occur in the same terms as Gentile salvation, by faith in Jesus as their crucified Messiah."[21] They maintain that another Jewish age will never exist.

The Thousand Years. Historic premillennialism teaches that Christ will reign on earth for one thousand literal years following the church age.

Pre or Post? As its name implies, historic premillennialism teaches Christ will return before the millennium.

Optimistic or Pessimistic? Historic premillennialism says the kingdom of God will triumph on earth *after* the church age. In the meantime, the kingdom will lose influence because the church cannot make disciples of the nations at present. Ladd makes this plain: "Since these enemies [of the church] are spiritual enemies—Satanic enemies—this is a victory that neither men nor the church can win. It can only be done by a direct act of God."[22] He says, "The central theology of the coming of the heavenly Son of Man is that men cannot build the Kingdom of God, nor can history produce it."[23] Ladd summarizes the historic premillennial position: "The Kingdom will not triumph in this age."[24] This view is pessimistic regarding the kingdom's influence in the church age.

Conclusion. Figure 1-4 shows the major tenets of historic premillennialism:

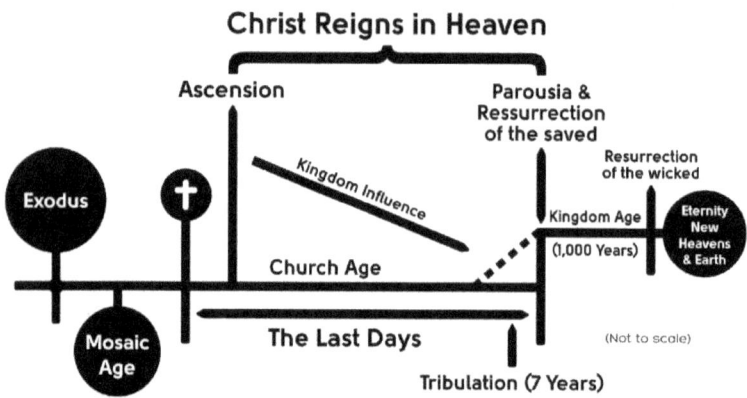

Figure 1-4. Historic Premillennialism

Dispensational Premillennialism

The above three prophetic systems have enjoyed seasons of popularity throughout church history. Dispensational premillennialism, however, rose to prominence in the nineteenth century through the teaching of John Nelson Darby. It gained a large following after C. I. Scofield published his study Bible in 1909. Dispensationalism served as the foundation for several best-selling books, including Hal Lindsey's *The Late Great Planet Earth* and Tim LaHaye's *Left Behind* series. This view finds support at the academic level from theologians at the Dallas Theological Seminary: John Walvoord, Charles Ryrie, and J. Dwight Pentecost, for example.

According to dispensationalism,

> The promises made to Abraham and David are unconditional and have had or will have a literal fulfillment. In no sense have these promises made to Israel been abrogated or fulfilled by the Church, which is a distinct body in this age having promises and a destiny different from Israel's. At the close of this age, premillennialists believe that Christ

> will return for His Church, meeting her in the air (this is
> not the Second Coming of Christ), which event, called the
> rapture or translation, will usher in a seven-year period
> of tribulation on the earth. After this, the Lord will re-
> turn to the earth (this is the Second Coming of Christ)
> to establish His kingdom on the earth for a thousand
> years, during which time the promises to Israel will be
> fulfilled.[25]

Debates exist within dispensationalism regarding the relationship between the church and the "great tribulation": will God remove (i.e., rapture) the church from the earth before, during, or after the tribulation? Such internal questions do not affect our analysis of this prophetic model.

Israel After the Flesh. Dispensationalism says God still honors his covenant with "Israel after the flesh" (1 Cor 10:18). This belief lies at the heart of the system and distinguishes it from all other prophetic models. "The *essence* of dispensationalism is the distinction between Israel and the church."[26] Only this view teaches a future Jewish age: "The New Covenant theocracy of Israel will retain its distinctive Israelite characteristics—a promised land, a temple, appropriate animal sacrifices, and an earthly Zadokian priesthood (subordinate to Jesus Christ)."[27]

The Thousand Years. No ambiguity exists among dispensational writers: the future reign of Christ will last a thousand literal years.

Pre or Post? Dispensationalism agrees with historic premillennialism: the second coming of Christ will occur before the millennium.

Optimistic or Pessimistic? Dispensationalism's pessimism about the church age is more pronounced than that of any other system. It says, "This [church] age is ... under the domination of Satan, its god, in a unique and unprecedented way."[28] According to this model, the church will fail in its quest to "make disciples of all nations" before the second coming of Christ.

Conclusion. Dispensationalism adds a few key features to the historic premillennial model. It divides the return of Christ at the end of the church age into a "secret coming" in the air and then the official second coming (the *parousia*) after a seven-year period of tribulation. It also divides this time of suffering into two distinct phases, each lasting three and one-half years. During the first phase, the antichrist will make a peace covenant with Israel. In the second half of the tribulation, the antichrist will turn on Israel and start a time of unparalleled suffering that commentators often call the "great tribulation."

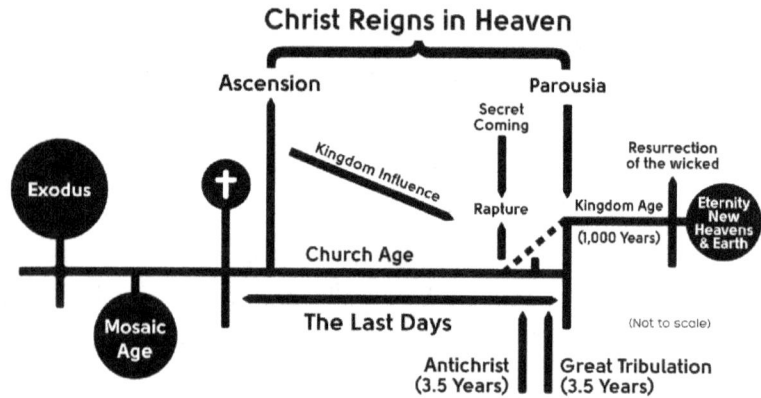

Figure 1-5. Dispensational Premillennialism

Comparison

Table 1-1 uses our four evaluation criteria to summarize the basic differences between the existing prophetic models.

The four evaluation criteria are binary: each has two possible answers. For example, "Israel after the flesh" either has a unique covenant with God or she does not. Therefore, the four criteria can produce sixteen combinations.[29] This fact may raise a question in your mind: since

No.	Criteria	Amill.	Postmill.	Premill. (Hist.)	Premill. (Disp.)
1	Does fleshly Israel (1 Cor 10:18) now have a unique covenant?	No	No	No	Yes
2	Is the "thousand years" of Rev 20—the millennium—literal?	No	Yes/No (two forms)	Yes	Yes
3	Does the second coming (*parousia*) occur before or after the millennium?	After	After	Before	Before
4	Will the existing kingdom of God be triumphant *in history*?	No	Yes	No	No

Table 1-1. Summary of Existing Prophetic Models

the existing prophetic models claim only five of them,[30] could another prophetic model use one of the other combinations? This book answers in the affirmative and, after revealing a prophetic model with redefined "last days," I will return to this chart to show how this is possible.

Notes

1 Craig L. Blomberg and Sung Wook Chung, "Introduction," in *A Case for Historic Premillennialism: An Alternative to "Left Behind" Eschatology*, eds. Craig L. Blomberg and Sung Wook Chung (Grand Rapids: Baker Academic, 2009), xii. I will often shorten the last-named model to dispensationalism.
2 Rev 20:2–7. "Millennial" comes from two Latin words meaning "one thousand" and "year."
3 Dispensationalism emerged during the nineteenth century.
4 See, for example, Max R. King, *The Cross and the Parousia of Christ: The Two Dimensions of One Age-Changing Eschaton* (Grand Rapids: Parkman Road Church of Christ, 1987), 213.
5 Russell, *The Parousia*, 514.
6 As I stated in the Preface, I reject Russell's interpretation of certain key passages and several of his conclusions.
7 A term Paul uses in 1 Cor 10:18.
8 Kim Riddlebarger, *A Case for Amillennialism: Understanding the End Times* (Grand Rapids: Baker, 2003), 32.
9 Riddlebarger, *A Case for Amillennialism*, 312.
10 William E. Cox, *Amillennialism Today* (Phillipsburg, NJ: Presbyterian and Reformed, 1966), 1.
11 Cox, *Amillennialism*, 58.
12 Floyd E. Hamilton, *The Basis of Millennial Faith* (Grand Rapids: Wm. B. Eerdmans, 1942), 34-36.
13 Cox, *Amillennialism*, 5.
14 I first thought of using diagrams like this while reading Max R. King, *The Cross and the Parousia of Christ*.
15 Ian H. Murray, *The Puritan Hope: A Study in Revival and the Interpretation of Prophecy* (Carlisle, PA: The Banner of Truth Trust, 1975), 89–95, 129–84.
16 Keith A. Mathison, *Postmillennialism: An Eschatology of Hope* (Phillipsburg, NJ: P&R, 1999), 10.
17 Cf. Murray, *The Puritan Hope*, 47.
18 Erroll Hulse, *A Christianized World? The Post-Millennial Universal Reign of Christ*, 2nd ed. (Toronto: Toronto Baptist Seminary and Bible College, October 17–21, 1988): 141.
19 Blomberg and Chung, "Historic Premillennialism," xii.
20 Stanley J. Grenz, *The Millennial Maze: Sorting Out Evangelical Options* (Downers Grove, IL: IVP Academic, 2007), 138.
21 George Eldon Ladd, "Historic Premillennialism," in *The Meaning of the Millennium: Four Views*, ed. Robert G. Clouse (Downers Grove, IL: IVP Academic, 1996), 28.

22 George Eldon Ladd, *The Last Things: An Eschatology for Laymen* (Grand Rapids: Eerdmans, 1978), 47.
23 Ladd, *The Last Things*, 65.
24 Ladd, *The Last Things*, 107-08.
25 Charles Caldwell Ryrie, *The Basis of the Premillennial Faith* (Neptune, NJ: Loizeaux Bros., 1953), 12.
26 Charles C. Ryrie, *Dispensationalism* (Chicago: Moody Publishers, 1995), 41 (emphasis added).
27 John C. Whitcomb, "Millennial Sacrifices," in *The Popular Encyclopedia of Bible Prophecy*, eds. Tim LaHaye and Ed Hindson (Eugene, Oregon: Harvest House, 2004), 228.
28 J. Dwight Pentecost, *Things to Come: A Study in Biblical Eschatology* (Grand Rapids: Zondervan, 1964), 132.
29 For readers interested in the math, r variables which can take n values will produce $n \cdot n \ldots n = n^r$ total possibilities. In this case, $r = 4$ and $n = 2$, so $2^4 = 16$.
30 Amillennialism, historic premillennialism, and dispensational premillennialism claim one combination each; postmillennialism claims two.

CHAPTER TWO

Benefits of a Better Model

COPERNICUS' MODEL of the solar system brought incalculable benefits, many outside the field of astronomy. These advantages were the fruits of a fresh way of *thinking* about God's creation. Copernicus' controversial theory spurred scientists, like Galileo Galilei and Johannes Kepler, to examine his ideas, and something important happened as they did so—the scientific revolution began, first in physics, then in other areas of science.

Similarly, a better prophetic model will benefit the church in various ways as she ponders God's revelation in the Scriptures. I will discuss some of the most significant benefits under five headings, the names of which form the acrostic VALUE: Vision, Apologetics, Legacy, Understanding, and Experience. These benefits are the "value proposition" for the new prophetic model in this book.

Vision

Solomon stresses the church's need for a *vision*: "Where there is no vision, the people perish" (Prov 29:18). Duane A. Garrett says, "The word for ['vision'] is commonly associated with the visions of the prophets and stands for the importance of prophetic exhortation to the community."[1] Without such prophetic encouragement, the people "perish" or "are discouraged,"[2] but, with it, they persevere.

I will reiterate a point I made in the previous chapter: I am speaking of a prophetic vision for the kingdom of God *in history*. All existing prophetic models teach that the kingdom will have overcome all its enemies when the eternal state arrives. But all models do not do a suitable job of relating that victory to the present work of Christians. An improved prophetic model can make a strong contribution in this regard.

Other belief systems have well-defined visions for history. "Islam," according to Efraim Karsh, "envisages a global political order in which all humankind will live under Muslim rule as either believers or subject communities."[3] Secular humanists also have a vision for the here-and-now: "Humanism ... stands for the building of a more humane society through an ethic based on human and other natural values in the spirit of reason and free inquiry through human capabilities."[4]

God gave Israel such a vision during the Exodus from Egypt: "I will bring you in unto the land, concerning the which I did swear to give it to Abraham, to Isaac, and to Jacob; and I will give it you for an heritage: I am the LORD" (Exod 6:8). God's vision for Israel was never in doubt, but the people were slow to believe God would bless them to achieve it. After wandering forty years in the wilderness for their unbelief, they entered the land and began fighting the necessary battles. Many years later, the vision became reality; the land was theirs (cp. Josh 23:14).

In each of these examples—Islam, humanism, and Israel—the people's vision direct(ed) their actions. Donald S. Whitney uses a powerful metaphor to illustrate the principle at work here:

> Imagine six-year-old Kevin, whose parents have enrolled him in music lessons. After school every afternoon, he sits in the living room and reluctantly strums "Home on the Range" while watching his buddies play baseball in the park across the street. That's discipline without direction. It's drudgery.
>
> Now suppose Kevin is visited by an angel one afternoon during guitar practice. In a vision he's taken to

Carnegie Hall. He's shown a guitar virtuoso giving a concert. Usually bored by classical music, Kevin is astonished by what he sees and hears. The musician's fingers dance excitedly on the strings with fluidity and grace. Kevin thinks of how stupid and klunky his hands feel when they halt and stumble over the chords. The virtuoso blends clean, soaring notes into a musical aroma that wafts from his guitar. Kevin remembers the toneless, irritating discord that comes stumbling out of his.

But Kevin is enchanted. His head tilts slightly to one side as he listens. He drinks in everything. He never imagined that anyone could play the guitar like this.

"What do you think, Kevin?" asks the angel.

The answer is a soft, slow, six-year-old's "W-o-w!"

The vision vanishes, and the angel is again standing in front of Kevin in his living room. "Kevin," says the angel, "the wonderful musician you saw is you in a few years." Then pointing at the guitar, the angel declares, "But you must practice!"

Suddenly the angel disappears and Kevin finds himself alone with his guitar. Do you think his attitude toward practice will be different now? As long as he remembers what he's going to become, Kevin's discipline will have a direction, a goal that will pull him into the future. Yes, effort will be involved, but you could hardly call it drudgery.[5]

Kevin's vision of his future changed his estimation of his current task; daily practice was no longer drudgery. If the angel had shown him an incompetent musician, this transformation would not have happened. A vision inspires, motivates, encourages, and controls the routine tasks necessary to achieve it.

An improved prophetic model will clarify God's vision for the church in history. This clarity will then give deepened meaning to the routine tasks necessary for the people of God to achieve that vision. A better model will create a smooth path between prophetic vision and vocation. It will say to God's people what Caleb and Joshua said to Israel: "If the LORD delight in us, then he will bring us into this land, and give it us; a land which floweth with milk and honey" (Num 14:8).

Apologetics

A better prophetic model will assist Christians in *apologetics* by giving them better arguments with which to defend the faith. The apostles command Christians to "earnestly contend for the faith which was once delivered unto the saints" (Jude 3) and to "sanctify the Lord God in your hearts: and be ready always to give an answer to every man that asketh you a reason of the hope that is in you with meekness and fear" (1 Pet 3:15). God's people need a better prophetic model for apologetics like astronomers needed the Copernican model to explain planetary movements.

This is no insignificant matter. Opponents of Christianity often exploit the weaknesses of the existing prophetic models. The atheist Bertrand Russell, for example, rejected Christianity because of two prophecies in Matthew's gospel. He explained his logic to the South London Branch of the National Secular Society:

> Having granted the excellence of these maxims, I come to certain points in which I do not believe that one can grant either the superlative wisdom or the superlative goodness of Christ…. I am concerned with Christ as He appears in the Gospels, taking the Gospel narrative as it stands, and there one does find some things that do not seem to be very wise. For one thing, he certainly thought that His second coming would occur in clouds

of glory before the death of all the people who were living at that time. There are a great many texts that prove that. He says, for instance, "Ye shall not have gone over the cities of Israel till the Son of Man be come" [Matt 10:23]. Then he says, "There are some standing here which shall not taste death till the Son of Man comes into His kingdom" [Matt 16:28]; and there are a lot of places where it is quite clear that He believed that His second coming would happen during the lifetime of many then living. That was the belief of His earlier followers, and it was the basis of a good deal of His moral teaching. When He said, "Take no thought for the morrow," and things of that sort, it was very largely because He thought that the second coming was going to be very soon, and that all ordinary mundane affairs did not count. I have, as a matter of fact, known some Christians who did believe that the second coming was imminent. I knew a parson who frightened his congregation terribly by telling them that the second coming was very imminent indeed, but they were much consoled when they found that he was planting trees in his garden. The early Christians did really believe it, and they did abstain from such things as planting trees in their gardens, because they did accept from Christ the belief that the second coming was imminent. In that respect, clearly He was not so wise as some other people have been, and He was certainly not superlatively wise.[6]

Russell accused Jesus of uttering false prophecies, making himself a false prophet instead of the divine Son of God. Many Christians cannot meet such challenges because the existing prophetic models do not provide coherent explanations for the passages Russell used. These models not only fail to explain these passages, they lead honest critics to conclusions like those Russell reached. R. C. Sproul emphasizes the gravity of this situation:

> It is my fear that evangelicals today tend to underplay the significance of the problems inherent in Russell's assumptions. Too often we take a facile approach to the problem that reveals our failure to feel the weight of such objections. This becomes particularly acute when we realize the extent to which these problems have contributed to the entire modern controversy over the inspiration of Scripture and the person and work of Christ.[7]

The need for a better prophetic model is not limited to external challenges; leading thinkers *within* the church sometimes undermine the historic Christian faith through prophetic errors. Sherman E. Johnson wrote a widely used evangelical commentary in which he (like Russell) charges Jesus with making erroneous prophetic statements. Regarding Jesus' prophecy in Matthew 16:28, Johnson said,

> *The prediction was not fulfilled*, and later Christians found it necessary to explain that it was metaphorical and had been fulfilled at Pentecost. John 21:22–23 deals with a similar promise that the "beloved disciple" would not die, and tries to explain it as a misunderstanding. It would not be strange if Jesus believed that within a generation the kingdom would be manifested in full glory, for certainly most early Christians and many Jews thought so. The thought-forms of the day were what we call "eschatological";[8] God had created the world as we know it, and he would bring it to an end.... We cannot decide with certainty exactly what Jesus thought would happen in the future, and it is not important that we should.[9]

Johnson made a similar observation about Jesus' prophecy in Matthew 24:34:

> Matthew cannot have thought of this generation as lasting only thirty or forty years after the Crucifixion. He probably believed, however, that the end would come

BENEFITS OF A BETTER MODEL

> before all of Jesus' hearers had died (cp. 16:28). The saying may be essentially genuine but its exact force is uncertain.[10]

Some Christian scholars concede Bertrand Russell's major objection against the Christian faith to salvage something of value from Jesus' teaching. Edwin Freed says, "The early church, in fact, found much of his teaching that applied to the present useful even *after time had proven Jesus wrong* about the nearness of the End."[11] Writers of this ilk think Jesus left some practical teachings that can benefit Christians, but he erred in his prophetic statements. I maintain that practical advice from a fallible teacher is not the authoritative word of God.

Samuel Lee mentions writers much closer to my conservative hometown:

> It is a conviction very common that the Apostles were in error. The more frank and out-spoken admit this in so many words: while others less open-hearted say the same thing, though indirectly and with more or less of ambiguity. As belonging to these classes are such illustrious names as Locke, Watts, Jonathan Edwards, Barnes, Conybeare, Olshausen, Arnold, Bush, Hudson.[12]

Lee then provides quotes from these writers to establish his point; I will give just three. He cites Isaac Watts:

> The Christians of the first age did generally expect the second coming of Christ to judgment, and the resurrection of the dead, in that very age wherein it was foretold. St. Paul gives us a hint of it in 2 Thess. 2: 1, 2.[13]

Lee provides the following passage by W. J. Conybeare:

> We know that our Saviour himself had warned his disciples that 'of that day and that hour knoweth no man, no, not the angels of heaven, but the Father only;' and we find these words remarkably fulfilled by the fact that the early church, and *even the Apostles themselves, expected*

> *their Lord to come again in that very generation. St. Paul himself shared in that expectation.*[14]

He quotes at length from a well-known commentator:

> Rev. Albert Barnes in his "Commentary" on 1 Cor. 15:51, says, "I do not know that the proper doctrine of inspiration suffers, if we admit that the Apostles were ignorant of the exact time when the world would close; or even that in regard to the precise period when that would take place, *they might be in error.*[15]

Lee shows how these men (and the others) tried to explain how the apostles could teach their erroneous beliefs about the return of Christ without destroying the inspiration of Scripture. He argues that this is not possible, and I agree; these beloved writers believed in the inerrancy of the Bible, but held prophetic views that undermined that belief. He says,

> These extracts are from men of eminent talent. And for the very reason that they are such, they thus speak. It is the only inference that a rigid logic can draw from their premises. And they who are the most unequivocal and explicit, evince the most candor, and the control in highest degree, of the true principles of interpretation. There is no escape from this conclusion, if the premises are conceded. These premises are that "the Coming of the Son of Man," and "the Coming of the Lord" are the same; and that with these "the end of the world," "the Judgment," and "the Resurrection," are associate events; and that by the end of the world (*aiōn*) is meant the physical catastrophe. This conceded, and *it must be* that the Apostles expected the great event in their day. If this be not so, then we know nothing of the opinions of the Apostles and of the Saviour by what he or they have said. We admire the courage of such men as have given a frank utterance to a meaning, which the application of their own principles must of necessity

find in the language of the Bible. The caution and reserve with which some writers utter this same belief, show that they were not satisfied with their own findings, nor with the principles by which they were led, or rather driven to them. We wonder that they did not throw away at once, both their conclusions and their premises, and enter upon an *original* investigation of the Sacred Volume.[16]

I cannot imagine a greater challenge to the faith than that presented by the statements Lee cites. If Jesus was mistaken about prophecy, if Matthew and the apostles believed a fundamental prophetic error, and if they taught their errors as truth for Christians to believe and act upon, where does that leave "the faith once delivered to the saints"? Not in the category of "inerrant"! This book will show that the error lies not in Jesus and the apostles, but in *assumed* and erroneous prophetic models. A better model will eliminate this problem and strengthen the church's apologetic witness.

Legacy

An improved prophetic model will show the church's vision for the future, but it will also explain her *legacy*. From ancient times, God's people have linked the story of their heritage to their future. Moses rehearsed Israel's past: God had given them the law at Horeb; punished them for their unbelief at Kadesh Barnea; sustained them for forty years in their wilderness wanderings; defeated the kings of neighboring nations; and brought them to the border of the Promised Land a second time (Deut 1–3). Moses used this legacy to encourage Israel to pursue God's vision for her future: "Go in and possess the land which the LORD sware unto your fathers, Abraham, Isaac, and Jacob, to give unto them and to their seed after them" (Deut 1:8).

About a thousand years later, Israel's leaders repeated this formula. The nation had returned from Babylon after spending seventy years in exile because of her rebellion against God. The Levites again rehearsed

Israel's legacy: God had called Abraham out of idolatry and made a covenant with him, saying his descendants would inherit "the land of the Canaanite, the Hittite, the Amorite, the Perizzite, the Jebusite, and the Girgashite" (Neh 9:8). The Levites repeated the story Moses had told about God redeeming Israel from Egyptian bondage, giving the law to her at Mount Sinai, etc. (Neh 9:9–14). Then the Levites updated the story: God had blessed Israel to take possession of their land as Moses said they would (Neh 9:22–25), but "they did evil again before" God (Neh 9:28) and, because of this, God had sent them into Babylonian captivity. In his great mercies, God "did not make an end of them or forsake them" (Neh 9:31); instead, he brought them back into their land. The prophets of the day—Haggai, Zechariah, and Malachi—linked this legacy to Israel's future:

> Rejoice greatly, O daughter of Zion; shout, O daughter of Jerusalem: behold, thy King cometh unto thee: he is just, and having salvation; lowly, and riding upon an ass, and upon a colt the foal of an ass. And I will cut off the chariot from Ephraim, and the horse from Jerusalem, and the battle bow shall be cut off: and he shall speak peace unto the heathen: and his dominion shall be from sea even to sea, and from the river even to the ends of the earth. (Zech 9:9–10)

About four hundred years later, Stephen used this pattern just before his martyrdom (Acts 6:8–7:53). He repeated Israel's time-honored story about Abraham, Moses, and the Exodus from Egypt (Acts 7:2–36). He mentioned the exile to Babylon just as the Levites had done (Acts 7:43). Then Stephen also advanced Israel's story: Moses had "said unto the children of Israel, A prophet shall the Lord your God raise up unto you of your brethren, like unto me; him shall ye hear" (Acts 7:37; cp. Deut 18:15–19). Stephen said Jesus was the prophet of which Moses spoke and Israel's story would continue in him: "Jesus of Nazareth shall destroy this place [i.e., the temple and its precincts], and shall change the customs which Moses delivered us" (Acts 6:14).[17]

I wish to state this most emphatically: a prophetic model must tell *Israel's* story from beginning to end; her historical legacy must give way seamlessly to her future vision. The existing prophetic models tell Israel's story in different ways. An improved model will clarify Israel's legacy-to-vision story and show the church's place in it.

Understanding

The Scriptures contain many admonitions for Christians to deepen their *understanding*. For example, Paul says, "Brethren, be not children in understanding ... but in understanding be men" (1 Cor 14:20). He admonishes Timothy to "consider what I say; and the Lord give thee understanding in all things" (2 Tim 2:7).

The above discussions show that a better prophetic model will deepen our understanding of the church's vision, apologetics ministry, and legacy. I will here add three additional subjects: time statements, model documentation, and the gospel.

Time Statements. Jesus once baffled some of his disciples with a time statement: "A little while, and ye shall not see me: and again, a little while, and ye shall see me, because I go to the Father." The disciples said, "What is this that he saith, A little while? we cannot tell what he saith" (John 16:16, 18). Later, Jesus and his apostles made many similar time statements in prophetic passages. They did so positively and emphatically: they did not say their predictions *might* happen soon; they taught that they *would* do so. Commentators who use the existing prophetic models have the same problem as the disciples: such "little while" statements in prophetic contexts puzzle them. Here are a few such statements:

> From that time Jesus began to preach, and to say, Repent: for the kingdom of heaven is at hand.... And as ye go, preach, saying, The kingdom of heaven is at hand.... For verily I say unto you, *Ye shall not have gone over the cities of Israel, till the Son of man be come.* (Matt 4:17; 10:7, 23)

> Verily I say unto you, There be some standing here, *which shall not taste of death, till they see the Son of man coming in his kingdom.* (Matt 16:28)

> Now all these things happened unto them for ensamples: and they are written for our admonition, *upon whom the ends of the world are come.* (1 Cor 10:11)

> For *yet a little while, and he that shall come will come*, and will not tarry. (Heb 10:37)

> The Revelation of Jesus Christ, which God gave unto him, to shew unto his servants things *which must shortly come to pass*.... Blessed is he that readeth, and they that hear the words of this prophecy, and keep those things which are written therein: *for the time is at hand.* (Rev 1:1, 3)

> And he saith unto me, Seal not the sayings of the prophecy of this book: for *the time is at hand*.... And, behold, *I come quickly.* (Rev 22:10, 12)

These statements—especially those in Revelation—contrast with Daniel's last vision (Dan 10–12): "The message was true, but the appointed time was long" (Dan 10:1 NKJV). A divine messenger told Daniel to "shut up the words, and seal the book, even to the time of the end" (Dan 12:4). Daniel and Revelation speak of the same events; how can one be sealed because the time was long and the other be *un*sealed because the time was short?

Proponents of the existing prophetic models have created explanatory devices to account for such texts. These mechanisms resemble those required to allow the Ptolemaic model in astronomy to explain planetary motion. They include: *double sense* (or *dual fulfillment*)—the idea that a prophecy can have multiple fulfillments; *elastic time*—the belief that time statements in prophetic contexts are not literal because "soon" can mean a long time and vice versa; and *telescopic* or *prophetic perspective*—the belief that the prophets sometimes spoke of distant future events as near without an awareness of lengthy periods of intervening history.

These problematic devices do not flow from a correct (or necessary) interpretation of the biblical texts. Rather, the prophetic systems need them to yield acceptable results. Commentators have proclaimed the need for these mechanisms for centuries; few modern interpreters question their existence.[18]

Adherents of the existing prophetic models use their corrective devices erratically, a practice not found among their astronomical counterparts. Ptolemaic astronomers invented corrective devices to make their system work, then used them consistently. The adjusting devices were a permanent part of the astronomical model. Interpreters of prophecy, however, use their corrective devices randomly—*all* prophecies do not have dual fulfillments, for example. They use corrective devices only if a prophecy does not fit their prophetic model. If the passage presents no time-statement difficulty, they ignore the corrective devices without fanfare.

These corrective devices obscure a fundamental flaw in the underlying prophetic models. In astronomy, the new Copernican model eventually abolished the need for the ancient astronomical devices required to make the Ptolemaic system work. For interpreting prophecy, an improved model will eliminate the unnecessary corrective devices and allow God's people to understand time statements as Jesus and the apostles intended.

Documentation. When I worked as an engineer, I disliked using a formula that I could not develop from scratch. I thought my lack of understanding about how the equation came into existence might cause me to misapply it. I carried this mindset into the study of prophecy. This caused me great angst because I could not find documentation regarding the derivation of the current prophetic models. This is a glaring deficiency in my estimation; if I cannot trace the development of these models from Scripture, how can I apply them with confidence?

Christian thinkers developed these models (except dispensationalism[19]) over the centuries on a piecemeal basis. They stitched together individual prophecies such that the end products resemble patchwork quilts made from materials on hand as chilly weather approaches. Some modern writers lament this situation. Thomas Ice, for example, while defending his futuristic system against a rival view, said, "hardly anybody has thought through how you inductively develop Futurism from the Bible."[20] George E. Ladd made a similar observation after providing a list of scholars that support his position: "None of these nor any other premillennial scholar has written a comprehensive critical study of the New Testament doctrine of the kingdom of God."[21] Louis Berkhof says Kleifoth "complained about the fact that there had never yet appeared a comprehensive and adequate treatise on eschatology as a whole."[22] This state of affairs prompted Robert L. Reymond to say, "with such eschatological confusion running rampant today ... never has the need been greater to return to Scripture and to see what God's Word says concerning this vital, all-important, capstoning locus of theology."[23]

Full documentation regarding how the current models came into existence does not exist, at least not in readily available formats. Today's Christian reader cannot find the prophetic equivalent to Copernicus' explanation of his astronomical system in his book *De revolutionibus*. A new prophetic model would have an immediate advantage over the other systems—Christians could examine the documentation that verifies its truth claims.

The Gospel. Prophetic models are important because they affect how Christians understand the gospel. Jesus and the apostles described their message in terms of prophetic fulfillment; theirs was the gospel *of the kingdom* (Matt 4:23; 9:35; 24:14). The arrival of God's kingdom lay at the heart of the apostolic message (e.g., Acts 8:12; 14:22; 19:8; 20:25; 28:23,

31). This caused C. H. Dodd to say, "The Gospel of primitive Christianity is a Gospel of realized eschatology."[24] Christians depend on prophetic models to explain which prophecies are in the "realized" category and which are not.

Many Christians truncate the "good news" by defining the gospel as just Christ's death for sins, his burial, and his resurrection (1 Cor 15:1–11). This is the critical first part of Paul's definition, but only the first part; his gospel expands to include the reign of Christ during which he subdues all his enemies. Paul's "good news" includes Christ's defeat of the last enemy, death, in the bodily resurrection (1 Cor 15:12–58). Robert L. Reymond recognized this larger scope: "The proclamation of eschatological matters [including the resurrection] was … *a vital, integral aspect* of Paul's 'gospel,' which eschatologically oriented gospel was … also preached by the other apostles."[25]

The full preaching of the gospel must include a proclamation about the kingdom of God. The existing prophetic models describe that kingdom in divergent ways. They thus present varying accounts of the gospel of the kingdom. An improved prophetic model will allow Christians to better understand this vital element in "the gospel of the grace of God" (Acts 20:24). I will say more about the prophetic content of the gospel in Chapter 13.

Experience

Prophetic models are not just theoretical; they affect how Christians *experience* God. God tells his people to test their experiences using the written Word, even when deceivers tempt them to do otherwise: "To the law and to the testimony: if they speak not according to this word, it is because there is no light in them" (Isa 8:20). A prophetic model is a lens through which Christians see the Word; therefore, it regulates the experiences they deem valid. I will briefly discuss two such experiences and show how prophetic interpretation affects each experience.

Drinking Spiritual Water. The Old Testament prophets used powerful images to describe how God's people would one day experience his presence. Several of these pictures involved *refreshing water*: "I will pour water upon him that is thirsty, and floods upon the dry ground: I will pour my spirit upon thy seed, and my blessing upon thine offspring: And they shall spring up as among the grass, as willows by the water courses" (Isa 44:3–4; cp. Isa 55:1; 58:11; Zech 13:1; 14:8–9). Jesus also used this metaphor: "Whosoever drinketh of the water that I shall give him shall never thirst; but the water that I shall give him shall be in him a well of water springing up into everlasting life" (John 4:14; cp John 7:38).

Christians of all ages have believed these promises of reviving water belong to them in the present age, but how does this belief fit into the current prophetic models? This question arises from the fact that the river that supplies this water is in the "new heaven and a new earth" that exist after "the first heaven and the first earth [have] passed away" (Rev 21:1). In this new environment, Jesus promises to "give of the fountain of the water of life freely to him who thirsts" (Rev 21:6).

In the new heaven and earth, John sees the new Jerusalem—"the bride, the Lamb's wife" (Rev 21:9) "descending out of heaven from God" (Rev 21:10) and describes her glory (Rev 21:11–27). John says an angel then showed him the source of the water Jesus had mentioned in John:

> And he shewed me a pure river of water of life, clear as crystal, proceeding out of the throne of God and of the Lamb. In the midst of the street of it, and on either side of the river, was there the tree of life, which bare twelve manner of fruits, and yielded her fruit every month: and the leaves of the tree were for the healing of the nations. (Rev 22:1–2)

This river of the "water of life" only exists in the new heavens and earth. The existing prophetic models equate the new heavens and earth to a future age, either to the thousand-year reign of Christ mentioned in Revelation 20 or to the eternal state. Therefore, according to these models, the refreshing water of which the prophets and Jesus spoke pertain to a future age.

This logic produces an erroneous conclusion—Christians know the life-giving water God promised belongs to the present age. They need a better prophetic model—one that validates the experience of drinking this heavenly water now.

Seeking Spiritual Gifts. Should Christians desire to experience the miraculous spiritual gifts Paul describes in 1 Corinthians 12–14? Sincere Christians give different answers to this question, but most of them agree that Paul sets an ending-point for the supernatural gifts:

> Charity never faileth: but whether there be prophecies, they shall fail; whether there be tongues, they shall cease; whether there be knowledge, it shall vanish away. For we know in part, and we prophesy in part. But *when that which is perfect is come*, then that which is in part shall be done away. (1 Cor 13:8–10)

The crucial question is this: has "that which is perfect" (Gk. *teleios*) come since the time Paul wrote these words? If not, Paul's admonition requires today's Christians to seek miraculous spiritual gifts: to "follow after charity, and desire spiritual gifts" (1 Cor 14:1). However, if "that which is perfect" has already come, then such spiritual gifts have "vanish[ed] away" (1 Cor 13:8), and Christians should not seek to experience them.

The prophetic model through which one filters this question determines its answer. Paul discusses the cessation of supernatural gifts in a context that includes a series of end-time statements: "This I say, brethren, the time is short" … "the form of this world is passing away" … "the ends of the ages have come" (1 Cor 7:29, 31; 10:11 NKJV). He then says the supernatural gifts would cease "when that which is perfect is come" (1 Cor 13:10). Modern Christians need a prophetic model that explains the relationship between these statements, one that helps them determine whether Paul's admonition to seek the supernatural gifts is still valid.

Conclusion

Copernicus knew he was risking much by publishing his revised model of the solar system. He suspected many academics and churchmen would ostracize him because he was challenging their long-cherished paradigms, but he persisted. Eventually, Copernicus' system proved to be correct, and his insights produced great blessings for following generations.

The need for a better model with which to interpret biblical prophecies is great; the current alternatives do not provide the explanations Christians need. Henry Alford, the well-known premillennial commentator already mentioned, acknowledged this need in his commentary on Matthew's gospel:

> I thought it proper to state … that I did not feel by any means that full confidence which I once did in the exegesis, [concerning] prophetical interpretation, here given.… But *I had no other system* to substitute, and some of the points here dwelt on seem to me as weighty as ever.[26]

Many Bible students identify with this feeling of inadequacy when interpreting prophecy. They despair of finding an accurate and understandable solution, so they humorously describe themselves as "*pan*millennialists"—they believe God will make "everything *pan* out in the end."[27] (I suspect even the most ardent advocates of the existing systems can sympathize with such sentiments.) This resignation is tragic, but it gives challenge, excitement, and urgency to the task at hand—to find a prophetic model that improves our vision, apologetics, legacy, understanding, and experience

This book calls for a reexamination of the piecemeal systems the church has inherited; it questions their underlying hidden assumptions. It asks the reader to lay aside his prejudices—to the greatest extent possible—and allow the Scriptures to reveal the model God placed in them. A fresh proposal will, undoubtedly, face strong resistance from some who support the older systems, but the potential for long-term good outweighs the risks of short-term opposition.

Notes

1 Duane A. Garrett, *Proverbs, Ecclesiastes, Song of Songs*, vol. 14 of *New American Commentary* (Nashville: Broadman & Holman, 1993), 231.

2 The English Standard Version's marginal reading.

3 Efraim Karsh, *Islamic Imperialism* (New Haven, CT: Yale University Press, 2006), 62.

4 "IHEU Minimum Statement on Humanism," Humanists International, General Assembly, (1996): https://humanists.international/policy/iheu-minimum-statement-on-humanism/.

5 Donald S. Whitney, *Spiritual Disciplines for the Christian Life*, rev. ed. (Colorado Springs, CO: NavPress, 2014), 15–16.

6 Bertrand Russell, *Why I Am Not a Christian: And Other Essays on Religion and Related Subjects*, ed. Paul Edwards (New York: Simon & Schuster, 1957), 17–18.

7 R. C. Sproul, *The Last Days According to Jesus*, 3rd ed. (Grand Rapids: Baker, 1998), 17.

8 Eschatology is, technically, the study of last things but is commonly expanded to include other subjects. I prefer the broader term "prophecy" which includes eschatology proper.

9 Sherman E. Johnson, "The Gospel According to St. Matthew," in *The Interpreter's Bible*, ed. George Arthur Buttrick (Nashville: Abingdon, 1951), 7:457 (emphasis added).

10 Johnson, "Matthew," 7:551.

11 Edwin D. Freed, *The New Testament: A Critical Introduction* (Belmont, CA: Wadsworth, 1986), 82 (emphasis added). Conservative writers sometimes say the apostles imbibed Jesus' error: "Paul believed Jesus would return soon, and history would come to an end." [Thomas R. Schreiner, *Spiritual Gifts: What They Are & Why They Matter* (Nashville: Broadman & Holman, 2018), 150.] Such statements compromise the doctrine of the inerrancy of Scripture.

12 Samuel Lee, *Eschatology; or, the Scripture Doctrine of the Coming of the Lord, the Judgment, and the Resurrection* (Boston: J. E. Tilton, 1859), 55.

13 Lee, *Eschatology*, 55.

14 Lee, *Eschatology*, 60 (emphasis in original).

15 Lee, *Eschatology*, 61 (emphasis in original).

16 These quotes are from Lee, *Eschatology*, 69–70 (emphasis in original).

17 Jesus had preached the same message earlier (e.g., Matt 24:1–3; John 4:21–24).

18 A recent work by a dispensational premillennialist asserts that a "telescoping phenomena" is common in the prophets and is a key concept in determining their meaning. No defense for this statement is given other than a reference to two prophecies where "telescoping" is necessary *if* the interpretive system itself is correct. This is a classic example of circular reasoning. See Paul N. Benware,

Understanding End Times Prophecy: A Comprehensive Approach (Chicago: Moody, 2006), 29–30.

19 For a brief history of dispensationalism, see William E. Cox, *An Examination of Dispensationalism* (Phillipsburg, NJ: Presbyterian and Reformed, 1963), 1–16.

20 Thomas Ice, "The Destructive View of Preterism" (paper presented at The 2nd Annual Meeting of the Conservative Theological Society, Ft. Worth, TX, August 3, 1999)

21 George E. Ladd, *Crucial Questions About the Kingdom of God* (Grand Rapids: Eerdmans, 1954), 48.

22 As documented by Kenneth L. Gentry, Jr., *He Shall Have Dominion: A Postmillennial Eschatology*, 2nd ed. (Tyler, TX: Institute for Christian Economics, 1992), 3.

23 Robert L. Reymond, *A New Systematic Theology of the Christian Faith* (Nashville: Thomas Nelson, 1998), 986.

24 C. H. Dodd, *The Apostolic Preaching and Its Developments*, 2nd ed. (New York: Harper & Brothers, 1954), 85.

25 Reymond, *Systematic Theology*, 1035–36.

26 Henry Alford, *Alford's Greek Testament: An Exegetical and Critical Commentary*, 4 vols. (Grand Rapids: Baker, 1980), 1:257 (emphasis added).

27 This is a primary target audience for this book!

CHAPTER THREE

Discovering a Better Model

RECOGNIZING THE DEFICIENCIES of the existing prophetic models is easy; offering a better one is not. Copernicus needed minor work to decry the errors in the Ptolemaic model, but he had to devote an enormous part of his life to documenting and defending a better system.

This chapter will show my strategy for discovering a better prophetic model. "Discover," I say, not "build" or some other construction term. The reason is that, like Copernicus, I want to find the best way to describe something that already exists. He did not create a model of the solar system; he discovered the model God used at creation. My effort is analogous to his: I want to find the prophetic model the Holy Spirit used as he inspired the Scriptures. I do not want to build one myself.

If my goal is to discover the prophetic model God has embedded in his Word, it seems wise to begin by examining a strategic passage in that Word. By strategic I mean one that contains many prophetic elements, and that has the potential to reveal a basic prophetic framework.

Most authors who write about the existing prophetic systems follow a different script. They typically begin with some combination of the following elements: a discussion of interpretive principles and methods; an analysis of the history of prophetic interpretation; critiques of other systems; the author's explanation of his prophetic model; etc. After this, the writer uses his model to interpret selected biblical passages. This method runs the danger of creating an interpretive mold and then casting Scripture into it.[1] A better approach is to let the Scriptures govern the discovery of a prophetic model, not make them submit to one that is already established.

The Beginning Point

The approach I am taking—going to Scripture first—places tremendous importance on selecting the starting passage. I will use four criteria for making that selection: (1) the initial passage should be in the New Testament; (2) it should contain a minimum amount of figurative language; (3) it should be lengthy; and (4) it should influence the rest of the New Testament. The following paragraphs will justify these criteria and use them to suggest the optimum starting place.

In the New Testament. The search for a new prophetic model should begin in the New Testament rather than the Old. The apostles lend credence to this criterion: Paul says the prophetic mystery "in other ages was not made known unto the sons of men, as it is now revealed unto his holy apostles and prophets by the Spirit" (Eph 3:5); Peter says the Old Testament prophets were

> Searching what, or what manner of time the Spirit of Christ which was in them did signify, when it testified beforehand the sufferings of Christ, and the glory that should follow. Unto whom it was revealed, that not unto themselves, but unto us they did minister the things, which are now reported unto you by them that have preached the gospel unto you with the Holy Ghost sent down from heaven; which things the angels desire to look into. (1 Pet 1:10–12)

The apostles were uniquely qualified to interpret the prophets' writings. Their Jewish background made them familiar with those writings; Jesus' teaching revealed their meaning. Luke says, "Beginning at Moses and all the prophets, he [Jesus] expounded unto them in all the scriptures the things concerning himself.... Then opened he their understanding, that they might understand the scriptures.... [He said] ye are witnesses of these things" (Luke 24:27, 45, 48).

After Jesus taught the apostles how to interpret the prophets, God gave the Holy Spirit to them to ensure they would transmit their knowledge to the church. The Spirit led them into all truth (John 16:13) and enabled them to speak "none other things than those which the prophets and Moses did say should come" (Acts 26:22). In this way, the apostles bequeathed a canon of writings (the New Testament) to the church that explains Old Testament prophecies. In it, they "declared fulfillments; they defined terms; they made new and important revelations; they left many examples of interpretive technique; they dealt thoroughly with the fundamental covenants ... and they discuss the future with satisfying fullness."[2]

God authorized the New Testament writers to not only complete but also interpret the Old Testament sacred predictions.[3] Therefore, their writings provide the only firm basis for understanding prophecy. George Eldon Ladd says, "The Old Testament prophets must be interpreted in light of their fulfillment in the person and mission of Jesus.... The final word in doctrine, whether in Christology or eschatology, must be found in the New Testament."[4] A famous saying attributed to Augustine summarizes this point: "The new is in the old concealed; the old is in the new revealed."

In one sense, the Bible is a drama in which there is a "developing Plot, the unfolding of an end which is not discernible from the beginning."[5] Peter W. L. Walker says, "Biblical theology requires that the Old Testament material be interpreted through the prism of the New."[6] The New Testament is the best place to look for a better prophetic model.

Minimal Figurative Language. The beginning passage should contain a minimum amount of figurative language. Figures of speech can convey truth in powerful and interesting ways. Scripture contains many of these linguistic devices; the Holy Spirit takes pleasure in their use. But the Bible also shows the inherent challenges figurative language can present. A few examples will illustrate this point.

Jesus once used a *parable* (a common figure of speech) to illustrate his point about soon-coming judgment (John 9:39). But the Pharisees "understood not what things they were which he spake unto them" (John 10:6). On another occasion, the Lord told his disciples the reason he spoke in parables: "Unto you it is given to know the mystery of the kingdom of God: but unto them that are without, all these things are done in parables: that seeing they may see, and not perceive; and hearing they may hear, and not understand; lest at any time they should be converted, and their sins should be forgiven them" (Mark 4:11–12).

Jesus told his disciples that a time would come when he would "no longer speak … in figures of speech." This promise caused them to exclaim, "Ah, now you are speaking plainly and not using figurative speech!" (John 16:25, 29 ESV).

Figurative language challenges both sinner and saint, so prophetic passages with sizeable amounts of it are not suitable places to search for a better prophetic model. Better to recognize a basic interpretive guideline: "Scripture interprets Scripture (or, 'obscure passages in Scripture must give way to clear passages')."[7]

This rule suggests the book of Revelation is not the best place to start. There, God *signified* his message through "various emblems, signs, and visions, represented and set before John."[8] These figures of speech "take more reflection and imagination to interpret than strict grammatical interpretation."[9] This need for imagination often causes commentators to reach contradictory opinions of Revelation's symbols: one scholar, for example, thinks the rider on a white horse in Revelation 6:2 "symbolizes the proclamation of the gospel of Christ in all the world";[10] another says "the conqueror mentioned here is the future world ruler, sometimes referred to as Antichrist."[11] The large number of such symbols in Revelation makes its underlying prophetic model difficult to see; so we need to start our search in a passage with fewer of them.

Lengthy. The new prophetic model should come from a lengthy prophetic passage. Revelation is the longest New Testament prophetic passage, but, as we have seen, its figurative language militates against it. John MacArthur mentions another possibility:

> Other than the book of Revelation, the largest and most important prophetic portion of the New Testament is Matthew 24–25, known as the Olivet Discourse. It is the second-longest message of Christ recorded in scripture ... the longest answer He ever gave to any question recorded in the New Testament.[12]

The other two synoptic gospels also contain accounts of Jesus' Olivet Discourse (Mark 13:1–37 and Luke 21:5–36). Writers refer to this speech as "Christ's Eschatological Discourse" or as his "Discourse on Last Things." Milton Terry calls it the "Apocalypse of the Gospel."[13] It "is Jesus' longest, most important and detailed discussion of eschatology."[14] These characteristics commend this passage as a starting point for discerning a new prophetic model.

The Olivet Discourse also satisfies the second criterion. It is a straightforward dialog between Christ and his disciples that uses little figurative language. As a bonus, "There is not a single figure employed whose use has not been already sanctioned and its meaning determined in the Old Testament."[15]

Influential. The starting point for seeking a better prophetic model should be a passage that influences other New Testament prophetic passages. This test also recommends the Olivet Discourse; it contains subject matter the apostles subsequently placed in their writings. In this Discourse, Jesus answered the disciples' question about the end of the age (Matt 24:3); the apostles later wrote about this subject (e.g., 1 Cor 10:11; Heb 9:26). The Discourse lists the signs that would transpire before the end of the age (e.g., Matt 24:14, 24); the apostles followed suit (e.g., 1 John 2:18). Jesus described a period of intense trials associated with the age-ending events (Matt 24:21); the apostles followed his lead (e.g., 1 Tim 2:16).

This pattern caused Milton Terry to say the apostles based their prophetic doctrine squarely on Jesus' emphatic statements in the Olivet Discourse.[16] D. A. Carson agrees: "The discourse itself is undoubtedly a source for the Thessalonian Epistles and Revelation.... If so then we may say that Jesus himself sets the pattern for the church's eschatology."[17] Henry Alford agreed with Isaac Williams who called the Olivet Discourse "the anchor of apocalyptic interpretation"; he then added his own opinion that it is "the touchstone of apocalyptic systems."[18] Donald A. Hagner applies this principle to a specific passage: "So too in 2 Thess. 2:4 Paul depends on the prophecy of Jesus [in the Olivet Discourse], employing the same Danielic symbol, when he refers to the antichrist to come."[19] The Olivet Discourse is the fountain from which many other New Testament prophecies flow.

Conclusion. These four principles—preferences for the New Testament, for non-figurative language, for a longer passage, and for a passage with significant influence—show that the Olivet Discourse is the best passage in which to look for a better prophetic model. I have provided the full text of the three accounts of the Olivet Discourse in Appendices B, C, and D.

A New Name

This is a somewhat awkward place to introduce the name for the new prophetic model; its major characteristics, which determine that name, are not yet on the drawing table. But without a name, I am restricted to using terms like "the prophetic model," "my framework," etc. This makes the discussion too vague; I need a specific and descriptive name to clarify the abstract and general terms I have used to this point.

What does one do when no suitable name is available? Invent one! Here, the invention does not require a tremendous amount of creativity. The name of the new model should simultaneously identify it with the other prophetic systems and also distinguish it from them.

As I mentioned earlier, the other prophetic models create their names by attaching a Latin prefix to the base word *millennial*: *pre*millennial, *post*millennial, and *a*millennial. Following this pattern will link the alternative model to the pre-existing ones: it will be a form of "millennialism," but what is the best Latin prefix?

A unique characteristic of the new model is its proclivity to translate the Greek word *parousia* as "presence." It says Christians now live in the *parousia* (i.e., presence) of Christ.[20] The preposition "in" has the same meaning in English and Latin. Making this word a prefix to the base word (*millennial*) yields the term *in*millennial; so the name of the new model becomes *inmillennialism*. This name achieves both my objectives: it links the new model to the existing systems but also distinguishes it from them.

Notes

1 I'm not accusing previous writers of insufficient biblical commitment; I am suggesting methodological improvements are possible.
2 Russell Bradley Jones, *The Latter Days* (1947; repr., Grand Rapids: Baker, 1961), 23–24.
3 Jones, *The Latter Days*, 21.
4 Ladd, *The Last Things*, 18.
5 W. Graham Scroggie, *The Unfolding Drama of Redemption: The Bible as a Whole* (Grand Rapids: Zondervan, 1976), 33.
6 Peter W. L. Walker, *Jesus and the Holy City: New Testament Perspectives on Jerusalem* (Grand Rapids/Cambridge: William B. Eerdmans, 1996), 309.
7 Bernard Ramm, *Protestant Biblical Interpretation: A Textbook of Hermeneutics*, 3rd ed. (Grand Rapids: Baker, 1970), 104.
8 John Gill, *An Exposition of the Old and New Testaments*, 9 vols. (1809–10; repr., Paris, AR: The Baptist Standard Bearer, 1989), 9:683 (commentary on Rev 1:1).
9 Ramm, *Protestant Biblical Interpretation*, 143–44.
10 George Eldon Ladd, *A Commentary on the Revelation of John* (Grand Rapids: Eerdmans, 1974), 99.
11 John F. Walvoord, "Revelation," in *The Bible Knowledge Commentary: An Exposition of the Scriptures*, eds. J. F. Walvoord and R. B. Zuck (Wheaton, IL: Victor, 1985), 2:947.
12 John MacArthur, *The Second Coming: Signs of Christ's Return and the End of the Age* (Wheaton, IL: Crossway Books, 1999), 69–70.
13 Milton S. Terry, *Biblical Apocalyptics: A Study of the Most Notable Revelations of God and of Christ* (1898; repr., Grand Rapids: Baker, 1988), 213.
14 Jonathan Menn, *Biblical Eschatology* (Eugene, OR: Resource Publications, 2013), 94.
15 J. Marcellus Kik, *An Eschatology of Victory* (Nutley, NJ: Presbyterian and Reformed, 1975), 156.
16 Milton S. Terry, *Biblical Hermeneutics: A Treatise on the Interpretation of the Old and New Testaments*, 2nd ed. (n.d.; repr., Grand Rapids: Academie Books, n.d.), 457.
17 D. A. Carson, "Matthew," in *Matthew, Mark, Luke*, vol. 8 of *The Expositor's Bible Commentary*, ed. Frank E. Gaebelein (Grand Rapids: Zondervan, 1984), 489.
18 Henry Alford, *The Epistle to the Hebrews, the Catholic Epistles, and the Revelation*, vol. 2.2 of *The New Testament for English Readers* (London: Rivingtons, 1866), 352.
19 Donald A. Hagner, *Matthew 14–28*, Word Biblical Commentary, ed. Bruce M. Metzger (Dallas: Word, 1998), 700.
20 The following chapters will provide support for this assertion.

CHAPTER FOUR

The Prophecy

WE ARE NOW READY to look for a better prophetic model in the Olivet Discourse. Each synoptic gospel—Matthew, Mark, and Luke—contains the following elements: (1) Jesus' prophecy of the temple's destruction; (2) the disciples' two questions about that prophecy; and (3) Jesus' response to their questions. I will use Matthew's account as the basis for our study of the Olivet Discourse because of four of its unique characteristics: it alone (1) uses the Greek word *parousia* regarding the "coming" of Christ; (2) refers to the "end of the age"; (3) contains certain parables; and (4) mentions the sheep and goats judgment. Each of these will enhance the prophetic model we seek. I will use the accounts in Mark and Luke to emphasize and enhance our discoveries in Matthew. (Please see Appendices B, C, and D for the full texts.)

The following outline summarizes the Olivet Discourse:[1]

I. Jesus prediction of the temple's destruction (Matt 24:1-2)

II. The disciples' two questions regarding *when* and the *sign* (Matt 24:3)

III. Jesus' response to the *sign* question (Matt 24:4–31)

    A. Phase 1: preliminary signs (Matt 24:4–14)—the beginning of birth pains (v. 8)

    B. Phase 2: later sign (Matt 24:15–26)—the period of "the end" (v. 14)

  C. Phase 3: immediate signs (Matt 24:27–31)—the end itself (v. 29)

IV. Jesus' response to the *when* question (Matt 24:32–36)

V. Jesus' exhortations to watchfulness (Matt 24:37–25:46)

This outline will serve two purposes. First, it will provide a tracking mechanism; as we work through the Olivet Discourse, I will occasionally insert it into my comments and highlight the current topic in bold text. Second, repeating the outline will emphasize the unity of the Olivet Discourse, counterbalancing the temptation to slice it into pieces that deal with different subjects. Succumbing to this temptation has caused many prophecy students to misunderstand the prophetic framework Jesus is using. I want to avoid this mistake.

An often-overlooked characteristic of the Olivet Discourse also highlights its cohesiveness: it is a chiasm. A *"chiasm* (or chiasmus) is [a] common structural device in which the word order of a parallel line is the reverse of its predecessor *(a b / b' a*). A line drawn between the parallel elements would form an X—the Greek letter *chi* from which the device draws its name."[2] Many English-language readers are familiar with parallelism, a literary technique that places thoughts in a pattern like A-A', B-B', C-C'. Here is a simple example that shows the two parallel thoughts in Isaiah 1:10:

 A. Hear the word of the LORD, ye rulers of Sodom;

 A'. Give ear unto the law of our God, ye people of Gomorrah.

A chiasm presents thoughts in a pattern like A-B-C-C'-B'-A'.[3] Matthew's use of a chiastic structure is not surprising; there "are chiastic structures that underlie entire passages and even entire books," and it "was a common literary technique in the ancient Near East."[4] We can show Matthew's account of the Olivet Discourse as an extended chiasm:[5]

 A. *Exhortation*: observe!—the temple will fall (Matt 24:1–2)

  B. *When question*: what will be the time? (Matt 24:3a)

   C. *Sign question*: what will be the sign? (Matt 24:3b)

   C'. *Sign answer*: the signs of associated events, symbols (Matt 24:4–31)

B'. *When answer: this* is the time (Matt 24:32–36)

A'. *Exhortation*: observe! (Matt 24:37–25:46); watch! (Matt 24:42, 43; 25:13)

The chiastic correspondences of parts—A to A', B to B', etc.—function like powerful bands to hold the Olivet Discourse together. We must allow this unity to control our efforts to discover a prophetic model unless we find compelling reasons to rupture it. To underscore the importance of this observation, I will list it as our first Key Point:[6]

KEY POINT #1

The Olivet Discourse is a unit; a single subject controls it from beginning to end. This fact governs our interpretation of it.

Jesus initiated the Olivet Discourse by predicting the temple's destruction. The accounts in Matthew, Mark, and Luke are similar:

> And Jesus went out, and departed from the temple: and his disciples came to him for to shew him the buildings of the temple. And Jesus said unto them, See ye not all these things? verily I say unto you, There shall not be left here one stone upon another, that shall not be thrown down. (Matt 24:1–2)

> And as he went out of the temple, one of his disciples saith unto him, Master, see what manner of stones and what buildings are here! And Jesus answering said unto him, Seest thou these great buildings? there shall not be left one stone upon another, that shall not be thrown down. (Mark 13:1–2)

> And as some spake of the temple, how it was adorned with goodly stones and gifts, he said, As for these things which ye behold, the days will come, in the

which there shall not be left one stone upon another, that shall not be thrown down. (Luke 21:5–6)

Before ascending the Mount of Olives, Jesus had often rebuked Israel for her unfaithfulness to God's covenant. These utterances formed a major part of Jesus' teachings; he uttered over thirty such threats of judgment. His prophecy of the temple's collapse—given on Tuesday of Passion Week in AD 30[7]—was the last in his series of woes against the apostate nation. N. T. Wright makes the following observation about it:

> In the sad, noble, and utterly Jewish tradition of Elijah, Jeremiah and John the Baptist, Jesus announced the coming judgment of Israel's covenant god on his people, a judgment consisting of a great national, social and natural disaster comprehensible only in theological terms.[8]

This prophecy of the temple's destruction is the subject of the Olivet Discourse. The following principles emphasize the importance of this fact:

> The interpreter is always bound to consider how the subject lay in the mind of the author, and to point out the exact ideas and sentiments intended.... The real meaning intended by the author, and that only, is to be set forth.[9]

> [The] theme of the immediate context regulates the meaning of the individual words, phrases, clauses, and sentences within the specific passage under study.[10]

The temple's destruction is the subject in Jesus' mind; it is the theme that gives meaning to what he says in the Olivet Discourse. I will have several occasions to consider whether Jesus or the disciples interject another subject into their discussion; for now, I will consider this to be the only theme.

My engineering background engendered a love for diagrams; they can encapsulate an author's points.[11] I will here begin developing one for inmillennialism similar to those I provided above for the existing prophetic models. The initial diagram is simple, showing only Jesus' prophecy about the temple:

Figure 4-1. The Subject of the Olivet Discourse

The rest of the Olivet Discourse will increase the number of elements in the diagram; another passage outside the Olivet Discourse will then furnish the parts necessary to depict the complete inmillennial model. This approach will allow you to see the various parts of the prophetic model as they appear.

KEY POINT #2

The subject of the Olivet Discourse is Jesus' prophecy of the temple's destruction and matters related to that event.

In the next three chapters, I will examine the two questions the disciples asked in response to this prophecy.

Notes

1 The divisions shown here generally follow the pericopes found in *The Holy Bible: English Standard Version* (Wheaton: Standard Bible Society, 2016).

2 William W. Klein, Craig L. Blomberg, and Robert L. Hubbard Jr., *Introduction to Biblical Interpretation*, ed. Kermit A. Ecklebarger (Dallas: Word, 1993), 237.

3 James B. Jordan, *Through New Eyes: Developing a Biblical View of the World* (Brentwood, TN: Wolgemuth & Hyatt, 1988), 55.

4 Klein, Blomberg, and Hubbard Jr., *Introduction to Biblical Interpretation*, 237–38, 238n75.

5 I am indebted to Matt Carpenter, a former fellow-pastor, for drawing my attention to this arrangement.

6 Appendix A contains a list of these Key Points.

7 A. T. Robertson, *A Harmony of the Gospels for Students of the Life of Christ* (New York: Harper, 1922), 173.

8 N. T. Wright, *Jesus and the Victory of God*, vol. 2 of *Christian Origins and the Question of God* (Minneapolis: Fortress Press, 1996), 185.

9 Terry, *Biblical Hermeneutics*, 596.

10 Klein, Blomberg, and Hubbard Jr., *Introduction to Biblical Interpretation*, 163.

11 Clarence Larkin put many elaborate diagrams in his book *Dispensational Truth*; he, too, was an engineer.

CHAPTER FIVE

The Two Questions: Similarities

THE LORD'S announcement of the temple's coming destruction provoked two questions from the apostles, one related to the *time*[1] of its fulfillment and the other to its *sign*. The bold print in our outline shows their place in Matthew's Olivet Discourse:

I. Jesus' prediction of the temple's destruction (Matt 24:1–2)

II. The disciples' two questions: regarding *when* and the *sign* (Matt 24:3)

III. Jesus' response to the *sign* question (Matt 24:4–31)

    A. Phase 1: preliminary signs (Matt 24:4–14)—the beginning of birth pains (v. 8)

    B. Phase 2: later sign (Matt 24:15–26)—the period of "the end" (v. 14)

    C. Phase 3: immediate signs (Matt 24:27–31)—the end itself (v. 29)

IV. Jesus' response to the *when* question (Matt 24:32–36)

V. Jesus' exhortations to watchfulness (Matt 24:37–25:46)

Here are the two questions as they occur in the synoptic gospels:

> And as he sat upon the mount of Olives, the disciples came unto him privately, saying, Tell us, *when* shall these things be? and what shall be the *sign* of thy coming, and of the end of the world? (Matt 24:3)

> And as he sat upon the mount of Olives over against the temple, Peter and James and John and Andrew asked him privately, Tell us, *when* shall these things be? and what shall be the *sign* when all these things shall be fulfilled? (Mark 13:3–4)

> And they asked him, saying, Master, but *when* shall these things be? and what *sign* will there be when these things shall come to pass? (Luke 21:7)

These questions reflect the disciples' deep interest in Jesus' prediction; they had never known life without the temple. Throughout the Olivet Discourse, Jesus clarifies his prophecy and encourages his disciples to remain faithful as the catastrophe would draw near.

The When Question: Similarities

I will now separate the questions and discuss the similarities between the three gospel accounts. In the next two chapters, I will review the differences related to the sign question in Matthew's account.

The disciples' first question was about time:

When shall these things be? (Matt 24:3)

When shall these things be? (Mark 13:4)

When shall these things be? (Luke 21:7)

This question relates solely to the subject introduced by the Lord's prophecy; the words "these things" refer to the circumstances and events surrounding the temple's destruction. The disciples did not ask about the end of the church age, the climax of history, the collapse of the physical universe, or anything else; they wanted to know when the temple would fall.

KEY POINT #3

The disciples ask two questions; their when question relates to the subject of the Olivet Discourse—the temple's destruction and matters related to that event.

The Sign Question Similarities: Mark and Luke

Let us now turn our attention to the disciples' *sign* question. Matthew's version of it diverges from the other two, so I will consider it in the following sections. Here is the *sign* question as it appears in Mark and Luke:

> What shall be the *sign* when all these things shall be fulfilled? (Mark 13:4)

> What *sign* will there be when these things shall come to pass? (Luke 21:7)

Mark and Luke make the subject of the disciples' *sign* question identical to the subject of their *when* question: their term "these things" relates to the temple's destruction. These verses in the original Greek contain a word that highlights this point, a word translated in only a few versions, including the following ones:

> Peter, and James, and John, and Andrew, were questioning him by himself, "Tell us when these things shall be? and what is the sign when all these may be *about to be fulfilled* (Gk. *mellō*[2])?" (Mark 13:3–4 YLT)

> So they asked Him, saying, "Teacher, but when will these things be? And what sign will there be when these things *are about to take place* (Gk. *mellō*)?" (Luke 21:7 NKJV)

The Greek word *mellō* means "*to be about* to do anything."[3] It shows that the disciples expected the temple's fall to occur soon after whatever sign Jesus might give them. They were not asking for—and Jesus did not give—a sign separated from the temple's destruction by a lengthy period.

We can add this to our growing list of interpretive guidelines that should govern our interpretation of the Olivet Discourse:

KEY POINT #4

The disciples' sign question relates to the subject of the Olivet Discourse—the temple's destruction and matters related to that event.

Conclusion

The Holy Spirit inspired three accounts of the disciples' two questions, producing six combinations in all. To this point, we have seen that five combinations—the *when* question in all three synoptic gospels plus the *sign* question in Mark and Luke—are almost identical; they all relate to the temple's destruction. The significance of this agreement will soon become obvious.

Notes

1 I will hereafter use "time question" and "when question" as equivalents.
2 Most Bible versions leave this important Greek verb untranslated in prophetic contexts.
3 Joseph Thayer and James Strong, *Thayer's Greek-English Lexicon of the New Testament: Coded With Strong's Concordance Numbers* (Milford, MI: Mott Media, 1982), 396.

CHAPTER SIX

The Sign Question in Matthew: The End of the Age

MATTHEW'S TENDENCY to provide more details for the Olivet Discourse than Mark or Luke first shows itself in the disciples' *sign* question. They present a single query:

> What shall be the *sign* when all these things shall be fulfilled? (Mark 13:4)
>
> What *sign* will there be when these things shall come to pass? (Luke 21:7)

But he divides it into two parts:

> What will be the *sign* of Your coming (Gk. *parousia*), and
> of the end of the age (Gk. *aiōn*)? (Matt 24:3 NKJV)

Matthew replaces "these things" with "Your coming" and "the end of the age."

The previous Key Points suggest "these things"—the events surrounding the temple's fall—relate in some organic way to Jesus' coming and the end of the age. The temple's demise is the subject in all three records of the disciples' *when* question and in two accounts of their *sign* question. There is no obvious reason in the Olivet Discourse to this point (i.e., Matt 24:1–3) to think this is not the subject in Matthew's account of the *sign* question, too. Without such reasons, I will assume the three synoptic writers are reporting the same *sign* question, but that Matthew is reporting a more detailed version of it than Mark or Luke. The following diagram shows this relationship:

```
Jesus' Parousia +                           "These Things" About the
The End of the Age      ◄──────────►        Temple's Destruction
    (Per Matthew)                              (Per Mark & Luke)
```

Figure 6-1. The Sign Question – Matthew vs. Mark & Luke

Most commentators reject this straightforward connection. D. A. Carson, for example, says, "'The end of the age' ... look[s] to final judgment and the consummation of all things.... [And] *parousia* is closely tied with ... the end of human history."[1] Writers make such statements because their prophetic models force them to do so. Their models cause them to interpret the phenomena a certain way; they *think* they see *pro*grade movement in which the disciples' *when* question suddenly jumps forward into the distant future. This is the theological inverse of the *retro*grade movement Ptolemaic astronomers thought they saw when planets seemed to move backwards.

This erroneous perception causes important (and unnecessary) questions to arise: Why does this prograde movement happen in Matthew but not in Mark and Luke? Why does Jesus, in his responses, seem to bounce between the temple's fall and the end of history? Like their astronomical counterparts, commentators invent creative ways to answer questions of this sort. This is a futile exercise; the prophetic elements in the Olivet Discourse are not behaving like the commentators think. A better prophetic model will show their true motion, eliminating the perceived problems and the need for creative devices to solve them. In short, faulty prophetic models generate erroneous assumptions about the *sign* question in Matthew—*that* is the problem.

In Chapter 2 regarding the benefits of a better model, I showed how atheists and some Christians charge Jesus and the apostles with error regarding prophecy. Bad assumptions about the disciples' *sign* question in Matthew open the door for such charges. John MacArthur, for example, says the disciples asked their *sign* question out of confusion: "The destruction of the temple made no sense at all to the disciples."[2] Other writers extrapolate this point of view; they say the disciples never recovered from their confusion and continued to mingle end-of-history prophecies with events in their immediate future.

Quite the contrary, the disciples knew what Jesus' prophecy meant and understood the theological ramifications of it. I will attempt to sustain my contrarian view by presenting the prophetic equivalent to Copernicus' explanation of retrograde motion: a simple explanation of the disciples' *sign* question in Matthew that accounts for its unique form. My proposal (in this chapter and the next) will reveal several important components of the improved prophetic model we seek; it will also reveal part of the reason for the subtitle of this book. I will begin with the second part of the *sign* question in Matthew: why did the disciples equate the temple's fall to "the end of the age?"

The End of an Age

To clear the disciples from the charge of confusion, I will first stress that they asked about the end of an *age*: "What will be the sign ... of the end of the age (Gk. *aiōn*)? (Matt 24:3 NKJV). The Greek word *aiōn* means "a segment of time as a particular unit of history,"[3] or something similar. The disciples were not asking about the end of the cosmos (Gk. *kosmos*), the reality John describes when he says, "the world (Gk. *kosmos*) was made by [Jesus]" (John 1:10).

Some English translations—including our beloved Authorized Version—create confusion about this difference by translating both *kosmos* and *aiōn* as "world." The distinction between these words is not absolute—the ideas they represent can overlap—but the general distinction between them is important, for, as Richard C. Trench says, "In all those passages which speak of the end ... *there are none which speak of the end of the kosmos.*"[4] Those passages are speaking about the end of an *age*.

A popular Mayan prophecy illustrates the necessity of maintaining this distinction. The prophecy foretold the end of the "world" on December 21, 2012. Many people understood this to be a prediction about the destruction of the *physical* world—the *kosmos*. As the specified date approached, well-informed people attempted to clarify its meaning: the prophecy was about the end of *a period*—an *aiōn*. Here is one explanation:

> Is 2012 going to be the "End of The World?" No, not in terms of the complete destruction of the Earth and some kind of annihilation scenario. 2012 is not bringing the end of the planet. When we contemplate the expression "end of the world" let us realize the term "world" can refer to a cycle; a period of time; a world age era. Therefore 2012 is signaling the completion of one World Age Cycle, transiting into an emerging New World Age to come.[5]

I am not suggesting this pagan prophecy was accurate; I cite it to emphasize the importance of distinguishing between the Greek words *kosmos* and *aiōn*. We cannot understand the disciples' sign question in Matthew 24:3 and Jesus' response to it without recognizing the differences between them.

It is sometimes difficult to keep this distinction in mind because prophets often speak about *age* transitions in cataclysmic terms—as if they were talking about the end of the *physical* creation. This is true across a broad spectrum of ancient cultures and beliefs, including the prophets in Israel. Jesus also did this in the Olivet Discourse, as we will see below. We should not mistake prophetic images of the end of an age for prophecies about the end of creation.

The disciples' *sign* question in Matthew relates to the end of a specific *age*, not to the end of the physical universe.

The Two-Age Framework

From ancient times, the Jews thought within a two-age framework that defined all history. Recognition of this perspective is fundamental to the correct interpretation of the New Testament. Geerhardus Vos says:

> In New Testament eschatological[6] teaching a general development in a well-defined direction is traceable. The starting-point is the historico-dramatic conception of the two successive ages. These two ages are distinguished as … "this age," "the present age" … and … "that age," "the future age".… To each age belongs its own characteristic order of things.[7]

According to Kim Riddlebarger, "These two eschatological ages can … be seen as the basic eschatological framework taught by both Jesus and Paul."[8]

The disciples had heard Jesus teach from this two-age framework: "Anyone who speaks a word against the Son of Man, it will be forgiven him; but whoever speaks against the Holy Spirit, it will not be forgiven him, either in *this age* or in *the age to come*" (Matt 12:32 NKJV). They knew he meant forgiveness for this sin would not come in either segment of Jewish history; it would *never* be forgiven.[9]

Another disciple, the apostle Paul, later spoke from this perspective. He said God had exalted Jesus above "every name that is constantly being named, not only in *this age*, but also in *the one about to come* (Gk. *mellō*)."[10] The apostle meant God had exalted Jesus above all others for all time.

For the disciples, these two ages comprised all history.

Which Age?

To which of the two ages were the disciples referring when they asked about "the end of the age" in Matthew 24:3? Milton Terry helps answer this question: "The period which preceded the coming of the Messiah was spoken of as *this age*; that which followed his coming was *the age to come*."[11] John Gill provides additional insights in his comments on Habakkuk: "At the end of the Jewish state, both civil and ecclesiastic, the Messiah should appear, as he did, which is called the end of the world … when a new world began, the world to come, the Gospel dispensation."[12] Gill uses "world" to mean "age," but his point is clear: the prophets taught that the end of "this age"—speaking from the disciples' perspective—would occur when the Messiah appeared. The disciples believed the prophets; they also believed Jesus was the Messiah of whom the prophets had spoken. Peter spoke for them when he said to Jesus, "You are the Messiah!" (Matt 16:16 HCSB). So, they were not confused when they asked about "the end of the age"; they meant "the end of the Jewish state."

I will use the term "Mosaic age" to mean "the period which preceded the coming of the Messiah" (Terry) and "the Jewish state" (Gill). This is consistent with the theological literature where it designates the period from Israel's Exodus from Egypt under Moses to the coming of Christ.[13] The disciples thought of themselves as living in the Mosaic age; they framed their questions about the temple's fall from this perspective. John Lightfoot is correct when he says, "the end of the age" in Matthew 24:3 means *"the end of the Jewish age, or world"*;[14] the disciples meant the end of the Mosaic age.

KEY POINT #5

Matthew recorded the disciples' sign question in the Olivet Discourse within a framework of age transition: the Mosaic age was giving way to the messianic age.

The Temple as Symbol

The disciples had an excellent reason to connect the temple's destruction to the end of the Mosaic age: the temple and its system of sacrifices was the ultimate symbol of that age. As N. T. Wright says,

> The temple ... formed in principle the heart of Judaism, in the full metaphorical sense: it was the organ from which there went out to the body of Judaism, in Palestine and in the Diaspora, the living and healing presence of the covenant God. The temple was thus also, equally importantly, the focal point of the

Land which the covenant God had promised to give to his people.[15]

For the disciples, the temple was "the central institution of Judaism, the living and breathing embodiment of the divine presence.... [It] was the singular point on which Israel fixed its national hopes and from which it derived its national identity. The temple was the balance on which Israel's fortunes hung."[16] When the disciples heard Jesus say the temple would fall, they knew that the age it symbolized—the Mosaic age—would simultaneously end. This accounts for the form of their *sign* question in Matthew: Is the temple going to fall? Then what will be the *sign* of the end of the Mosaic age for which it stands? (cp. Matt 24:3).

The New Testament provides evidence that supports this explanation. After Jesus' resurrection, the disciples stood in the temple and taught the people (Acts 5:25, 42). The Jewish leaders charged Stephen with speaking "blasphemous words against Moses, and against God ... against *this holy place* [i.e., the temple], and the law ... that this Jesus of Nazareth shall destroy *this place*, and shall change *the customs which Moses delivered us*" (Acts 6:11, 13–14). For Stephen and other first-century Jews, the temple's destruction implied the destruction of the entire Mosaic order; the temple's fall meant the end of the Mosaic age during which that order prevailed.

This understanding creates a perfect harmony in all three synoptic accounts of the disciples' *sign* question in the Olivet Discourse: Mark and Luke make it relate to the "these things" regarding the temple's destruction; Matthew makes it relate to the end of the Mosaic age for which the temple stood. There is no reason to make the disciples' question relate to the end of history, the destruction of the physical cosmos, or any other subject.

Conclusion

When Jesus foretold the temple's fall, the disciples knew they were living in the "last days" of the Mosaic age. They wanted to know *when* that would occur—how long did they have?—and the *sign* that it would happen. Understanding Matthew's record of their questions this way allows me to update our developing prophetic model:

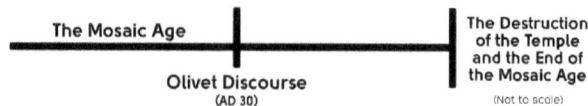

Figure 6-2. Inmillennialism through the End of the Mosaic Age

This diagram does not depict the time that would elapse between the Olivet Discourse and the end of the Mosaic age; that would be to anticipate Jesus' answer to the disciples' *when* question. It aims to show the understood causal relationship between the temple's fall and the end of the age embedded in the disciples' *sign* question.

KEY POINT #6

In Matthew's account of the sign question, "the end of the age (Gk. aiōn*)" means the end of the Mosaic age that would come when the temple fell.*

The proposition that the temple's destruction would end the Mosaic age seems intuitive enough, but what about the other part of the *sign* question in Matthew? How does the temple's fall relate to the coming of Christ?

Notes

1 Carson, "Matthew," 497.
2 MacArthur, *The Second Coming*, 76.
3 Frederick W. Danker et al., eds., *Greek-English Lexicon of the New Testament and Other Early Christian Literature*, 3rd ed. (Chicago: University of Chicago Press, 2000), 32.
4 Richard Chenevix Trench, *Synonyms of the New Testament* (Grand Rapids: Eerdmans, 1953), 214 (emphasis and transliteration added).
5 "Is 2012 Going to be the 'End of the World?'," http://mayas2012ingles.blogspot.com/2011/04/is-2012-going-to-be-end-of-world.html.
6 Eschatology is the study of last things; I will use it in a broader sense to mean the study of prophecy.
7 Geerhardus Vos, "Eschatology of the New Testament," in *The International Standard Bible Encyclopaedia*, ed. James Orr (Grand Rapids: Wm. B. Eerdmans, 1956), 2:980.
8 Riddlebarger, *A Case for Amillennialism*, 89.
9 Jesus refers to this two-age model in other places (e.g., Luke 18:29–30, 35; 20:34–36). The explanation of these passages from an inmillennial perspective is beyond the scope of this book.
10 Kenneth S. Wuest, *The New Testament: An Expanded Translation* (Grand Rapids: Eerdmans, 1961), 450 (Eph 1:21).
11 Terry, *Biblical Apocalyptics*, 247–48.
12 Gill, "Exposition," 6:619 (commentary on Hab 2:3).
13 For example: John MacArthur, *The MacArthur Topical Bible: New King James Version* (Nashville: Word, 1999), 417. Also see Geerhardus Vos, *Biblical Theology, Old and New Testaments* (Grand Rapids: Wm. B. Eerdmans, 1948), 304.
14 John Lightfoot, *A Commentary on the New Testament From the Talmud and Hebraica*, ed. Robert Gandell, 4 vols. (1859; repr., Peabody, MA: Hendrickson Publishers, 1997), 3:135 (emphasis his).
15 N. T. Wright, *The New Testament and the People of God*, vol. 1 of *Christian Origins and the Question of God* (Minneapolis: Fortress Press, 1992), 226.
16 Nicholas Perrin, *Jesus the Temple* (Grand Rapids: Baker Academic, 2010), 6, 8.

CHAPTER SEVEN

The Sign Question in Matthew: The Coming of Christ

I SENSE some momentum here: in all three accounts of the Olivet Discourse, the disciples' *when* question relates to the "these things" of the temple's fall; in Mark and Luke, their single *sign* question also relates to "these things"; and in Matthew, the second part of their bifurcated *sign* question also pertains to the temple's fall as the event that would end the Mosaic age. This impetus will help us understand the other part of the disciples' *sign* question in Matthew: "What shall be the sign of thy coming (Gk. *parousia*)?" (Matt 24:3).

I will begin with a simple question: if the disciples knew the temple's fall would end the Mosaic age, did they not also know it would signal the "age to come?" Nicholas Perrin recognizes the logic of this question: "If the old order was on its way out, that meant that a new order ... was on its way in."[1] The disciples' two-age model of history required the beginning of "a new world ... the Gospel dispensation"[2] as the old world of the Mosaic age passed away. They knew, as Milton Terry says, "the age to come, the Messianic time ... would follow immediately after the termination of the pre-messianic age."[3] Based on these observations, I propose an affirmative answer: yes, since the disciples associated the Lord's "coming" with the temple's fall and the end of the Mosaic age, they also associated it with the start of the new age. They were, perhaps, mistaken about some *characteristics* of the kingdom, but they knew Jesus would soon sit in the glory of the new age (e.g., Mark 10:35–45).

I will explore the implications of this observation by defining an important term: I will use "messianic age" to describe the second age in the Jewish two-age model of history. Some writers use this term to designate a future (to us) age of one thousand literal years, but I will use it as Terry does in the quote above and as A. T. Robertson does in his comments on Luke 4:19: "*The acceptable year of the Lord* ... [means] the Messianic age has come";[4] it is the "church age" in which we now live.

The Greek word the disciples used for "coming"—*parousia*—shows they were asking about the messianic age. Most writers who adopt one of the existing models say the *parousia* is a point-in-time (i.e., punctiliar) event at the end of the church age. This is a mistake; another Greek word—*erchomai*—would have met the disciples' needs if that was their meaning. The disciples used *parousia* because of its unique capabilities that go far beyond "coming." I will show the relationship between these two words in the next section.

Inmillennialism stands alone in its assertion that the disciples were right to see an unbreakable link between a triad of events: the temple's fall, the end of the Mosaic age, and the extended *parousia* of Christ. This linkage will have a tremendous role in the discovery of an improved prophetic model, so I will provide supporting evidence for its existence.

Parousia vs. Erchomai; Presence vs. Coming

In Matthew 24:3, the disciples use *parousia* (presence), not *erchomai* (coming) in their sign question. Standard dictionaries and lexicons often define *parousia* as "*the state* of being present at a place, presence;"[5] "to be present;"[6] or something similar. W. E. Vine says, "Parousia literally signifies 'a being with,' 'a presence.' Not infrequently it is so rendered. *It thus denotes a state*, not an action. We never read of a parousia to, always of a parousia with."[7] The "state" of interest to the disciples in the Olivet Discourse was the messianic age that would replace the Mosaic age.

Antonyms often clarify word meanings. Most Bible translations and commentators translate *parousia* as "coming"; but if this were correct, its opposite would be "going," but the Scriptures never use this word as the opposite of *parousia*. Since *parousia* means "presence," its antonym is "absence." The Apocrypha provides an example of this when it speaks of people who flattered a king "that was *absent*, as if he were *present* (*parousia*)."[8] The apostle Paul gives another example in his letter to the Philippians: "Wherefore, my beloved, as ye have always obeyed, not as in my *presence* (Gk. *parousia*) only, but now much more in my *absence* (Gk. *apousia*), work out your own salvation with fear and trembling" (Phil 2:12). He provides a third example in his letter to the Corinthians:

> For his letters, say they, are weighty and powerful; but his bodily *presence* (Gk. *parousia*) is weak, and his speech contemptible. Let such an one think this, that, such as we are in word by letters when we are *absent* (Gk. *apeimi*), such will we be also in deed when we are *present* (Gk. *pareimi*[9]). (2 Cor 10:10–11)

The antonyms of *parousia* in these passages conform to Milton Terry's succinct observation: "The word [*parousia*] ... means presence as opposed to absence."[10] *Parousia* signifies a state of being present, not a point-in-time action like "coming"; its antonym is "absence," not "going."

Scholars of the highest rank confirm "presence" is the primary meaning of *parousia*. The McReynolds English Interlinear Bible supplies "presence" for every occurrence of *parousia* in the New Testament. Israel P. Warren says, "The Revised Version, in every instance where it does not put *presence* into the text as the representative of *parousia*, inserts the marginal note, 'Gr. *presence*,' thus affirming that such is its real meaning."[11] Robert Young and Philip Schaff translate the disciples' *sign* question in Matthew 24:3 using this meaning: "What is the sign of thy *presence*?"[12] and "What shall be the *sign* of thy presence?"[13]

Warren amasses an impressive amount of support for "presence" as the primary meaning of *parousia*. He says, "It is found but twice in the Septuagint (2 Macc. 8:12; 15:21), and there only in its ordinary secular meaning"[14] of presence. Warren's first reference in Maccabees says: "Now when word was brought unto Judas of Nicanor's coming, and he had imparted unto those that were with him that the army was *at hand* (Gk. *parousia*; present), they that were fearful, and distrusted the justice of God, fled" (2 Macc 8:12–13). This example illustrates the meaning of *parousia*; it also shows how the context in which it occurs can emphasize a particular part of the period of "presence." Nicanor's point-in-time "coming" caused the army to be "at hand" (*parousia*; present); this setting emphasizes the beginning of the army's *parousia*.

A passage may also stress events that occur during or at the conclusion of the period of "presence" under consideration. In all cases, however, *parousia* carries the idea of presence; it is never a point-in-time action alone. This word means "presence, arrival; a coming *which includes the idea of* a permanent dwelling from that coming onwards."[15] James M. Campbell provides an excellent summary: "*Parousia* does not mean 'coming.' It means 'presence,' and nothing but 'presence.' ... The implication in the word is that the one who was approaching has arrived and is now present. His coming has resulted in the presence, or, rather, it has merged into the presence."[16]

Adolf Deissmann provides several examples from ancient sources that confirm *parousia* means presence. Here is how he describes one of them:
> I have found another characteristic example in a petition, *circa* 113 B.C., which was found among the wrappings of the mummy of a sacred crocodile. A *parousia* of King Ptolemy, the second who called himself *Soter* ("saviour"), is expected, and for this occasion a great requisition has been issued for corn, which is being collected at Cerceosiris by the village headman and the elders of the peasants. Speaking of this and another delivery of corn, these officials say:—
>> ... and applying ourselves diligently, both night and day, unto fulfilling that which was set be-

fore us and the provision of 80 artabae[17] which was imposed for the *parousia* of the king ...[18]

These Egyptian peasants did not toil day and night to supply provisions for the mere "coming"—a point-in-time action—of the king; they did so to sustain him during his "presence"—a state of being—for an extended period. The basic meaning of *parousia* is "presence," not "coming."

Why did the disciples not use the Greek word *erchomai*, a word that can mean "coming" and often refers to the coming of Christ in other Scriptures? Were they using this particular word for variety, or is there a more significant reason for their word choice?

Many English translations (and commentaries) hinder our ability to answer such questions because they use "coming" for both words in prophetic contexts. Here is an example from later in the Olivet Discourse:

> As the lightning cometh (Gk. *exerchomai*) out of the east, and shineth even unto the west; so shall also the coming (Gk. *parousia*) of the Son of man be.... Then shall all the tribes of the earth mourn, and they shall see the Son of man coming (Gk. *erchomai*) in the clouds of heaven with power and great glory. (Matt 24:27, 30)

Translations like this ignore significant differences between these words: one is a noun, the other is a verb; one describes a state of being, the other an action; etc. I, therefore, will repeat a sentence from my discussion about the word "world" almost verbatim: some English translations—including our beloved Authorized Version—create confusion about these differences by translating both *parousia* and *erchomai* as "coming."

Erchomai is a verb with a wide range of meanings—*The Theological Dictionary of the New Testament* devotes nineteen pages to its word group! For my purposes, the most important features are that it depicts a point-in-time (punctiliar) action and almost always "has the senses of 'to come' and 'to go.'"[19]

How can we understand the relationship between these two words? One of my Greek students once made a keen observation: "an *erchomai* (coming) is necessary for a *parousia* (presence) to exist." He was right, for "parousia signifies 'becoming present' and 'being present' for a longer or shorter period."[20] *Erchomai* represents the action of "becoming present" without implying a stay for a period. Paul made another statement about his *parousia* with the Philippians that illustrates this point (and validates my student's summary):

> And having this confidence, I know that I shall *abide and continue with you* all for your furtherance and joy of faith; that your rejoicing may be more abundant in Jesus Christ for me by my *coming* (Gk. *parousia*) to you again. Only let your conversation be as it becometh the gospel of Christ: that whether I *come* (Gk. *erchomai*) and see you, or else be absent, I may hear of your affairs, that ye stand fast in one spirit, with one mind striving together for the faith of the gospel. (Phil 1:25–27)

Paul must "go" (Gk. *erchomai*) to Philippi for his "presence" (Gk. *parousia*) to be there; only then could he "abide and continue" with the saints there. Sadly, the translations obscure this relationship.

I will add a corollary to my student's insight: to have a *parousia* (presence), there must be an *erchomai* (coming), but there can be an *erchomai* (coming) without a *parousia* (presence). To illustrate my addition, I will relate an incident that occurred while I was writing these lines: our mail person came to our door and left a few items. In Greek, I could use *erchomai* to describe this event, but I would not refer to it as a *parousia*; the mail person "came," but not for a "visit."

The disciples knew Jesus' "coming" (*erchomai*; Matt 24:30) would bring the temple's destruction, the end of the Mosaic age, and result in his ongoing "presence" (*parousia*; Matt 24:3, 27, 39) with his churches throughout the messianic age. *Parousia* was, perhaps, the *only* word the disciples could have used to counterbalance "the end of the (Mosaic) age" in their *sign* question. Since they did, it will not surprise us when Jesus uses it in his response (Matt 24:27, 37, 39).

The following diagram illustrates the relationship between *erchomai* (coming) and *parousia* (presence):

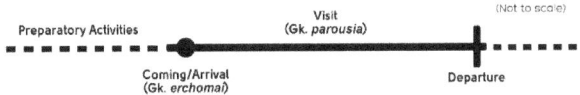

Figure 7-1. The Relationship between *Parousia* and *Erchomai*

The Parousia as an Age

Of particular importance to our prophetic model is the fact that a *parousia* can show the beginning of a new age:

> *Parousia* means, on the one hand, presence (with certain effects following) ... and, on the other hand, it means arrival, someone's coming in order to be present. Technically the noun is used for the arrival of a ruler.... In Greece *a new era* was reckoned from the *parousia* of Hadrian, and special advent coins were struck, in various places to commemorate the *parousia* of an emperor.[21]

Deissmann provides several ancient sources that show a *parousia* can start an age. Here are some examples:

> It is the legitimate continuation of the Hellenistic usage that in the Imperial period the *parousia*[22] of the sovereign should shed a special brilliance. Even the visit of a scion of the Imperial house, G. Caesar (4 A.D.), a grandson of Augustus, was, as we know from an inscription, made the beginning of *a new era* in Cos.... How deeply a *parousia* stamped itself on the memory is shown by *the eras* that were reckoned from parusiae....[23]
> We find that in Greece *a new era was begun* with the first visit of the Emperor Hadrian in the year 124.[24]

Some modern dispensational writers recognize that *parousia* can represent an age. A. R. Fausset, in his comments on 1 Corinthians 15:23, says, "Christ's second coming is not a mere *point* of time, but a *period*."[25] William MacDonald writes:

> *Parousia* ... means a *presence* or a *coming alongside*. Vine says it denotes both an arrival and a consequent presence. When we think of the Lord's coming, we should think of it not only as a momentary event but as a period of time.
>
> Even in English, the word *coming* is used this way. For instance, "Christ's coming to Galilee brought healing to multitudes." Here we do not mean the day He arrived in Galilee but the whole period of time He spent in that area. So when we think of Christ's coming, we should think of a period of time rather than an isolated event. Now if we take all the occurrences of *parousia* in the NT, we find that they describe a period of time with (1) a beginning, (2) a course, (3) a manifestation, and (4) a climax....
>
> When we think of Christ's coming, we should think of a period of time rather than an isolated event.... This climax of Christ's *parousia* is after the Millennium and at the inauguration of the eternal state.[26]

I disagree with MacDonald's view of the millennium but appreciate his insights regarding Christ's *parousia*, especially his recognition that its climax will inaugurate the eternal state. When Jesus answers the disciples' questions in the Olivet Discourse, he will end by speaking of the last judgment (Matt 25:31–46); Christ's *parousia*—his presence with his church as it now exists—will continue until that event.

Some non-dispensational writers agree. Ezra P. Gould comments on Mark 14:62: "the coming is not a single event, any more than the sitting on the right hand of power.... [It is a] period."[27] Joseph L. Mangina mentions that Karl Barth held a view similar to the one I am advocating: "Barth expands the category of *parousia* to include Easter and Pentecost as well; the *parousia* is not limited to his final return."[28]

Barth's expansion makes *parousia* represent the entire messianic age as it does in inmillennialism.

When I was developing my ideas about Christ's *parousia*, I rejoiced exceedingly to learn that Israel P. Warren had reached the same conclusion. His words, written in the nineteenth century, could be my own:

> For myself I freely say, that, having reflected much upon all these ways, and having tried in vain to feel satisfied with any other, I can find none which seems so simple, so accordant with common sense, so perfectly able to meet all the conditions of the problem and to exalt and honor our Lord himself, as that which regards the Parousia *as covering a vast period of duration, beginning with the generation when he was on earth, and lasting long enough to include all those great events which are to make up the history of time.*[29]

This view means the disciples were not confused when they asked Jesus about his *parousia* in connection with the temple's fall and "the end of the (Mosaic) age" (Matt 24:3). They knew a new age (or era) must take its place; their King's presence—his *parousia*—would start the new messianic age. And, unlike the Roman kings, King Jesus' presence would not end; he would be present with his people throughout the entire new age—he is King (and Priest) "not after the law of a carnal commandment, but after the power of an endless life" (Heb 7:16).

KEY POINT #7

In Matthew's account of the sign question, "the parousia of Christ" means Christ's presence with his people in the messianic age; it does not refer to a point-in-time event in our future (or past).

The Parousia as the Kingdom Age

So far, in our examination of the *sign* question in Matthew, we have seen that the disciples: (1) thought in terms of two ages; (2) understood that the temple's fall would end the Mosaic age; (3) knew the messianic age would succeed the Mosaic age; and (4) used *parousia* to describe Christ's presence with his church in the messianic age.

The disciples also knew the new age as the "kingdom of God"[30] that the prophets had foretold. Daniel, for example, had said: "And in the days of these kings shall the God of heaven set up a kingdom, which shall never be destroyed: and the kingdom shall not be left to other people, but it shall break in pieces and consume all these kingdoms, and it shall stand for ever" (Dan 2:44). The disciples also knew John the Baptist had announced the kingdom's arrival in their near future: "Repent ye: for the kingdom of heaven is at hand" (Matt 3:1–2). And, on multiple occasions, Jesus had taught the disciples about this new age. At the beginning of his ministry, he had echoed John's message: "Repent: for the kingdom of heaven is at hand" (Matt 4:17). Later, Jesus had sent them to preach that the new age was near: "These twelve Jesus sent forth, and commanded them, saying, Go … to the lost sheep of the house of Israel. And as ye go, preach, saying, The kingdom of heaven is at hand" (Matt 10:5–7). Jesus had explicitly taught the disciples that his coming would start this new age: "Verily I say unto you, There be some standing here, which shall not taste of death, till they see the Son of man *coming* (Gk. *erchomai*) in his kingdom" (Matt 16:28). The disciples were aware of the soon-coming kingdom age; they used the word *parousia* to describe the kingdom, a word that provided a counterbalance for the "end of the (Mosaic) age" in their *sign* question.

That Christ's *parousia* (presence) exists in the kingdom of God is not surprising; as we have seen, this word "became the official term for a visit of a person of high rank, esp. of kings and emperors visiting a province."[31] Jesus had promised to come "in his kingdom" before all of the disciples tasted death, or, in more positive terms, while some of them were still living. The word *parousia* represents the presence of King Jesus in the new age; it was the ideal word for the disciples to use to designate the kingdom of God in their *sign* question.

The link between the *parousia* of the Son of Man and the establishment of his kingdom is of utmost importance: "The motifs of Son of Man and kingdom of God … are the two most frequent and important phrases (and, we would argue, theologically loaded phrases) in the Synoptic Jesus tradition."³² This link is vital to our understanding of the Olivet Discourse; it is also vital to our understanding of the kingdom of God in the rest of the New Testament.

KEY POINT #8

Mark and Luke relate the sign question to the events surrounding the temple's fall; Matthew relates it to the results—the end of the Mosaic age and the start of the messianic age. The Scriptures refer to the new age as the kingdom of God, the kingdom of heaven, the age to come, the parousia of Christ, et al.

The Parousia as the New Covenant Presence

Parousia was the best word for the disciples to use in their *sign* question for another important reason: it signifies God's *covenantal* presence with his people. During the Exodus, God had promised to be present with his people in the Mosaic age:

> I will dwell among the children of Israel, and will be their God. And they shall know that I am the LORD their God, that brought them forth out of the land of Egypt, that I may dwell among them: I am the LORD their God. (Exod 29:45–46)

Joseph Plevnik shows how Flavius Josephus (AD 37–100)—the famous Jewish historian who witnessed the temple's fall—uses *parousia* to describe God's covenant-presence with Israel.³³ He cites a passage that describes the scene at Mt. Sinai in which the Hebrews were reveling in an idolatrous orgy: "Thunder, with its thunderbolts, were sent down, and declared God to be there present (Gk. *parousia*) in a gracious way to such as Moses desired he should be gracious."³⁴ Josephus is not using *parousia* to describe a "coming" of God into Israel's camp; he is using it to signify the divine "presence" already among them.

N. T. Wright notes that Josephus uses *parousia* in a passage about Elisha. Josephus says, "he besought God to make manifest to his servant his power and presence (Gk. *parousia*), so far as was possible, in order to the inspiring him with hope and courage."[35] Wright says, "Here *parousia* is simply 'presence'—'the fact that he was there all along'—rather than 'arrival'."[36]

These passages show that the Jews of Jesus' generation used *parousia* to describe God's presence with Israel in the Mosaic age. It was natural for the disciples to use this word to represent Jesus' covenant presence with his people in the messianic age.

Typology makes this apparent: in the Mosaic age, Israel had "the bread of the Presence" (Exod 25:30 ESV; *passim*). At the dawn of the messianic age, Jesus said: "I am the bread of life. He who comes to Me shall never hunger" (John 6:35). "The bread of the Presence" was the type; Jesus was the antitype. Such imagery suggests the disciples were thinking of Jesus' *parousia* as his covenant presence during the messianic age.

Another line of reasoning supports this idea: God's Mosaic-age shekinah was in the physical temple at Jerusalem—the temple Jesus said would fall. Anthony J. Saldarini says,

> Shekinah [is] a Hebrew word from the root 'to dwell' that is translated as the 'Presence' of God…. God's presence was seen in the cloud that led the Israelites in the desert and in the tent of meeting in the desert. The Priestly writer's word for the tent of meeting, the *mishkan* or 'tabernacle,' comes from the same root as *Shekinah*. The glory of God, which filled the Temple, was his *Shekinah* and when the Temple was destroyed, God's *Shekinah* left the Temple.[37]

When the disciples heard Jesus' prophecy, they may have wondered, What will replace the shekinah of God once the temple falls? As you contemplate the possibility of them asking this question, consider a pertinent comment by Hermann Cremer: "Ewald acutely says … 'The [*parousia* of Christ] perfectly corresponds with the [Shekinah] of God in the O. T.,—the permanent dwelling of the King, where His people ever behold Him, and are ever shielded by Him."[38] The disciples later spoke of God dwelling in the church as the messianic-age temple (e.g., Eph 2:21; 1 Pet 2:5); it seems fitting, therefore, to assume they were thinking of the *parousia* (presence) of Christ as the messianic-age shekinah of God when they asked their *sign* question.

The disciples knew that, through the prophet Jeremiah, God had promised to establish a better covenant than the one he had made with Israel in the Exodus:

> Behold, the days come, saith the LORD, that I will make a new covenant with the house of Israel, and with the house of Judah: not according to the covenant that I made with their fathers in the day that I took them by the hand to bring them out of the land of Egypt; which my covenant they brake, although I was an husband unto them, saith the LORD: but this shall be the covenant that I will make with the house of Israel; After those days, saith the LORD, I will put my law in their inward parts, and write it in their hearts; and will be their God, and they shall be my people. And they shall teach no more every man his neighbour, and every man his brother, saying, Know the LORD: for they shall all know me, from the least of them unto the greatest of them, saith the LORD: for I will forgive their iniquity, and I will remember their sin no more. (Jer 31:31–34; cp. Heb 8:8–13; 10:8–9, 16–17)

The disciples knew that, by sending Jesus, God had "raised up an horn of salvation ... to remember his holy covenant" (Luke 1:69, 72). They knew God's covenant presence—his *parousia*—had dwelt with Israel in the physical temple; they knew his covenant presence under the new covenant—the *parousia* of Christ—would be far more glorious.

The existing prophetic models misplace Christ's *parousia*; they take the start of this "state of being" out of its proper historical location—in the "last days" of the Mosaic age—and make the entire *parousia* a point-in-time event at the end of the church age. This mistake robs *parousia* of its rich associations with God's covenant presence in both ages; it minimizes the temple's fall as a pivotal event in the transition from God's old-covenant presence to Christ's new-covenant presence with his people.

Inmillennialism suggests that a better prophetic model will restore the *parousia* of Christ to its rightful place.

Objections

Writers who hold the current prophetic models almost always agree that the disciples erred by connecting Jesus' coming (Gk. *parousia*) to the temple's fall. They reject the notion that *parousia* can represent an age. Frederic Louis Godet, for example, chided another commentator for proposing this idea: "Van Hengel has unfortunately thought of applying the word *Parousia* to the epoch of Christ's presence on the earth."[39] Godet takes the traditional view and speaks of "the *moment* of the Parousia."[40] This esteemed writer died in 1900, just eight years before Deissmann first published his *Light From the Ancient East*; one wonders if its many examples of *parousia* in ancient writings would have convinced Godet that this word does not signify a point-in-time event. In any case, Godet did not feel the need to establish his view; he simply asserted it.

Some writers are condescending in their opposition to the idea that *parousia* represents an age. George N. H. Peters, for example, says: "It is too late in the day ... for a Divine to make the Parousia an entire dispensation—the Christian."[41] Peters makes this statement while denouncing Israel P. Warren's book, *The Parouisa*. Even though Peters is extremely detail-oriented—his three-volume work on the kingdom has 2,175 pages!—he offers no arguments to support his too-late-in-the-day rejection of Warren's position.

That commentators like Peters reject *parousia* as an age is regrettable; this view explains the form of the disciples' *sign* question in Matthew

24:3 better than the existing paradigms. Failure to give *parousia* its principle meaning hinders our ability to understand that question and Jesus' response; it blocks the discovery of a full-orbed framework for prophecy.

These rejections are like Ptolemaic astronomers telling Copernicus it was "too late in the day" for him to make the sun the center of the solar system, even though his proposal better explained the phenomena! Let us not invalidate an improved prophetic model just because other models have prevailed a thousand years.

Conclusion

I will use the definition of *parousia* as "presence" to update the diagram of our burgeoning prophetic model. I will elevate the line representing the *parousia* (presence) of Christ to show its superiority to the Mosaic age (cp. Matt 11:9–11):[42]

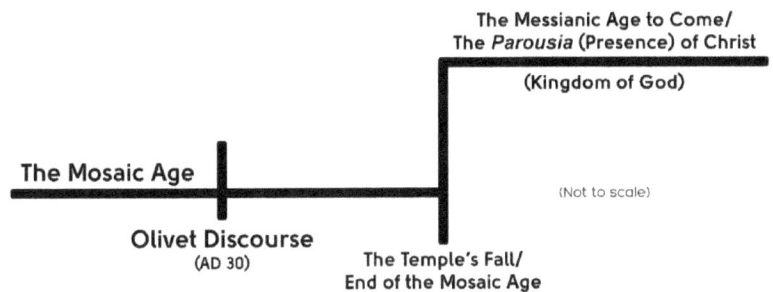

Figure 7-2. Inmillennialism through the Sign Question

The disciples knew Jesus' coming would end the Mosaic age and start the kingdom age. The Mosaic presence (*parousia*) of God with Israel would yield to the messianic presence (*parousia*) of Christ with his people. The temple's destruction would proclaim to observers for all time that the transition had occurred.

I can now summarize Matthew's prologue to the Olivet Discourse (Matt 24:1–3): Jesus says the temple will fall; the disciples ask *when* this will occur and for a *sign* of its fulfillment. The accounts of the Olivet Discourse in Mark and Luke raise no issues about their subject: the disciples want to know about things related to the temple's fall. The same is true of the *when* question in Matthew 24:3a. The *sign* question in Matthew 24:3b carries the same subject but focuses on the results of the temple's demise: it would end the Mosaic age and complete the transition to the messianic-age *parousia* (presence) of Christ with his church. As Ezra P. Gould says, "The way in which the temple's destruction, the reappearance of Jesus, and the consummation of the age are introduced in [Matt 24: 2–3] shows conclusively that in that Gospel the three are all treated as parts and titles of the one event."[43] There is no justification for making the "coming" of Christ—his *parousia*—a single event at the end of the church age.

Here is my amplified version of the disciples' questions:

> Now as He sat on the Mount of Olives, the disciples came to Him privately, saying, "Tell us, *when* will these things [related to the temple's fall] be? And what will be the sign of Your coming [that is, Your presence in the messianic age], and of the end of the [Mosaic] age?" (Matt 24:3 NKJV)

The following chapters will examine whether we must insert additional elements to produce the desired prophetic model.

Notes

1 Perrin, *Jesus the Temple*, 37.
2 Gill, "Exposition," 6:619 (commentary on Hab 2:3).
3 Terry, *Biblical Apocalyptics*, 248.
4 Archibald Thomas Robertson, *Word Pictures in the New Testament*, 6 vols. (Nashville: Broadman, 1930–33), 2:57.
5 Danker et al., eds., *Greek-English Lexicon*, 780 (emphasis added).
6 Albrecht Oepke, "παρουσία, κτλ," in *Theological Dictionary of the New Testament*, ed. Gerhard Friedrich, trans. Geoffrey W. Bromiley (Grand Rapids: Eerdmans, 1964–76), 5:859.
7 W. E. Vine, *Collected Writings of W. E. Vine*, 5 vols. (Nashville: T. Nelson, 1996), 5:149 (emphasis added).
8 W. R. Churton, *The Uncanonical and Apocryphal Scriptures* (London: J. Whitaker, 1884), Wis 14:17.
9 *Pareimi* is the verb form of the noun *parousia*. [Oepke, "παρουσία, κτλ," 5:858. See also Ethelbert W. Bullinger, *A Critical Lexicon and Concordance to the English and Greek New Testament* (London: Bagster, 1971), 169.]
10 Terry, *Biblical Apocalyptics*, 246.
11 Israel P. Warren, *The Parousia: A Critical Study of the Scripture Doctrines of Christ's Coming; His Reign as King; the Resurrection of the Dead; and the General Judgment*, 2nd ed. (Portland, ME: Hoyt, Fogg & Dunham, 1884), 24–25.
12 Robert Young, *The Holy Bible*, 3rd ed. (Edinburgh: G. A. Young & Co., 1898), Matt 24:3.
13 Philip Schaff, *The Oldest Church Manual Called the Teaching of the Twelve Apostles*, 2nd ed. (Edinburgh: T. & T. Clark, 1887), 216 (emphasis in original).
14 Israel P. Warren, *The Parousia: A Critical Study of the Scripture Doctrines of Christ's Coming; His Reign as King; the Resurrection of the Dead; and the General Judgment* (Portland, ME: Hoyt, Fogg & Dunham, 1879), 9.
15 Bullinger, *Lexicon*, 169 (emphasis in original).
16 James M. Campbell, *The Presence* (New York: Eaton & Mains, 1911), 114.
17 In ancient Egypt, a unit of dry capacity, about 30–40 liters.
18 Adolf Deissmann, *Light From the Ancient East; the New Testament Illustrated By Recently Discovered Texts of the Graeco-Roman World*, trans. Lionel R. M. Strachan, 4th ed. (1922; repr., Grand Rapids: Baker, 1978), 369.
19 Johannes Schneider, "ἔρχομαι, κτλ," in *Theological Dictionary of the New Testament*, ed. Gerhard Kittel, trans. Geoffrey W. Bromiley (Grand Rapids: Eerdmans, 1964–76), 2:666.
20 Geerhardus Vos, *The Pauline Eschatology* (Phillipsburg, NJ: P&R, 1994), 75.
21 Georg Braumann, "παρουσία," in *The New International Dictionary of New Testament Theology*, ed. Colin Brown (Grand Rapids: Zondervan, 1976), 2:898.
22 I have universally replaced Deissmann's "parusia" with "*parousia*."

23 This is a theoretical plural form of *parousia*, "Parousia is a word that has no plural." [John A. T. Robinson, *Jesus and His Coming* (Philadelphia: Westminster Press, 1979), 185.]
24 Deissmann, *Light*, 370–72.
25 Robert Jamieson, A. R. Fausset, and David Brown, *A Commentary, Critical, Experimental and Practical on the Old and New Testaments*, 3 vols. (n.d.; repr. Grand Rapids: Eerdmans, 1976), 3.3:329 (1 Cor 15:23) (emphasis in original).
26 William MacDonald, *Believer's Bible Commentary: Old and New Testaments*, ed. Arthur Farstad (Nashville: Thomas Nelson, 1995), 2030–31.
27 Ezra P. Gould, *The Gospel According to St. Mark*, The International Critical Commentary, eds. Alfred Plummer and Samuel R. Driver (New York: Charles Scribner's Sons, 1896), 252.
28 Joseph L. Mangina, *Karl Barth: The Ecumenical Promise of His Theology* (Burlington, VT: Ashgate, 2004), 118.
29 Warren, *The Parousia* (1879), 78–79 (emphasis added).
30 I take "kingdom of God" and "kingdom of heaven" to be interchangeable terms.
31 Danker et al., eds., *Greek-English Lexicon*, 781.
32 Ben Witherington, III, *The Jesus Quest: The Third Search for the Jew of Nazareth* (Downers Grove, IL: InterVarsity, 1995), 95.
33 Joseph Plevnik, *Paul and the Parousia: An Exegetical and Theological Investigation* (Eugene, OR: Wipf & Stock, 2014), 5.
34 Flavius Josephus, *The Works of Flavius Josephus*, trans. William Whiston, 4 vols. (Grand Rapids: Baker, 1974), 2:192 (A.J. 3.80). Cf. 2 Kgs 6:15–19.
35 Josephus, "The Works of Flavius Josephus," 3:11 (A.J. 9.55).
36 N. T. Wright, *Paul and the Faithfulness of God*, vol. 4 of *Christian Origins and the Question of God* (Minneapolis: Fortress Press, 2013), 1083n168.
37 Anthony J. Saldarini, "Shekinah," in *Harper's Bible Dictionary*, ed. Paul J. Achtemeier (San Francisco: Harper & Row, 1985), 938.
38 Hermann Cremer, *Biblico-Theological Lexicon of New Testament Greek*, trans. William Urwick, 4th English ed. (New York: Charles Scribner's Sons, 1895), 238 (my translations of Ewald's Greek and Hebrew).
39 Frederic Louis Godet, *Commentary on First Corinthians* (1889; repr., Grand Rapids: Kregel, 1977), 784.
40 Godet, *Commentary on First Corinthians*, 137 (emphasis added).
41 George N. H. Peters, *The Theocratic Kingdom of Our Lord Jesus, the Christ, as Covenanted in the Old Testament and Presented in the New Testament*, 3 vols. (1884; repr., Grand Rapids: Kregel, 1972), 2:221.
42 Again, this diagram is designed to show the relationship of the events, not anticipate Jesus' answer to the *when* question.
43 Gould, *Mark*, 243.

CHAPTER EIGHT

Response: Preliminary Signs

WITH A BASIC prophetic model now in hand, I am ready to examine Jesus' responses to the disciples' two questions. I have two primary goals: (1) to see if Jesus says anything that invalidates the foundational model that I documented in the last chapter, and (2) to find additional details for the model. In this chapter and the two following, I will discuss Jesus' answer to the disciples' two-part *sign* question (Matt 24:4–31). I will assume, based on the previous chapters, that this question relates to the temple's fall and nothing else. Our chiastic arrangement of the Olivet Discourse emphasizes this point; here it shows our current passage in bold type:

    A. *Exhortation*: observe!—the temple will fall (Matt 24:1–2)

        B. *When question*: what will be the time? (Matt 24:3a)

            C. *Sign question*: what will be the sign? (Matt 24:3b)

            C'. *Sign answer*: the signs of associated events, symbols (Matt 24:4–31)

        B'. *When answer*: *this* is the time (Matt 24:32–36)

    A'. *Exhortation*: observe! (Matt 24:37–25:46); watch! (Matt 24:42, 43; 25:13)

Jesus' answers to the *sign* question create two literary patterns: First, he moves from *general to specific geographical regions*. The first signs, which I will call "Phase 1: preliminary signs" (Matt 24:4–14), would happen across the Roman Empire. They would include religious deceptions, wars, earthquakes, etc. that could happen in any empire at any time. They would also include signs that would affect the disciples as they ministered "in all the world" (Matt 24:14) during the age-transition period. The Lord next mentions the sign that would happen in Israel and Jerusalem; I will refer to it as "Phase 2: later sign" (Matt 24:15–26; cf. Luke 21:20, 24). To describe the fall of the temple itself and the consequences of that event, Jesus gives what I will call "Phase 3: immediate signs" (Matt 24:27–31). The signs move from "all the world" to Israel and Jerusalem, and, finally, to the Temple Mount. This general-to-specific pattern points the reader (and hearer) to the specific location of the catastrophic event Jesus foretold—the temple's fall.

The second sign-pattern is Jesus' movement from *literal to figurative language*. At first, he uses straightforward prose to describe the wars, famines, persecutions, etc., the disciples would witness. As he comes closer to the temple's destruction, Jesus creates a crescendo of literary images drawn from the writings of the prophets. He uses the strongest images available in the passage about God's judgment on Jerusalem and the temple: lightning, feasting vultures, cosmic collapse, etc.

I advocated starting our search for a prophetic model in the Olivet Discourse, in part because it contains a minimum amount of figurative language. But I also want to emphasize that the figurative language Jesus uses produces a striking and dramatic effect as he is concluding his list of signs—a memorable flourish at just the right moment. Prose is incapable of creating this effect. The temple's fall would symbolize the end of the world for unbelieving Jews; they could not see the Jerusalem above, its temple, or Jesus as the ultimate Prophet, Priest, and King. Jesus used the traditional dramatic imagery to convey what the temple's fall meant to such persons.

These two literary patterns in Jesus' sign-answers point to the temple's fall, not to events at the end of the church age or the end of human history.

In this chapter I will examine the first group of signs Jesus gave, shown here in bold type in our outline of the Olivet Discourse:

I. Jesus prediction of the temple's destruction (Matt 24:1-2)
II. The disciples' two questions regarding *when* and the *sign* (Matt 24:3)
III. Jesus' response to the *sign* question (Matt 24:4–31)
    A. Phase 1: preliminary signs (Matt 24:4–14)—the beginning of birth pains (v. 8)
    B. Phase 2: later sign (Matt 24:15–26)—the period of "the end" (v. 14)
    C. Phase 3: immediate signs (Matt 24:27–31)—the end itself (v. 29)
IV. Jesus' response to the *when* question (Matt 24:32–36)
V. Jesus' exhortations to watchfulness (Matt 24:37–25:46)

Jesus arranged these preliminary signs in two groups: those that were general (Matt 24:4–8) and those that would affect the disciples and their mission during the last days of the Mosaic age (Matt 24:9–14).

General Preliminary Signs

The general preliminary signs of the age-transition[1] period are of three types: religious deceptions, political and military unrest, and physical disturbances. Jesus said these would exist during the entire period between the Olivet Discourse and the temple's fall.

Religious Deceivers. Jesus' first preliminary sign involved religious deception: "And Jesus answered and said unto them, Take heed that no man deceive you. For many shall come in my name, saying, I am Christ; and shall deceive (Gk. *planaō*[2]) many" (Matt 24:4–5).

Religious deceivers had plagued Israel throughout her history: Balaam, the for-hire prophet, had caused the people to sin through wicked counsel (Num 31:16). False prophets had assured Israel that God would not judge her covenant unfaithfulness. Jeremiah had complained about such deceivers when he announced God's soon-coming judgment of Israel at the hands of the Babylonians:

> Then said I, Ah, Lord GOD! behold, the prophets say unto them, Ye shall not see the sword, neither shall ye have famine; but I will give you assured peace in this place. Then the LORD said unto me, The prophets prophesy lies in my name: I sent them not, neither have I commanded them, neither spake unto them: they prophesy unto you a false vision and divination, and a thing of nought, and *the deceit of their heart.* (Jer 14:13–14)

That religious deception would exist during the transition period was nothing new; it would not show that the end of the Mosaic age had arrived.[3]

Extra-biblical records mention deceivers throughout the Roman Empire during this period. Justin Martyr mentioned some while defending Christians before the Romans:

> After Christ's ascension into heaven the devils put forward certain men who said that they themselves were gods; and they were not only not persecuted by you, but even deemed worthy of honours. There was a Samaritan, Simon, a native of the village called Gitto, who in the reign of Claudius Cæsar, and in your royal city of Rome, did mighty acts of magic, by virtue of the art of the devils operating in him. He was considered a god, and as a god was honoured by you with a statue, which statue was erected on the river Tiber, between the two bridges, and bore this inscription, in the language of Rome:— "Simoni Deo Sancto," "To Simon the holy God."[4]

G. K. Beale makes several keen observations in his commentary on Revelation about these deceivers:

> A part of the majority text tradition ... [renders Rev 13:13a] as, "he does great signs in order that *in deception* [*en planē*[5]] he should make fire descend from heaven." This is part of what Christ prophesied in Matt. 24:24:

> "false messiahs and false prophets will arise and will show great signs and wonders, so as to mislead, if possible, even the elect" (so likewise Matt. 7:15; 24:5, 11; 2 Thess. 2:9; 2 Pet. 2:1–3...).[6]

> The second beast's ability to "perform great signs" in [Rev. 13:14] and now its ability to give "breath" and power to speak to the first beast's image recall various pseudo-magical tricks, including ventriloquism, false lightning, and other such phenomena, that were effectively used in temples of John's time and even at the courts of Roman emperors and governors.[7]

Beale gives an impressive list of ancient sources that document the ability of magicians to create fire from heaven and make images move and speak.[8] Sir William Ramsay provides more evidence: "The State cultus in Asia, the most civilised and educated part of the Empire, recommended itself by tricks and pseudo-miracles, such as bringing down fire from heaven or making the Imperial image speak."[9] Gerhard Kittel says, "The presumed life of the image which enables it to speak (Rev. 13:15) reminds us of *many priestly devices to make images move*. Thus in the Mithras mystery the statue of the god with a lion's head was made to spit out fire by means of a concealed pipe ending in the mouth."[10]

Ramsay mentions one deceiver of special interest to us because of his proximity to the fulfillment of Jesus' prophecy. Vespasian and Titus—the Roman generals in command when the temple fell—had Apollonius of Tyana as their friend:

> [He] enjoyed widely the reputation of a magician. He had been well received in Rome, and was the friend of Vespasian, Titus and Nerva. His biographer Philostratus defends him from the charge of magic, but represents him as a worker of signs and wonders.... There is every reason to think that a man like Apollonius would use all his influence in favour of Vespasian and Titus.[11]

John Gill, in his comments on Matthew 24:5, provides a list of deceivers who had influence in Israel during this period:

> As there was a general expectation among the Jews of a Messiah; that is, of one that should arise and deliver them from the Roman yoke, which was the common *idea* tacked to that word; in this period of time, many set up themselves to be deliverers and redeemers of the people of Israel: who had each of them their followers in great numbers, whom they imposed upon, and brought to destruction. Of this sort was Theudas, not he that Gamaliel speaks of, Acts 5:36 for he was before this time; but one that was in the time of Claudius Caesar, when Cuspius Fadus was governor of Judea; who persuaded a great number to follow him to the river Jordan, which he promised to divide, by a word of command, and give them a passage over; and thereby, as the historian observes, ... he deceived many; which is the very thing that is here predicted [i.e., in Matt 24:5]: but he and his company were routed by Fadus, and his head cut off. There was another called the Egyptian, mentioned in Acts 21:38 who made an uproar, and led four thousand cut-throats into the wilderness; and this same man persuaded thirty thousand men to follow him to Mount Olivet, promising a free passage into the city; but he being vanquished by Felix, then governor of Judea, fled, and many of his followers were killed and taken: and besides, there were many more magicians and impostors, that pretended to signs and wonders, and promised the people deliverance from their evils, by whom they were imposed upon to their ruin. There were others also besides these, that set up for deliverers, who called themselves by the name of the Messiah. Among these, we may reckon Simon Magus, who gave

> out that he was some great one; yea, expressly, that he was the word of God, and the Son of God, which were known names of the Messiah; and Dositheus the Samaritan, asserted himself to be Christ; and also Menander affirmed, that no man could be saved, unless he was baptized in his name; these are instances before the destruction of Jerusalem, and confirm the prophecy here delivered.[12]

Jesus wanted the disciples to know that such deceivers would hinder their ministries during the last days of the Mosaic age, but that their opposition was *not* a sign of the temple's imminent fall.

I have given this lengthy list of deceivers and false prophets to show that there is nothing in Jesus' response that changes the subject of the Olivet Discourse; Jesus is speaking about the time between Passion Week and the temple's fall.

Social Unrest. Jesus' second preliminary sign concerned social unrest: "And ye shall hear of wars and rumours of wars: see that ye be not troubled: for all these things must come to pass, but the end is not yet. For nation shall rise against nation, and kingdom against kingdom" (Matt 24:6–7a).

The turmoil Jesus predicted came to pass: the Roman Empire suffered great and unexpected confusion before the temple fell. William Hendriksen says:

> When Jesus speaks these words [in the Olivet Discourse], the Roman empire has been enjoying a long era of peace. But about four decades later political turmoil [would] upset the great realm from one end to the other, so that Rome [would] see four emperors in one year: Galba, Otho, Vitellus, and Vespasian.[13]

John Gill, citing Josephus and other ancient writers, mentions a saying of the Jews that predicted the Messiah would come in a time of wars. Gill says:

> Here wars may mean the commotions, insurrections, and seditions, against the Romans, and their governors; and the intestine slaughters committed among them, some time before the siege of Jerusalem, and the destruction of it. Under Cumanus the Roman governor, a sedition was raised on the day of the passover, in which twenty thousand perished; after that, in another tumult, ten thousand were destroyed by cut-throats: in Ascalon two thousand more, in Ptolemais two thousand, at Alexandria fifty thousand, at Damascus ten thousand, and elsewhere in great numbers.[14]

Jesus' second sign pertained to the last days of the Mosaic age, but was not a sign of the imminent end of that age; nor was it a sign about the end of history.

Physical Disturbances. Jesus listed physical disturbances—natural upheavals with the potential to damage human life—as his third preliminary sign: "And there shall be famines, and pestilences, and earthquakes, in divers places" (Matt 24:7b). Some modern prophecy teachers (with their existing prophetic frameworks in hand) seem preoccupied—I could almost say obsessed—with current events of this type. They use seismological statistics to undergird their idea that earthquakes characterize *our* era to an unprecedented degree. Other data seem to support their teaching that other disasters are more frequent in *our* day than ever before. But these teachers ignore the fact that the Lord was not talking about our day; he was listing events that would define the period before the temple's destruction, not those that would happen two millennia later.

Both Scripture and history corroborate the Lord's words concerning these phenomena. Luke mentions famines in the book of Acts: "And there stood up one of them named Agabus, and signified by the Spirit that there should be great dearth [i.e., famine] throughout all the world: which came to pass in the days of Claudius Caesar" (Acts 11:28). Gill says there were earthquakes "at Crete, and in divers cities in Asia, in the times of Nero: particularly the three cities of Phrygia, Laodicea, Hierapolis, and Colosse; which were near to each other, and are all said to perish this way, in his reign; 'and Rome itself felt a tremor, in the reign of Galba.'"[15] Hendriksen provides historical information from extra-biblical sources: "During the period A.D. 60–80 famine, pestilence, fire, hurricane, and earthquake ravaged the empire, as Renan points out in *l'Antichrist*."[16] Descriptions like these, though not as titillating as recent data from the Richter scale, confirm the accuracy of Jesus' prediction in its historical context.

Jesus informed the disciples that such events would occur during their years of ministry. They would not, however, be the unmistakable prelude to the climactic end of the age—the temple's fall.

Birth Pains. As a summary statement, Jesus said these preliminary signs were *"the beginning of the birth pains"* (Matt 24:8 ESV).[17] The disciples knew that the prophets had used this imagery to depict God's judgment on nations: on Israel's enemies, and on Israel herself. Isaiah, for example, used it to describe God's coming judgment of Babylon: "And they shall be afraid: pangs and sorrows shall take hold of them; they shall be in pain *as a woman that travaileth*: they shall be amazed one at another; their faces shall be as flames" (Isa 13:8). Jeremiah likewise used it regarding the decimation of two other nations: "The mighty men's hearts in Moab at that day shall be as the heart of *a woman in her pangs*" (Jer 48:41), and "at that day shall the heart of the mighty men of Edom be as the heart of *a woman in her pangs*" (Jer 49:22).

The prophets had also used this imagery to describe God's past judgments of *Israel*. Here are a few examples that the disciples would have known: "Like as a woman with child, that draweth near the time of her delivery, *is in pain, and crieth out in her pangs*; so have we been in thy sight, O LORD" (Isa 26:17); "Our hands wax feeble: anguish hath taken hold of us, and pain, *as of a woman in travail*" (Jer 6:24); "For I have heard a voice *as of a woman in travail*, and the anguish as of her that bringeth forth her first child, the voice of the daughter of Zion, that bewaileth herself" (Jer 4:31); and,

> Now why dost thou cry out aloud? is there no king in thee? is thy counsellor perished? for *pangs have taken thee as a woman in travail*. Be in pain, and labour to bring forth, O daughter of Zion, like *a woman in travail*: for now shalt thou go forth out of the city, and thou shalt dwell in the field, and thou shalt go even to Babylon; there shalt thou be delivered; there the LORD shall redeem thee from the hand of thine enemies. (Mic 4:9–10)

That Jesus predicted the temple's fall and then used the familiar "birth pains" imagery to describe it would have arrested the disciples' attention. And perhaps, considering their knowledge of the messianic age, I can go further: the disciples knew the birth-pains imagery carried meaning beyond mere judgment. Isaiah, for example, had linked Israel's previous birth pains to her inability to achieve a specific outcome: "We have been with child, we have been in pain, we have as it were brought forth wind; *we have not wrought any deliverance in the earth; neither have the inhabitants of the world fallen*" (Isa 26:18).

Isaiah had used a powerful cluster of images: Israel's birth pains, a deliverance, and the subjugation of the nations. Without getting ahead of myself too much, I will point out that three days after Jesus gave the Olivet Discourse, he achieved, through his death on the cross, the deliverance Israel had failed to produce: he "delivered us from the wrath to come" (1 Thess 1:10). Jesus is "the Deliverer" (Rom 11:26), but what about the other two elements in Isaiah's cluster: Israel's birth pains and the subjugation of the nations? Jesus, in the Olivet Discourse, is telling the disciples about the birth pains; the preliminary signs he is listing would start Israel's final travail—they would be over when the temple fell. The subjugation of the nations—by making disciples of them—would follow during the messianic age, but that is a subject for a later section.

The signs Jesus is discussing at this point would be the "beginning of the birth pains" leading up to the age-changing event Jesus had foretold.

Specific Preliminary Signs

At this point in the Olivet Discourse, Jesus turns from general signs that might characterize any period to those that would affect the disciples and their work before the temple's fall. Jesus reminds the disciples that their transition-period ministry would be "a witness unto all nations" (v 14). The three signs he now gives relate to that mission: (1) persecution; (2) widespread apostasy; and (3) an accomplishment that must precede the end of the Mosaic age.

Persecution. Jesus' first ministry-related sign is Empire-wide *persecution*: "Then shall they deliver you up to be afflicted, and shall kill you: and ye shall be hated of all nations for my name's sake" (Matt 24:9). The Jews were the primary agents of this persecution, but the Gentiles also persecuted the disciples throughout the Roman Empire during the transition period. Luke's account of this persecution-sign shows these two agents: "They shall lay their hands on you, and persecute you, delivering you up to the [Jewish] synagogues, and into prisons, being brought before [Gentile] kings and rulers for my name's sake" (Luke 21:12).

The New Testament contains several references to the Jews persecuting the disciples. Earlier in his ministry, Jesus had sent the disciples to preach "to the lost sheep of the house of Israel," to tell them "the kingdom of heaven is at hand" (Matt 10:5–7). Some gladly received the disciples, but the majority violently rejected both the message and the messengers. The disciples had been like "sheep in the midst of wolves" (Matt 10:16). Even at that early date, Jesus had warned the disciples: "Ye shall be brought before governors and kings for my sake, for a testimony against them and the Gentiles" (Matt 10:18). And Jesus had told the disciples that they would "not have gone over the cities of Israel, till the Son of man be come (Gk. *erchomai*)" (Matt 10:23). The Jews opposed the gospel of the kingdom in Jesus' lifetime; they would continue to do so until the temple fell.

Jesus had emphasized this continuing persecution just hours before he gave the Olivet Discourse.[18] He had charged the scribes and Pharisees with being the sons of those who had killed the Old Testament prophets. Their former sins had partially filled the bowl of God's wrath; now, Jesus said, they would fill up that bowl by persecuting the disciples during the transition period. God would then judge Israel and leave their house (i.e., the temple) desolate (Matt 23:29–38). Jesus had linked the Jew's persecution of the disciples in the age-transition period to the temple's fall.

The New Testament shows the fulfillment of this persecution-sign. The Jews had synagogues in almost every nation, and they opposed the disciples wherever they preached the wonderful news of the coming kingdom age. In Jerusalem they put the disciples in prison (Acts 4:2–3; 12:5), beat them (Acts 5:40–41), stoned them (Acts 7:59), and killed them with swords (Acts 12:2). Later, when the disciples went to other parts of the Empire, the Jews followed them. In Iconium, "the unbelieving Jews stirred up the Gentiles, and made their minds evil affected against the brethren" (Acts 14:2). At Lystra, "certain Jews from Antioch and Iconium ... persuaded the people" to stone Paul (Acts 14:19).

The disciples wrote letters during the transition period that mention this Jewish persecution. Paul's first letter to the Thessalonians is one example:

> Ye, brethren, became followers of the churches of God which in Judaea are in Christ Jesus: *for ye also have suffered like things of your own countrymen, even as they have of the Jews: who both killed the Lord Jesus, and their own prophets, and have persecuted us*; and they please not God, and are contrary to all men: forbidding us to speak to the Gentiles that they might be saved, *to fill up their sins alway*: for the wrath is come upon them to the uttermost. (1 Thess 2:14–16)

In the Olivet Discourse, Jesus warned about these sufferings to prepare his disciples for what lay ahead. He wanted them to recognize that God intended to end the Mosaic age and establish the messianic age through their sufferings during the transition period. They learned the lesson; they understood that they "must through much tribulation enter into the kingdom of God" (Acts 14:22) before the temple's fall.

The Jews had persecuted the prophets, and they were about to kill the Lord Jesus; they would then fill up the cup of God's wrath against them by persecuting the disciples before the end of the Mosaic age (cf. Matt 23:32). That is why Paul could say: "I now rejoice in my sufferings for you, and *fill up in my flesh what is lacking in the afflictions of Christ*, for the sake of His body, which is the church" (Col 1:24). Christ's atonement on the cross was not lacking anything; it accomplished all that God meant for it to accomplish. Paul meant that the transition from the Mosaic age to the messianic age would not be complete until the Jews finished persecuting the disciples. Then, God would destroy the temple, leaving the church as the messianic-age temple in which Jesus's *parousia* (presence) would live. Paul knew the reason for his suffering as a minister of Christ.

Jesus linked his persecution-sign to the temple's fall, which was his subject in the Olivet Discourse; this sign has nothing to do with events at the end of history.

Widespread Apostasy. Jesus' second ministry-related sign was *widespread apostasy*:

> And then shall many be offended, and shall betray one another, and shall hate one another. And many false prophets shall rise, and shall deceive many. And because iniquity shall abound, the love of many shall wax cold. But he that shall endure unto the end, the same shall be saved. (Matt 24:10–13)

The previous signs—religious deceivers, civil unrest, physical disturbances, and persecution—would contribute to this falling away. The apostasy would be part of the "beginning of the birth pains" (Matt 24:8 NKJV), but would not show that the temple's fall was at hand.

The New Testament confirms this apostasy existed in the disciples' generation. Peter, for example, mentions it in his letters to Jewish Christians "scattered throughout Pontus, Galatia, Cappadocia, Asia, and Bithynia" (1 Pet 1:1). He tells them that "the end of all things is at hand … the time is come that judgment must begin at the house of God" (1 Pet 4:7, 17). The temple—the Old Testament house of God (e.g., 2 Chr 29:16)—would soon fall under God's judgment, signifying the end of the Mosaic age. Peter doubtless remembered Jesus' warning of apostasy before "the end" came when he wrote:

> But there were false prophets also among the people, even as there shall be false teachers among you, who privily shall bring in damnable heresies, even denying the Lord that bought them, and bring upon themselves swift destruction. And *many shall follow their pernicious ways*; by reason of whom the way of truth shall be evil spoken of. (2 Pet 2:1-2)

God had "bought" Israel from Egyptian bondage (e.g., Deut 32:6; Exod 15:16; Ps 74:2; 78:54; Isa 43:3–4), but false teachers had deceived many of them. Peter is saying a similar deception of those whom God had thus purchased will occur in his generation, fulfilling Jesus' sign.

The letter to the Hebrews, probably written between AD 64 and 68,[19] contains several warnings against this apostasy. It places them in a context almost identical to Jesus' Olivet Discourse: during the "last days" of the Mosaic age (Heb 1:2); when the inferior things of the Mosaic age were about to be removed (Heb 12:27); when the disciples were "receiving a kingdom" (Heb 12:28); when Jesus would come in "a little while" (Heb 10:37); and when God's judgment was "about to consume the adversaries" (Heb 10:27 HCSB)—elements that fit well on our current diagram of inmillennialism. Hebrews then emphasizes that earthly Jerusalem was not a "continuing city" (Heb 13:14). In this context, the Hebrew Christians must not draw back—apostatize—to perdition as many were doing (Heb 10:39). The Hebrews letter sees Jesus' apostasy-sign in the Olivet Discourse as a present danger.

Paul experienced the ravages of this widespread apostasy. In his second letter to Timothy, he said, "This thou knowest, that *all they which are in Asia* be turned away from me; of whom are Phygellus and Hermogenes" (2 Tim 1:15). He mentioned two false prophets, "Hymenaeus and Philetus; who concerning the truth have erred, saying that the resurrection is past already; and overthrow the faith of some" (2 Tim 2:17–18). Again, Paul poignantly wrote, "Demas hath forsaken me, having loved this present world, and is departed unto Thessalonica" (2 Tim 4:10). Paul said the Holy Spirit had confirmed the warning Jesus had given in the Olivet Discourse: "The Spirit speaketh expressly, that in the latter times some shall depart from the faith, giving heed to seducing spirits, and doctrines of devils" (1 Tim 4:1).

The apostasy-sign Jesus gave in the Olivet Discourse was for the last days of the Mosaic age; it was not a warning about apostasy at the end of history.

Preaching to All Nations. Jesus' last ministry-related sign involved gospel preaching: "This gospel of the kingdom shall be preached in all the world for a witness unto all nations; then shall the end come" (Matt 24:14). The fulfillment of this sign would point to the temple's sooncoming fall and "the end" of the Mosaic age.

This sign would involve preaching *the gospel of the kingdom*. In their *sign* question, the disciples associated the temple's fall with the end of the Mosaic age and the start of the messianic age, which they often called the kingdom of God. They had heard John the Baptist and Jesus preach about the kingdom; they, themselves, had preached this message to Israel. So the disciples were familiar with the subject of Jesus' ministry-sign: the proclamation of the "good news" that the long-promised age had arrived. The old Mosaic age would end when the temple fell; the kingdom of God would remain.

This preaching-sign would be *a witness unto all nations*. Jesus and his disciples had provided this witness to Israel alone for over three years (e.g., Matt 4:23; 9:35). And, Jesus had said, the disciples would continue to bear witness to Israel "till the Son of man be come" (Matt 10:7, 23). But during the period between the Olivet Discourse and the temple's fall, the disciples' preaching field would expand "unto all nations."

This broadened preaching would serve as *a witness* to the nations. In the Old Testament, God had used the prophets to call the nations to witness his judgments of apostate Israel. Micah provides one example:

> The word of the Lord that came to Micah ... which he saw concerning Samaria and Jerusalem. Hear, *you peoples, all of you; pay attention, O earth*, and all that is in it, and let the Lord God be *a witness* against you, the Lord from his holy temple. For behold, the Lord is coming out of his place, and will come down and tread upon the high places of the earth. And the mountains will melt under him, and the valleys will split open, like wax before the fire, like waters poured down a steep place. All this is *for the transgression of Jacob and for the sins of the house of Israel.* What is the transgression of Jacob? Is it not Samaria? And what is the high place of Judah? Is it not Jerusalem? Therefore I will make a heap in the open country, a place for planting vineyards, and I will pour down her stones into the valley and uncover her foundations.... Her wound is incurable, and it has come to Judah; it has reached to the gate of my people, to Jerusalem.... For the inhabitants of Maroth wait anxiously for good, because disaster has come down from the Lord to the gate of Jerusalem. (Mic 1:1–12 ESV)

God, through his prophet, provided a witness to the nations of his soon-coming judgment of apostate Israel.

The disciples' preaching in the last days of the Mosaic age would serve the same purpose—the nations must know that God was about to judge Israel again. This judgment would be more significant than any previous one: it would signify the transition to the messianic kingdom age.

This witness-preaching is not equivalent to the Great Commission. There, the objective is different: "make disciples of all the nations … teaching them to observe all things that [Jesus] commanded" (Matt 28:19–20 NKJV). Jesus' future disciples could accomplish this mission in the messianic age *because of* the things God was doing in the last days of the Mosaic age. The disciples must notify the nations that these things were happening; they must command "all men every where to repent" (Acts 17:30), believe the gospel of the kingdom, and submit to King Jesus.

Jesus said that when the disciples accomplished this preaching, *then shall the end come*. This does not mean the end of the messianic age, the end of history, or the end of the *kosmos*; it means the end of the Mosaic age connected with the temple's fall (Matt 24:1–3, 6, 13).

By this point, it will not surprise you to learn that the New Testament confirms the fulfillment of this sign, too. Paul confirmed it in his commendation of the Christians at Rome: "Your faith is spoken of *throughout the whole world*" (Rom 1:8). This means the "whole world" was aware, to some extent, of God's messianic-age temple. Later in the letter, Paul explains why most Jews had rejected the gospel of the kingdom. In his explanation, he refers to Psalm 19:4 as an accomplished fact: "But I say, Have they not heard? Yes verily, *their sound went into all the earth, and their words unto the ends of the world*" (Rom 10:18). By the time Paul wrote Romans, the gospel had reached "all the earth" and "the ends of the world." Then, in his benediction, Paul says:

> Now to Him who is able to establish you according to my gospel and the preaching of Jesus Christ, according to the revelation of the mystery which has been kept secret for long ages past, but now is manifested, and by the scriptures of the prophets, according to the commandment of the eternal God, *has been made known to all*

the nations, leading to obedience of faith; to the only wise God, through Jesus Christ, be the glory forever. Amen. (Rom 16:25–27 NASB)

Paul told the Colossians that the kingdom announcement had come to them as it had *"in all the world"* (Col 1:6); the disciples had, by this time, "preached to every creature which is under heaven" (Col 1:23). Just before "Paul's execution in A.D. 64 or 65,"[20] he "expounded and testified the kingdom of God" to the Jews in Rome. By that time, those Jews could say Christianity was a "sect … *every where* … spoken against" (Acts 28:22–23).

When the disciples finished writing their letters, they had preached "this gospel of the kingdom … in all the world for a witness unto all nations" (Matt 24:14); the end of the Mosaic age was about to come.

Conclusion

We have now surveyed all the "beginning of sorrows" signs Jesus said would occur before the temple fell. The New Testament Scriptures and ancient non-biblical sources provide abundant proof of their fulfillment during the disciples' generation. These preliminary signs fit well in the prophetic framework the Olivet Discourse has revealed to this point:

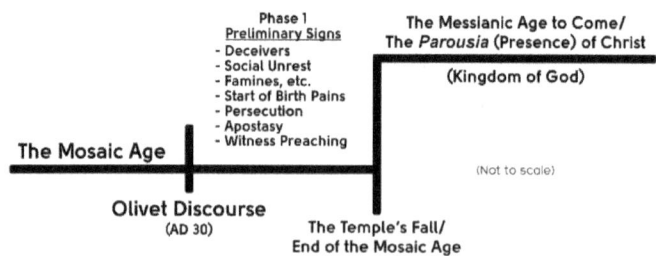

Figure 8-1. Inmillennialism through the Preliminary Signs

We are now ready to examine the signs Jesus gave that would occur just before the temple's fall.

Notes

1 I.e., from the Mosaic age to the messianic age.

2 This word is in the same group as *planētēs*, from which we get our English word planet. [Gerhard Kittel, Geoffrey W. Bromiley, and Gerhard Friedrich, eds., *Theological Dictionary of the New Testament* (Grand Rapids: Eerdmans, 1964–76), 6:228.] This reminds us of Copernicus and how his model restored order to the spheres orbiting our sun. May our emerging model of prophecy "restore order" to many of the biblical passages that seem to "deceive" us when we view them through the existing models!

3 The disciples' later writings demonstrate how some of Jesus' professed followers were deceived about this very thing. See, for example, 2 Thess 2:1–4.

4 Justin Martyr, "The First Apology of Justin," in *The Apostolic Fathers with Justin Martyr and Irenaeus*, ed. Alexander Roberts, James Donaldson, and A. Cleveland Coxe, vol. 1, The Ante-Nicene Fathers (Buffalo, NY: Christian Literature Company, 1885), 171.

5 Revelation uses the same word (*planaō*) as Jesus in the Olivet Discourse.

6 G. K. Beale, *The Book of Revelation: A Commentary on the Greek Text*, The New International Greek Testament Commentary (Grand Rapids: W. B. Eerdmans, 1999), 709.

7 Beale, *Revelation*, 711.

8 Other than the sources I quote here, Beale documents "miracles" of this type by repeatedly referring to Steven J. Scherrer, "Signs and Wonders in the Imperial Cult: A New Look At a Roman Religious Institution in the Light of Rev 13:13–15," *JBL* 103 (4) (Dec., 1984). He also lists pseudo-Clement, *Recognitions* 3.47; *Homilies* 2.32; Justin, *Apology I* 26; Irenaeus, *Contra Haereses* 1.23; Lucian, *Alexander* 24–33; *De Syria Dea* 10; Eusebius H.E. 2.13.1–4; Theophilus, *Ad Autolycum* 1.8; cf. the tradition about Simon Magus, who purportedly gave life to statues. [Beale, *Revelation*, 711n264.]

9 W. M. Ramsay, *The Letters to the Seven Churches of Asia and Their Place in the Plan of the Apocalypse* (1904; repr., Minneapolis: James Family, 1978), 99.

10 Gerhard Kittel, "εἰκών," in *Theological Dictionary of the New Testament*, ed. Gerhard Kittel, trans. Geoffrey W. Bromiley (Grand Rapids: Eerdmans, 1964–76), 388. Emphasis his.

11 Ramsay, *The Letters to the Seven Churches of Asia*, 102.

12 Gill, "Exposition," 7:285–86.

13 William Hendriksen, *Exposition of the Gospel According to Matthew*, New Testament Commentary (Grand Rapids: Baker, 1973), 852. Hendriksen observes these wars did not stop at the temple's destruction and, therefore, were not unique to what I am here calling the transition period. But this just proves Jesus' point—these things were *not* signs of the end of the Mosaic age.

14 Gill, "Exposition," 7:286 (commentary on Matt 24:6).
15 Gill, "Exposition," 7:286 (commentary on Matt 24:6).
16 Hendriksen, *Matthew*, 853.
17 The AV has "the beginning of sorrows."
18 Robertson, *A Harmony*, 169.
19 William L. Lane, *Hebrews 1–8*, Word Biblical Commentary, eds. David Allen Hubbard and Glenn W. Barker, reissue ed. (Dallas: Word, 1998), lxvi.
20 D. A. Carson, Douglas J. Moo, and Leon Morris, *An Introduction to the New Testament* (Grand Rapids: Zondervan, 1992), 192.

CHAPTER NINE

Response: Later Sign

JESUS HAS given preliminary signs that would show "the beginning of the birth pains" (Matt 24:8 ESV); now he gives a sign more closely associated with the temple's fall—a time of "great tribulation" (Matt 24:21). I will examine this sign by supplementing Matthew's description of it with details from Mark and Luke.

I will make three general observations about the "great tribulation" sign: First, it continues the *literary patterns* I mentioned earlier. It moves our focus farther down the *general-to-specific* geographic continuum: it is not a general sign that would affect the Roman Empire as a whole or the disciples' ministry in its various parts. Instead, this sign would occur within the land of Israel, particularly in Jerusalem. Jesus also changes *literary styles* as he describes this sign, moving from the prose of the earlier signs to more figurative expressions. He transitions from a literal description of the disciples' future afflictions (Gk. *thilipsis*; Matt 24:9) to a hyperbolic description of the "great tribulation (Gk. *thilipsis*)" as the greatest of all time (Matt 24:21). I will devote a section in this chapter to this hyperbole.

My second general observation is that this sign forces me to change my method of showing the fulfillment of Jesus' signs. Before, the New Testament Scriptures served as my primary source to show that Jesus' signs occurred before the temple fell. That will not be possible for the remaining signs because the New Testament does not provide a historical description of the temple's fall or the "great tribulation" that immediately preceded it. John A. T. Robinson recognizes this in his effort to establish dates for the New Testament books:

> One of the oddest facts about the New Testament is that what on any showing would appear to be the single most datable and climactic event of the period—the fall of Jerusalem ... and with it the collapse of institutional Judaism based on the temple—is never once mentioned as a past fact.[1]

I will, of necessity, use uninspired sources to show the fulfillment of Jesus' signs. But I will not be adrift in a sea of prophetic speculation; reliable historical sources—Josephus chief among them—will provide descriptions of the "great tribulation" that meet my needs.

My third general observation is that Jesus draws more heavily from the Old Testament prophets in this sign than in his earlier ones. The prophets had described abominations, God's vengeance, and the deliverance of Israel from tribulation; in the Olivet Discourse, Jesus is adding his voice to theirs as he tells how the "great tribulation" will fulfill their prophecies. They had told the story of God's dealings with Israel; Jesus is advancing the same story toward its climactic end.

Here is our outline of the Olivet Discourse that reminds us of our location (shown in bold):

I. Jesus prediction of the temple's destruction (Matt. 24:1-2)
II. The disciples' two questions regarding *when* and the *sign* (Matt. 24:3)
III. Jesus' response to the *sign* question (Matt 24:4–31)
    A. Phase 1: preliminary signs (Matt 24:4–14)—the beginning of birth pains (v. 8)
    B. Phase 2: later sign (Matt 24:15–26)—the period of "the end" (v. 14)
    C. Phase 3: immediate signs (Matt 24:27–31)—the end itself (v. 29)

IV. Jesus' response to the *when* question (Matt 24:32–36)
V. Jesus' exhortations to watchfulness (Matt 24:37–25:46)

In this chapter, I will discuss three aspects of the "great tribulation" sign: (1) the *desolation* it brought, (2) the *descriptions* it required, and (3) the *deliverance* it afforded.

Desolation

Jesus' "great tribulation" sign included a warning about the abomination of desolation that Daniel had foretold:

> When ye therefore shall see *the abomination of desolation*, spoken of by Daniel the prophet, stand in the holy place, (whoso readeth, let him understand:) then let them which be in Judaea flee into the mountains: let him which is on the housetop not come down to take any thing out of his house: neither let him which is in the field return back to take his clothes. And woe unto them that are with child, and to them that give suck in those days! But pray ye that your flight be not in the winter, neither on the sabbath day. (Matt 24:15–20)

When the disciples saw this abomination, they would know the temple's fall was at hand.

Daniel had described *three* temple desolations: which one did Jesus have in mind? In order of their historical fulfillment, the prophet had mentioned: (1) the desolation of the temple by the Babylonian armies (Dan 9:2, 17–18); (2) the "little horn" desolation (Dan 8:9–27; 11:31), and (3) the desolation of "the prince that shall come" (Dan 9:26–27; 12:11).[2]

The first desolation had already occurred in Daniel's day. It was the desolation Jeremiah had foretold while writing in "the years 627–587 B.C. (or perhaps a little later)."[3] He had said that God would send the king of Babylon against Israel: "And this whole land shall be a desolation, and an astonishment; and these nations shall serve the king of Babylon seventy years" (Jer 25:11). The date of the fulfillment is well known: "In 587 the Babylonian forces breached the walls of Jerusalem."[4]

Jeremiah had also said Israel would return to the land after the seventy years in exile (Jer 25:12; 29:10). While living in Babylon, Daniel read Jeremiah's prophecy and realized the seventy years were almost over; so he began praying that God would fulfill Jeremiah's prophecy (Dan 9:2–3). God answered his prayer: the Jews returned to their land, built the Second Temple,[5] and reinstated the daily sacrifices, reversing the effects of the first desolation in Daniel.

Daniel's second, "little horn," desolation was a future (to him) "transgression of desolation" (Dan 8:1, 13; 11:31). He predicted that the Jews would again restore the temple after this event happened: "Then shall the sanctuary be cleansed" (Dan 8:14). The tyrant Antiochus Epiphanes[6] abominated the temple in the month Tishri, 167 BC. Judas Maccabaeus became a Jewish hero when he accomplished "the rededication of the temple … on 25 Chislev (or 14 December) 164 B.C."[7] These events fulfilled Daniel's desolation prophecy of the "little horn."

When Jesus gave the Olivet Discourse, the disciples knew these two abominations and subsequent restorations had occurred—they celebrated the second one in the annual "feast of the dedication" (John 10:22). So they knew Jesus' reference to "the abomination of desolation spoken of by Daniel the prophet" pertained to Daniel's *third* abomination. The prophet had mentioned it twice:

> And after threescore and two weeks shall Messiah be cut off, but not for himself: and the people of the prince that shall come shall destroy the city and the sanctuary; and the end thereof shall be with a flood, *and unto the end of the war desolations are determined*. And he shall confirm the covenant with many for one week: and in the midst of the week he shall cause the sacrifice and the oblation to cease, and for *the overspreading of abominations he shall make it desolate*, even until the consummation, and that determined shall be poured upon the desolate. (Dan 9:26–27)

> And from the time that the daily sacrifice shall be taken away, and *the abomination that maketh desolate* set up, there shall be a thousand two hundred and ninety days. (Dan 12:11)

For over five centuries, Daniel's prophecy of a third abomination had remained unfulfilled; now, Jesus is saying, it would happen before the temple fell.

Two details of Daniel's third temple desolation are important for our prophetic model. First, *this desolation was to follow the Messiah's vicarious death*; he would "be cut off, but not for himself," *then* "the people of the prince that shall come shall destroy the city and the sanctuary … and … he shall cause the sacrifice and the oblation to cease, and for the overspreading of abominations he shall make it desolate" (Dan 9:26–27). Jesus is following this sequence in the Olivet Discourse as he responds to the disciples' sign question. He had told them he—as the Messiah—would die in Jerusalem and rise again the third day (e.g., Matt 16:21). After his resurrection, some disciples would witness Daniel's third abomination of desolation. The temple would fall, bringing the end of "the sacrifice and oblation." Both Daniel and Jesus say the Messiah would be "cut off," *then* the abomination of desolation would occur.

Second, in Daniel's prophecy of this desolation, *there was no promise of restoration*; he did not mention the continuation (or resumption) of the temple's sacrificial system as he had in the other two desolations. Instead, this prophecy of a third desolation emphasized its finality: a prince would destroy Jerusalem and "cause the sacrifice and the oblation to cease, and for the overspreading of abominations he shall make it desolate, *even until the consummation*, and that determined shall be poured upon the desolate" (Dan 9:27). This desolation would occur at "the time of *the end*" (Dan 12:9).[8]

Jesus again follows Daniel: he associates the abomination of desolation with "the end" and "the close of the age" (Matt 24:3 RSV). God had designed the temple in Jerusalem for the Mosaic age. Once that age ended, there would be no more need for the physical temple. The age of Christ's *parousia* (presence) would follow the abomination of desolation;

God has designed another temple appropriate for that age—Christ and his church (Matt 12:6; John 2:19–21; 2 Cor 6:16). It would have been improper, therefore, for Daniel (or Jesus) to foretell the resumption of the Mosaic-age daily sacrifices after *this* abomination of desolation. Once the Mosaic age ended, the physical temple in Jerusalem would no longer serve as the house of God.

With no promise of restoration, Jesus' reference to the abomination of desolation must have had an incredible effect on the disciples; this event would change their temple-centered world forever. Did they wonder how it would occur? If so, Jesus satisfied their curiosity: "And when ye shall see Jerusalem compassed with armies, then know that the desolation thereof is nigh" (Luke 21:20). Some disciples lived to see this siege.

In his book *The Wars of the Jews*, Josephus describes what happened: after Jesus' resurrection, the long-running Jewish resentment toward Roman occupation intensified to the point of open rebellion. In response, Roman armies invaded Judea from the North, continued south through the land, using "scorched earth" tactics, burning town after town and many square miles of countryside.[9] They eventually surrounded Jerusalem and destroyed the temple. Luke's account of the Olivet Discourse and Josephus' historical record led Matthew Poole to adopt the view of those

> who understand the abomination of desolation to be meant of the Roman armies, which being made up of idolatrous soldiers, and having with them many abominable images are therefore called the abomination … because they were to make Jerusalem desolate.… When, saith our Lord, you shall see the abominable armies stand in the holy place, that is, upon the holy ground, (as all Judea was), whoso readeth those prophecies of the prophet Daniel, let him understand, that as through the righteous judgment of God he once suffered the holy place to be polluted by the abominable armies of

> Antiochus, which he foretold, so he will again suffer the holy place to be polluted by the abominable armies of the Romans, who shall make the holy place desolate, which was prophesied by the prophet Daniel as well as the former. Therefore, saith our Saviour, when you see the Roman armies pitch their tents before Jerusalem, be you then assured God will give Jerusalem into their hands, and then all that I have foretold shall come to pass.[10]

The disciples who lived to see the Roman armies invade their land no doubt recalled their Lord's teaching about the abomination of desolation—they knew the temple's fall was at hand.

Daniel's third abomination of desolation and Jesus' reference to it fit well in our basic inmillennial prophetic model. If we try to project the words of Jesus onto an end-of-history tribulation that engulfs the entire world, his advice becomes trite. Who can escape a world-wide nuclear holocaust—as some envision the "great tribulation" to be—by heading to the hills before returning to their homes from their fields? Will the Mosaic-age restrictions on Sabbath-day travel be in effect then? Such questions are needless, for Jesus was speaking about first-century events in Israel connected with the temple's fall. Daniel's remaining abomination of desolation pertained to the disciples on the Mount of Olives, not to a generation in the far distant future.

Descriptions

Jesus shows the significance of the "great tribulation"—its immediate effects and its theological results—through his powerful *descriptions* of it. This time of upheaval would be: (1) the days of vengeance of which the prophets had spoken, and (2) the greatest tribulation of all time.

Days of Vengeance. Jesus used a powerful term to describe the "great tribulation" period: "For these be *the days of vengeance*" (Luke 21:22). He assumed his disciples (then and now) would understand the significance of this term concerning the "end of the (Mosaic) age" and the beginning of the messianic age; descriptions of it were "written in the law and in the prophets" (Acts 24:14).

In the law. God linked "the days of vengeance" to the end of the Mosaic age very creatively—he composed a song. Here is a conversation God had with Moses after Israel's forty-year journey in the wilderness, just before they entered the promised land:

> The LORD said unto Moses, Behold, thou shalt sleep with thy fathers; and this people will rise up, and go a whoring after the gods of the strangers of the land, whither they go to be among them, and will forsake me, and break my covenant which I have made with them.... Now therefore write ye this song for you, and teach it the children of Israel: put it in their mouths, that *this song may be a witness* for me against the children of Israel.... Moses therefore wrote this song the same day, and taught it the children of Israel.... [and said,] I know that after my death ye will utterly corrupt yourselves, and turn aside from the way which I have commanded you; and evil will befall you *in the latter days*; because ye will do evil in the sight of the LORD, to provoke him to anger through the work of your hands. (Deut 31:16, 19, 22, 29. See Appendix E for the entire song.)

Israel had this song to warn them of their future apostasy and God's latter-day judgment. If they heard this song, they would know their time was short.

The Scriptures provide the lyrics to this song in Deuteronomy 32:1–43. Here is a part of what Israel would hear in her "latter days": "O that they were wise, that they understood this, that they would consider *their latter end*.... To me belongeth *vengeance*, and recompence; their foot shall slide in due time: for the day of their calamity is at hand, and the things that shall come upon them make haste" (Deut 32:29, 35). Here is another verse: "Rejoice, O ye nations, with his people: for he will avenge the blood of his servants, and will render *vengeance* to his adversaries" (Deut 32:43; cp. Matt 23:30–38). For Jesus to equate the "great tribulation" period with "the days of vengeance" was for him to announce that Israel would hear the Song of Moses before the temple fell; that singing would be a *sign* of the temple's demise.

The disciples understood Jesus' lesson well; after his resurrection, they began to "sing" the Song of Moses by using it to teach important doctrinal lessons. In Romans 9–11, Paul posits and answers a pressing question: if Jesus is Israel's Messiah, why have so many Jews rejected the gospel of his kingdom? His answer includes a "verse" from the Song of Moses: "But I say, Did not Israel know? First Moses saith, I will provoke you to jealousy by them that are no people, and by a foolish nation I will anger you" (Rom 10:19; cf. Deut 32:21). Paul knew his mission to the Gentiles—the Song's "no people"—was God "provoking" Israel to jealousy in her "latter days."

The letter to the Hebrews also "sings" an impressive refrain from the Song of Moses. It views the law as a shadow "of the good things about to be" (Heb 10:1 Wuest).[11] Jesus had come to take away the law—God's Mosaic-age covenant—that he might establish God's new (and better) messianic-age covenant (Heb 10:9). The day in which "judgment and fiery indignation" would devour God's adversaries was approaching (Heb 10:25–27). The writer speaks of the coming of Christ: "For yet a little while, and he that shall come (Gk. *erchomai*) will come, and will not tarry" (Heb 10:37). It is in this context that the writer of Hebrews "sings" from the Song of Moses: "For we know him that hath said, Vengeance belongeth unto me, I will recompense, saith the Lord. And again, The Lord shall judge his people" (Heb 10:30; cf. Deut 32:35–36).[12] The term "his people" *must* mean God's Mosaic-age people—Israel after the flesh (1 Cor 10:18); God will never execute a vengeance-judgment against his messianic-age people, for he has already justified them—declared them not guilty—in Christ.

Jesus' vengeance-citation from the Song of Moses fits well in our rudimentary prophetic model. He gives the disciples a *sign* of the temple's fall: a time of "great tribulation" (Matt 24:21) near the end of the Mosaic age (Matt 24:1–3). The "great tribulation" would be "the days of vengeance" (Luke 21:22). This is where the Song of Moses had placed God's vengeance-judgment of Israel—in her latter days.

The disciples' "singing" of the Song of Moses also fits our model. They said God was provoking Israel by calling the Gentiles to salvation (Deut 32:21); the day of God's vengeance was coming on Israel (Deut 32:35–36); God was taking away the first (Mosaic) covenant, that he might establish the second (messianic) covenant; Jesus would come in "a very, very little while."[13] The disciples were singing the Song of Moses at just the right time.[14]

The following diagram shows the relationship between Israel's "latter days" and God's vengeance against them as foretold in the Song of Moses:

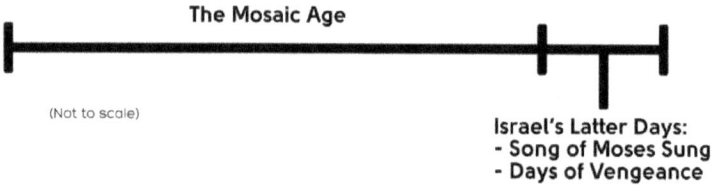

Figure 9-1. Israel's Latter Days as the End of the Mosaic Age

I will incorporate this diagram into our prophetic model after establishing another important relationship. See Appendix E for the full text of this song, selections from its introduction, instances of it being "sung" in the New Testament, and the only other direct reference to it by name in Scripture.

In the prophets. God had also linked "the days of vengeance" to the start of the messianic age. Isaiah provides an obvious example: the Messiah would say,

> The Spirit of the Lord GOD is upon me; because the LORD hath anointed me to preach good tidings unto the meek; he hath sent me to bind up the brokenheart-

> ed, to proclaim liberty to the captives, and the opening of the prison to them that are bound; to proclaim the acceptable year of the LORD, *and the day of vengeance* of our God. (Isa 61:1–2a)

The Messiah would do wonderful deeds *before* the "day[15] of vengeance" came. But Isaiah does not leave the matter there; *after* the day of vengeance, the Messiah would

> give unto them beauty for ashes, the oil of joy for mourning, the garment of praise for the spirit of heaviness; that they might be called trees of righteousness, the planting of the LORD, that he might be glorified. And they shall build the old wastes, they shall raise up the former desolations, and they shall repair the waste cities, the desolations of many generations. And strangers shall stand and feed your flocks, and the sons of the alien shall be your plowmen and your vinedressers. But ye shall be named the Priests of the LORD: men shall call you the Ministers of our God: ye shall eat the riches of the Gentiles, and in their glory shall ye boast yourselves. For your shame ye shall have double; and for confusion they shall rejoice in their portion: therefore in their land they shall possess the double: everlasting joy shall be unto them. For I the LORD love judgment, I hate robbery for burnt offering; and I will direct their work in truth, and I will make an everlasting covenant with them. And their seed shall be known among the Gentiles, and their offspring among the people: all that see them shall acknowledge them, that they are the seed which the LORD hath blessed. (Isa 61:2b–9)

Isaiah was giving a condensed description of the messianic age—the new covenant blessings that God would give mankind *after* the day of vengeance.

Over two years before giving the Olivet Discourse, Jesus had read from this passage (i.e., Isa 61) in his hometown synagogue as part of his first public address. He had stopped reading in mid-sentence, just before the reference to "the day of vengeance":

> And there was delivered unto him the book of the prophet Esaias. And when he had opened the book, he found the place where it was written, The Spirit of the Lord is upon me, because he hath anointed me to preach the gospel to the poor; he hath sent me to heal the brokenhearted, to preach deliverance to the captives, and recovering of sight to the blind, to set at liberty them that are bruised, to preach the acceptable year of the Lord. (Luke 4:17–19; cp. Isa 61:1–2a)

Jesus had said to the men of Nazareth, "This day is this scripture fulfilled in your ears" (Luke 4:21).

Jesus handled this passage with profound precision: God *had* already anointed him with the Holy Spirit; he *had* already preached to the poor, healed the blind, and announced the kingdom of God. These were already fulfilled, but "the day of vengeance" had *not* been fulfilled, and neither had the victories and restorations of the messianic age. Jesus stopped reading at just the right spot.

Jesus returns to this passage in the Olivet Discourse, picking up where he had stopped in Nazareth:

> These be the days of vengeance, that all things which are written may be fulfilled. (Luke 21:22; cp. Isa 61:2b)

Now—in his response to the disciples' request for a sign—Jesus proclaims Isaiah's "day of vengeance" will occur before the temple's fall. But that is not all: he also proclaims the fulfillment of the messianic-age blessings that will *follow* the days of vengeance. The days of God's vengeance against Israel must come so *"that all things which are written* [about the messianic age] *may be fulfilled."* The days of vengeance were not themselves the fulfillment of all things, but they were necessary *so that* all the promises of the messianic age might come.

Both events Jesus mentioned from Isaiah 61—his Spirit-anointed ministry about which he read at Nazareth and the "days of vengeance" about which he spoke in the Olivet Discourse—were necessary to establish the messianic age. "The days of vengeance" would destroy the temple and end the Mosaic age; they would simultaneously establish the messianic age. That is why Jesus says, "And when these things begin to come to pass, then look up, and lift up your heads; for *your redemption draweth nigh*" (Luke 21:28). As Geoffrey W. Grogan says, "The day of vengeance and the year of redemption belong together to the same complex of ideas."[16]

Another reference to the "day of vengeance" in Isaiah verifies these conclusions. The Messiah says in prospect, "The day of vengeance is in mine heart, and the year of my redeemed is come" (Isa 63:4). Regarding the terms "the day" and "the year" in this verse, Joseph A. Alexander refers to Hitzig's observation that this "is probably a reference to God's vengeance as a transitory act, and to his mercy as a lasting one."[17] Jesus's "great tribulation" sign—God's "days of vengeance" against Israel—would be of relatively short duration; "the year" of his redeemed would follow and comprise the entire messianic age.

The following diagram shows the relationship between Isaiah's "days of vengeance"[18] and the messianic age:

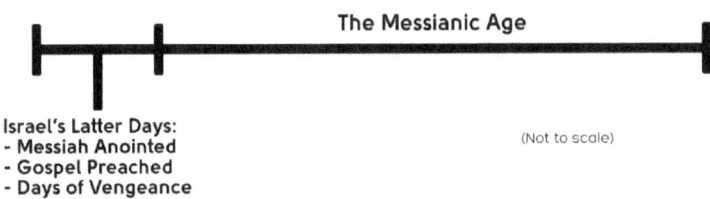

Figure 9-2. **Israel's Latter Days as the Beginning of the Messianic Age**

Conclusion. I will now combine the two diagrams in this section to show the *days of vengeance* and their relation to both ages of the traditional Jewish two-age model. The result looks strikingly similar to the prophetic model we have already discovered:

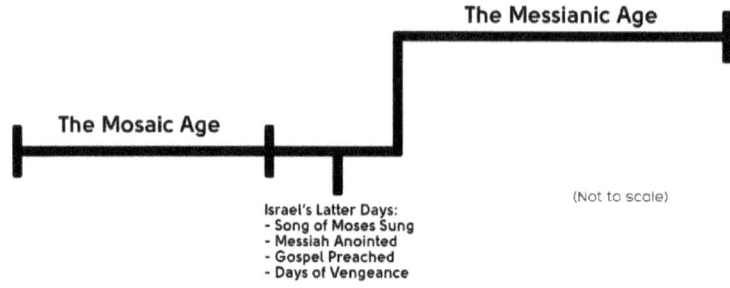

Figure 9-3. Israel's Latter Days and the Two Ages

Superlative Tribulation. Jesus elevates his "great tribulation" sign to the superlative degree: it would be tribulation "such as was not since the beginning of the world to this time, no, nor ever shall be" (Matt 24:21). As I mentioned earlier, this begins a shift in *literary styles* in the Olivet Discourse. Jesus transitions from unadorned prose to more figurative language to heighten the effect of the remaining signs. He finishes his sign-list with a panoply of sublime figures that may seem foreign to modern readers. But they were not strange to the disciples; they knew the prophets had repeatedly used these literary devices to describe God's previous judgments of Israel and other nations.

Jesus is describing the "great tribulation" by using a literary device we now call *hyperbole*. Ethelbert W. Bullinger, a linguistic authority of the highest rank, defines hyperbole as a figure of speech where "more is said than is meant to be literally understood, in order to heighten the sense."[19] Milton Terry, a widely respected authority on biblical interpretation, confirms that Jesus is using hyperbole here:

> The great tribulation and distress ... [in] the first two gospels ... may be regarded as hyperbolical; but it is no more extravagant than that of the Jewish historian Josephus, who says that "the multitude of those that per-

> ished exceeded all the destructions which either men or God ever brought upon the world," and describes the horrors of famine and pestilence and suffering within the city in most appalling detail.[20]

Jesus did not expect the disciples (or us) to understand him literally. He chose language that would impress the disciples with the gravity of what was to come, not send them to the record books of past tribulations to set their expectations.

Any attempt to interpret Jesus' language literally creates insurmountable difficulties. I will mention three. First, the question arises, *What metrics will we use* to gauge tribulation severity? We have no "suffering index" with which we can compare one tribulation to another, nothing like the Richter scale for afflictions. Should we use the percentage of population annihilated during the "great tribulation"? If so, how could this tribulation exceed the great flood, when the earth's entire population perished except for the eight members of Noah's family? If such questions and speculations seem juvenile, it is because Jesus never meant for us to ask them. He meant for his hyperbole to impress the hearer (or reader) with the severity of the event, not make him try to quantify the tribulation in modern scientific terms.

Second, interpreting Jesus' hyperbole literally *makes the Scriptures contradict themselves*: they say two separate events of the same nature are both the greatest of all time. For example, Joel described a day of the Lord in his near future:

> Blow a trumpet in Zion; sound an alarm on my holy mountain! Let all the inhabitants of the land tremble, for the day of the LORD is coming; it is near, a day of darkness and gloom, a day of clouds and thick darkness! Like blackness there is spread upon the mountains a great and powerful people; their like has never been before, nor will be again after them through the years of all generations. (Joel 2:1–2 ESV)

Some commentators believe this prophecy referred to literal locusts;[21] God would soon judge Israel by causing swarms of insects to invade the land. If this is Joel's meaning, his superlative statement—"their like has never been before, nor will be again after them"—conflicts with Moses' account of another locust plague: "And the locusts went up over all the land of Egypt, and rested in all the coasts of Egypt: very grievous were they; *before them there were no such locusts as they, neither after them shall be such*" (Exod 10:14). Two locust plagues cannot both be the greatest of all time in a literal sense.

Other writers think Joel was speaking figuratively: his vision was about the soon-coming (to him) invasion of human armies. John Gill believes Joel was speaking of the Babylonian armies.[22] Douglas Stuart says, "The foe is awesome ..., a massive empire army so great that its like cannot be imagined past or future."[23] This approach removes the contradiction between the statements Joel and Moses made about locusts, but it creates another, for Jesus now contradicts Joel by saying the "great tribulation"—caused by invading armies (Luke 21:20)—would be the greatest of all time. Two invasions by human armies cannot both be the greatest of all time in a literal sense.

Ignoring hyperbole makes Jesus appear to contradict Moses in another place. Moses told Pharaoh what was about to happen: "And there shall be a great cry throughout all the land of Egypt, *such as there was none like it, nor shall be like it any more*" (Exod 11:6). Which caused greater anguish, the "tribulation" in Egypt or the one in Jerusalem just before the temple fell?

Who was the wisest man of all time, Solomon or Jesus? God said to Solomon: "I have given thee a wise and an understanding heart; so that *there was none like thee before thee, neither after thee shall any arise like unto thee*" (1 Kgs 3:12). But Jesus described himself as being *"greater than Solomon"* (Matt 12:42).

Who was the greatest king in Israel, Hezekiah, who "trusted in the LORD God of Israel; so that *after him was none like him among all the kings of Judah, nor any that were before him*" (2 Kgs 18:5), or Josiah, of whom it was said that "like unto him was *there no king before him ... neither after him arose there any like him*" (2 Kgs 23:25)? The Scriptures contain other examples of apparent contradictions[24] like these.

We need not answer such questions; recognizing hyperbole in such passages removes the contradictions. In the Olivet Discourse, Jesus is using this well-established figure of speech to show that the "great tribulation" before the temple's fall would be of the severest magnitude imaginable. He did not intend for the disciples to search the record books, using some measure of tribulation-severity to test his prophecy. He meant for his hyperbole to impress the disciples' imaginations with the horrific nature of the coming event.

Third, a failure to recognize Jesus' use of hyperbole *disrupts the flow of Jesus' prophetic statements*. Modern interpreters who ignore the hyperbole in Matthew 24:21 think the tribulation associated with the temple's fall could not be "the greatest of all time." To buttress their case, they sometimes cite the Jewish holocaust in World War II as a greater tribulation. This thought process leads them to believe that an even greater tribulation must be in our future; *it* will be "the greatest of all time." They place this ultimate tribulation at the end of the church age, just before the millennium or the eternal state. But, as Craig L. Blomberg points out, if Jesus' "great tribulation" sign is a

> period of intense suffering just before the parousia, it would be so trite as to be pointless to say that such distress would never again be equaled [Matt 24:21]; of course it would never again be equaled, *because Christ's return will put an end to such a possibility!*[25]

D. A. Carson makes a similar observation:

> That Jesus in [Matt 24:21] promises that such "great distress" is never to be equaled implies that it cannot refer to the Tribulation at the end of the [church] age; for if what happens next is the Millennium or the new heaven and the new earth, it seems inane to say that such "great distress" will not take place again.[26]

Recognizing hyperbole eliminates the need to place the "great tribulation" in a place that makes Jesus' statement "so trite as to be pointless" or "inane"; it allows this sign to remain where Jesus placed it—just before the temple's fall.

Jesus' use of hyperbole to describe the "great tribulation" was fitting. Before they destroyed the temple, the Romans inflicted almost indescribable suffering on the Jews. Josephus provides an eyewitness account of the carnage; his summary contains language similar to that Jesus had used fifty years earlier:

> It is therefore impossible to go distinctly over every instance of these men's [the apostate Jews] iniquity. I shall therefore speak my mind here at once briefly:—That neither did any other city ever suffer such miseries, nor did any age ever breed a generation more fruitful in wickedness than this was, from the beginning of the world.[27]

Josephus was not a Christian, so he was not trying to support a prophetic framework; he certainly was not trying to verify Jesus' prophecy of the "great tribulation." His hyperbole was necessary to convey the horror of what he saw. He and Jesus both used this figure to describe superlative suffering—one in retrospect, the other in prospect.

The closer the signs of the temple's fall were to the event itself, the more elevated Jesus' language became. He uses hyperbole to describe the "great tribulation" instead of the simple prose he used for the previous signs; his next group of signs will contain literary devices more impressive still.

Deliverance

Jesus closes his explanation of the "great tribulation" sign with a promise to deliver the elect Jews from that catastrophe: "And except those days should be shortened, there should no flesh be saved: but for the elect's sake those days shall be shortened" (Matt 24:22). He also tells his disciples what they must do to be saved:

> And when ye shall see Jerusalem compassed with armies, then know that the desolation thereof is nigh. Then let them which are in Judaea flee to the mountains; and let them which are in the midst of it depart out; and let not them that are in the countries enter thereinto. (Luke 21:20–21)

The disciples may have questioned this plan: how would the days be shortened, and how could they escape *after* armies surrounded the city?

Almost forty years after Jesus gave the Olivet Discourse, Roman armies invaded Israel. The Jews had enough supplies inside Jerusalem to withstand the long siege they knew was coming. But warring factions developed inside the city; their infighting destroyed food and other necessities, reducing the time they could resist their enemies. As Jesus predicted, "those days [were] shortened."

The elect Jews—the Christians—escaped Jerusalem *after* the siege began through an amazing series of events. Josephus says the commanding Roman general, on the brink of Jerusalem's collapse, "retired from the city, without any reason in the world."[28] William Whiston, the editor of Josephus' works, tells how Jewish Christians in the city took advantage of this retreat and obeyed Jesus' command in the Olivet Discourse: "Jewish Christians fled to the mountains of Perea, and escaped this destruction."[29] By heeding Jesus' warning, "the elect" fled the city and escaped death.

Jesus had warned of another danger in Jerusalem:

> Then if any man shall say unto you, Lo, here is Christ, or there; believe it not. For there shall arise false Christs, and false prophets, and shall shew great signs and wonders; insomuch that, if it were possible, they shall deceive the very elect. Behold, I have told you before. Wherefore if they shall say unto you, Behold, he is in the desert; go not forth: behold, he is in the secret chambers; believe it not. (Matt 24:22–26)

Historians provide evidence that this sign occurred in Jerusalem during the "great tribulation." Josephus, an eyewitness to many of the tribulation events, shows how false prophets deceived the non-elect Jews:

> A false prophet was the occasion of these people's destruction, who had made a public proclamation in the city that very day, that God commanded them to get up upon the temple, and that there they should receive miraculous signs of their deliverance. Now, there was then a great number of false prophets suborned by the tyrants to impose upon the people, who denounced this to them, that they should wait for deliverance from God: and this was in order to keep them from deserting, and that they might be buoyed up above fear and care by such hopes. Now, a man that is in adversity does easily comply with such promises; for when such a seducer makes him believe that he shall be delivered from those miseries which oppress him, then it is that the patient is full of hopes of such deliverance. Thus were the miserable people persuaded by these deceivers.[30]

As David Brown says, "No one can read *Josephus'* account of what took place before the destruction of Jerusalem without seeing how strikingly this was fulfilled."[31]

John Lightfoot provides evidence from the Talmud[32] that shows the Jewish rabbis practiced sorcery and magical arts during this period, including bringing rain when they fasted and prayed. After providing several examples of this rabbinical magic, Lightfoot describes what happened in Jerusalem just before the Temple fell:

> False Christs broke out, and appeared in public with their witchcrafts, so much the frequenter and more impudent, as the city and people drew nearer to its ruin; because the people believed the Messias should be manifested before the destruction of the city; and each of them pretended to be the Messias by these signs. From

the words of Isaiah, "Before her pain came, she was delivered of a man child," the doctors concluded, "that the Messias should be manifested before the destruction of the city".... Mark that also; "The Son of David will not come, till the wicked empire [*of the Romans*] shall have spread itself over all the worlds nine months; as it is said, 'Therefore will he give them up, until the time that she which travaileth hath brought forth.'"[33]

Jesus' sign of false prophets just before the temple's fall occurred, just as he had predicted. Had the elect Jews—the followers of Christ—not exercised faith in Jesus' prophetic word, they, too, would have perished. Instead, they obeyed Jesus' instructions to "flee into the mountains," escaping destruction during the "great tribulation"; they remained on the earth to continue preaching the gospel of the kingdom.

Conclusion

History shows the accuracy of Jesus' "great tribulation" sign of the temple's fall; everything happened as he predicted. All the details I have considered so far fit well in the two-age prophetic model we have discovered to this point. Before concluding this chapter, I want to notice a few more incidental details that show the "great tribulation" was a first-century event, not something in *our* future.

The "great tribulation" would come upon people living in an agricultural society where many families lived in towns and villages but farmed land in the countryside. The disciples might learn of the approaching armies while "on a housetop" (Matt 24:17) because, as Hagner says, "the flat roof of the Palestinian house was a popular place to relax in the evening."[34] Or, if they hear of the invasion while tending their crops, Jesus says, "Neither let him which is in the field return back to take his clothes" (Matt 24:18). This lifestyle is foreign to most modern civilizations, especially in the West.

Jesus envisioned people trying to escape this time of suffering using primitive modes of transportation. He said flight will prove difficult for expectant mothers: "Woe unto them that are with child, and to them that give suck in those days!" (Matt 24:19). He told the disciples to pray that their "flight be not in the winter" (Matt 24:20a). Walking or riding an animal would be difficult for expectant mothers and more difficult for everyone during winter.

Jesus admonished the disciples to pray that their flight from Jerusalem not be "on the sabbath day" (Matt 24:20). Gary DeMar says,

> Jesus refers to the strict Sabbath laws that were operating in first-century Israel (Matt. 12:2, 10; Mark 2:24; 16:1; Luke 23:56; John 5:9, 16, 18; 9:16). Acceptable distances for travel on the Sabbath were measured in terms of a "Sabbath day's journey," approximately three-quarters of a mile as determined by Pharisaical law (Acts 1:12). The Christians would have been prohibited from traveling on the Sabbath by the religious leaders due to the distorted travel restrictions imposed upon the populace. During the Jewish and Idumean revolts against Rome (A.D. 66–70), Pella, a rock fortress hidden in the hill country approximately sixty miles northeast of Jerusalem, became a refuge for many fleeing Christians.[35]

The "great tribulation" would take place before the temple's fall ended the Mosaic age. D. A. Carson says, "The instructions Jesus gives his disciples about what to do in view of [Matt 24:15] are so specific that they must be related to the Jewish War."[36]

Within the lifetime of some disciples who heard the Olivet Discourse, Roman armies surrounded Jerusalem, polluted the holy place, and destroyed the temple. During the siege, the Christians escaped to the mountains; details of their flight agreed with those Jesus described in the Olivet Discourse. There is no reason to suppose Jesus was speaking about another event in their distant future.

The prophetic model we have discovered to this point accounts for all elements of the "great tribulation" sign: the abomination of desolation

RESPONSE: LATER SIGN

in Daniel; the "days of vengeance" in Moses and Isaiah; the hyperbole in Jesus' description; and the deliverance in Jesus' promise. I will update our diagram to show this sign:

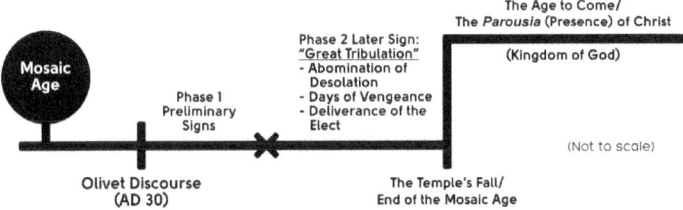

Figure 9-4. Inmillennialism through the Later Sign

Notes

1 John A. T. Robinson, *Redating the New Testament* (Eugene, OR: Wipf & Stock Pub, 2000), 13.

2 For a full discussion of these abominations, see James Farquharson, *A New Illustration of the Latter Part of Daniel's Last Vision and Prophecy* (London: Smith, Elder, and Co., 1838). A copy of this book in PDF format is available from American Vision.

3 Peter C. Craigie, Page H. Kelley, and Joel F. Drinkard Jr., *Jeremiah 1–25*, Word Biblical Commentary (Dallas: Thomas Nelson, 1991), xlv.

4 Craigie, Kelley, and Drinkard Jr., *Jeremiah 1–25*, xlvii.

5 This temple was the subject of Jesus' prophecy in the Olivet Discourse in AD 30. King Herod had almost completed his extensive enhancements to this structure by that time.

6 The identification of the little horn in Daniel's prophecy with Antiochus is common among scholars. See, for example, John E. Goldingay, *Daniel*, Word Biblical Commentary, ed. David A. Hubbard (Dallas: Word, 1989). The small horn growing from the Seleucid line was Antiochus IV.

7 For both desolation and restoration see Gleason L. Archer, Jr., "Daniel," in *Daniel–Minor Prophets*, vol. 7 of *The Expositor's Bible Commentary*, ed. Frank E. Gaebelein (Grand Rapids: Zondervan, 1986), 103. See 1 Macc 1:54 for the desolation (Archer provides pertinent details) and 1 Macc 4:52–53 for the cleansing. See also 2 Macc 5:20; 10:1–8.

8 For a defense of the assertion that Jesus referred to the desolation of Dan 12, see Farquharson, *Daniel's Last Prophecy*,

9 Josephus, "The Works of Flavius Josephus," 1:228 (B.J. 3.62–63), 1:236 (B.J. 3.132), 1:330 (B.J. 4.471), 1:336 (B.J. 4.489), 1:381 (B.J. 5.262). I thank Daniel Morais for most of these references, but without endorsing the site from which they are taken. ["The Destruction of Heaven and Earth and the New Heaven and Earth Explained!," Daniel Morais, https://revelationrevolution.org/the-destruction-of-heaven-and-earth-and-the-new-heaven-and-earth-explained/#_ednref11.]

10 Matthew Poole, *A Commentary on the Holy Bible*, 3 vols. (1685; repr., Carlisle, PA: The Banner of Truth Trust, 1962), 3:114.

11 Wuest, *Expanded Translation*, 527.

12 The disciples used the Song of Moses in several other places to similar effect. See the quotation of Deut 32:35 in Rom 12:19, and Deut 32:43 in Rom 15:10 and Heb 1:6. See Appendix E for other examples.

13 William Gouge, *Commentary on Hebrews* (1866; repr., Grand Rapids: Kregel, 1980), 748 (commentary on Heb 10:37).

14 The Song of Moses is mentioned by name in only one other passage of Scripture: Rev 15:3. See Appendix E.

15 Both singular (*day* of vengeance) and plural (*days* of vengeance) are used with the same point of reference. Cp. Amos 8:11, 13 and Luke 17:22, 24. [Walter L. Liefeld, "Luke," in *Matthew, Mark, Luke*, vol. 8 of *The Expositor's Bible Commentary*, ed. Frank E. Gaebelein (Grand Rapids: Zondervan, 1984), 997–98.]

16 Geoffrey W. Grogan, "Isaiah," in *Isaiah–Ezekiel*, vol. 6 of *The Expositor's Bible Commentary*, ed. Frank E. Gaebelein (Grand Rapids: Zondervan, 1986), 339.

17 Joseph Addison Alexander, *Commentary on the Prophecies of Isaiah*, ed. John Eadie (1875; repr., Grand Rapids: Zondervan, 1953), 2:399.

18 Other relevant passages depicting God's vengeance against Israel include Isa 6:9–12 (cp. Matt 13:14–15; Mark 4:12; Luke 8:10; Acts 28:26–27; Rom 11:8); Isa 63:4; Jer 5:28; Ezek 24:8; Dan 9:26–27; Hos 9:7 and Zeph 1:14–18. Not all these have explicit connections to either the end of the Mosaic age or the beginning of the messianic age.

19 Ethelbert W. Bullinger, *Figures of Speech Used in the Bible Explained and Illustrated* (Grand Rapids: Baker, 1968), 423. Bullinger did not list Matt 24:21 as an example of hyperbole.

20 Terry, *Biblical Apocalyptics*, 235.

21 Robert H. Gundry, *The Church and the Tribulation* (Grand Rapids: Zondervan, 1973), 90.

22 Gill, "Exposition," 6:462.

23 Douglas Stuart, *Hosea–Jonah*, Word Biblical Commentary (Dallas: Word, 2002), 250.

24 The examples here come primarily from John L. Bray, *Matthew 24 Fulfilled*, 5th ed. (Powder Springs, GA: American Vision, 2008), 93–94.

25 Craig L. Blomberg, "Matthew," in *Commentary on the New Testament Use of the Old Testament*, eds. G. K. Beale and D. A. Carson (Grand Rapids: Baker Academic, 2007), 88 (emphasis added). Blomberg thinks Christ's *parousia* is a future point-in-time event, contra inmillennialism. His point about the timing of the great tribulation remains valid for my purposes.

26 Carson, "Matthew," 501.

27 Josephus, "The Works of Flavius Josephus," 1:404 (B.J. 5.442).

28 Josephus, "The Works of Flavius Josephus," 1:204 (B.J. 2.540).

29 Josephus, "The Works of Flavius Josephus," 1:204n (B.J. 2:539n).

30 Josephus, "The Works of Flavius Josephus," 1:453 (B.J. 6.285–88).

31 Robert Jamieson, A. R. Fausset, and David Brown, *A Commentary, Critical, Experimental and Practical on the Old and New Testaments*, 3 vols. (n.d.; repr. Grand Rapids: Eerdmans, 1976), 3.1:193 (commentary on Mark 13:22).

32 Lightfoot, "A Commentary on the New Testament," 2:315–18. "The word Talmud or Thalmud, means to teach. And the Talmud contains the substance of the Jews' doctrine and traditions in religion and morality." [Robert Hawker, *The Poor Man's Concordance and Dictionary to the Sacred Scriptures* (London: Ebenezer Palmer, 1828), 878.]

33 Lightfoot, "A Commentary on the New Testament," 2:318 (emphasis in original).

34 Hagner, *Matthew 14–28*, 701.

35 Gary DeMar, *Last Days Madness: Obsession of the Modern Church*, 4th ed. (Atlanta: American Vision, 1999), 111.

36 Carson, "Matthew," 501.

CHAPTER TEN

Response: Immediate Signs

JESUS FORETOLD the temple's fall (Matt 24:1–2); the disciples, in response, asked for signs of that event. Jesus has given preliminary signs and a sign more closely associated with the temple's demise (i.e., the "great tribulation"). Now, he gives the signs that would occur immediately after the tribulation, those that would pertain directly to the temple's destruction:

> For as the lightning cometh out of the east, and shineth even unto the west; so shall also the coming of the Son of man be. For wheresoever the carcase is, there will the eagles be gathered together. *Immediately after the tribulation* of those days shall the sun be darkened, and the moon shall not give her light, and the stars shall fall from heaven, and the powers of the heavens shall be shaken: and then shall appear the sign of the Son of man in heaven: and then shall all the tribes of the earth mourn, and they shall see the Son of man coming in the clouds of heaven with power and great glory. And he shall send his angels with a great sound of a trumpet, and they shall gather together his elect from the four winds, from one end of heaven to the other. (Matt 24:27–31)

I will again use our outline to show (in bold) the location of these immediate signs in the Olivet Discourse:

I. Jesus prediction of the temple's destruction (Matt 24:1-2)
II. The disciples' two questions regarding *when* and the *sign* (Matt 24:3)
III. Jesus' response to the *sign* question (Matt 24:4–31)
    A. Phase 1: preliminary signs (Matt 24:4–14)—the beginning of birth pains (v. 8)
    B. Phase 2: later sign (Matt 24:15–26)—the period of "the end" (v. 14)
    C. Phase 3: immediate signs (Matt 24:27–31)—the end itself (v. 29)
IV. Jesus' response to the *when* question (Matt 24:32–36)
V. Jesus' exhortations to watchfulness (Matt 24:37–25:46)

This group of signs completes the literary trends I have been tracking. Jesus began his list with signs that would occur throughout the Roman Empire (e.g., earthquakes). He then gave a sign that related to the land of Israel and the city of Jerusalem (i.e., the "great tribulation"). Now, Jesus' signs concentrate on the Temple Mount: the events that happened there and the results. This completes the *general to specific* trend regarding geographic areas in which the signs would occur. The same is true for Jesus' shift from *literal to figurative* language: he used unadorned prose for his preliminary signs but used hyperbole for the "great tribulation." Now, for the immediate signs, Jesus relies more on figurative (apocalyptic) language to describe the temple's fall. Both trends make these immediate signs an impressive capstone for Jesus' list and bring attention to the temple itself.

Matthew's arrangement of the signs in Jesus' finale creates a chiasm:[1]

    A. *Lightning*: heavenly sign of danger (Matt 24:27).
        B. *Vultures*: earthly sign of carnage (Matt 24:28)
            C. *Cosmic collapse*: disintegration of a universe (Matt 24:29).
            C'. *Son of Man in heaven*: appearance of a universe (Matt 24:30a, c)

B'. *Mourning tribes*: earthly sign of sorrow (Matt 24:30b)

A'. *Angelic gathering*: heavenly sign of safety (Matt 24:31).

The signs in the outer couplet (A-A') would occur in the atmospheric regions: lightning flashes "out of the east, and shineth even unto the west" announce an approaching storm; angels would fly "from one end of heaven to the other" bringing the elect to safety. The middle couplet (B-B') draws attention to earthbound events: vultures feast and tribes mourn because of what has happened. The inner couplet (C-C') transcends earth and its atmosphere: the entire universe collapses, then the Son of Man is made to appear.[2]

We should not press these images too far toward physicality; their chief purpose is to elevate the importance of earthly phenomena, not describe their tangible characteristics. But prophetic images, especially those depicting catastrophes, often contain kernels of tangible reality that connect the images to the actual world. Embellishments around this tangible core produce the desired effect. I will mention some instances of these kernels as I discuss these signs.

Thankfully, the sign-figures Jesus uses for the temple's destruction come from the Old Testament Scriptures:[3] some from passages about God's previous judgments of Israel, others from descriptions of his judgments of other nations. *None* of these prophetic images appear for the first time in the Olivet Discourse, a fact that suggests the disciples understood the signs Jesus is giving; the prophets' previous use of these images had prepared the way for Jesus to connect them to the temple's fall.

If we can join the disciples in recognizing the role of these powerful images, we can test how well their presence in the Olivet Discourse fits within the prophetic model we have discovered.

Lightning

Jesus begins his last group of signs with lightning imagery: "for as the lightning doth come forth from the east, and doth appear unto the west, so shall be also the presence (Gk. *parousia*[4]) of the Son of Man" (Matt 24:27 YLT). This vivid and well-established simile[5] is a sign of God's presence as he judges his enemies—it suggests he uses the heavens to assist him in his works of devastation. In the Olivet Discourse, Jesus is using lightning to describe his presence (Gk. *parousia*) at the temple's destruction. He has just finished describing the presence and activities of false prophets during the "great tribulation" (Matt 24:23–26). Now, Jesus is saying "the presence of the Son of Man" will bring a sudden and obvious, lightning-like end to these deceivers.

Lightning is visible to the natural eye. Did Jesus mean that his physical body would be visible in the *parousia*? Most commentators say yes, but I will argue otherwise when we reach Matthew 24:30, where Jesus says the disciples would "*see* the Son of man coming in the clouds of heaven." For now, I will say that, in the Olivet Discourse, Jesus is using lightning as a simile for his divine *parousia* (presence) in judgment; he is not affirming the physicality of his presence. I will use several Old Testament passages to show this and to prepare the way for a more extensive discussion of visibility later.

David and Saul. David wrote a "song in the day that the LORD had delivered him out of the hand of all his enemies, and out of the hand of Saul" (2 Sam 22:1). He said God heard his prayer for help: "Then the earth shook and trembled; the foundations of heaven moved and shook, because he was wroth.... He bowed the heavens also, *and came down*.... He sent out arrows, and scattered them; *lightning*, and discomfited them" (2 Sam 22:8–10, 15; also Ps 18:6–9, 13). David was acknowledging the immediate presence of God in this deliverance, and he used lightning as a metaphor to describe it, but neither God's presence nor the lightning was a visible physical reality. David "saw" both through the events he experienced as God delivered him.

Egypt. David wrote another psalm in which he praised God for delivering Israel from Egyptian bondage:

> Thou hast with thine arm redeemed thy people, the
> sons of Jacob and Joseph. Selah. The waters saw thee,

> O God, the waters saw thee; they were afraid: the depths also were troubled. The clouds poured out water: the skies sent out a sound: thine arrows also went abroad. The voice of thy thunder was in the heaven: *the lightnings lightened the world*: the earth trembled and shook. Thy way is in the sea, and thy path in the great waters, and thy footsteps are not known. Thou leddest thy people like a flock by the hand of Moses and Aaron. (Ps 77:15–20)

Here, again, God was present in judgment and, as a result, "the earth trembled and shook." And, here again, lightning serves as an appropriate symbol of God's judgment of Egypt and deliverance of Israel. God led his people—the waters *saw* him—yet God left no footprints in the sand because his "footsteps are not known." The explanation is simple: God led Israel to safety *indirectly* through human agents—he led his "people like a flock *by the hand of Moses and Aaron*." Israel could "see" the lightning, discern God's judgment-presence, and observe his leadership, but not *directly* with their natural eyes.

Israel and Babylon. In Ezekiel, God used lightning imagery to describe a future (to him) judgment of Jerusalem:

> Son of man, set thy face *toward Jerusalem*, and drop thy word toward the holy places, and prophesy against the land of Israel, and say to the land of Israel, Thus saith the LORD; Behold, I am against thee, and will *draw forth my sword* out of his sheath, and will cut off from thee the righteous and the wicked. (Ezek 21:2–3)

A few verses later, God showed that this was no ordinary sword—it was his lightning-sword:

> And the word of the LORD came to me: Son of man, prophesy and say, Thus says the Lord, say: "A sword, a sword is sharpened and also polished, sharpened for slaughter, polished *to flash like lightning*!" (Ezek 21:8–10 ESV)

And, a few verses later still, God revealed that this instrument of death was "the sword of the king of Babylon" (Ezek 21:19).

God said he would *personally* fight against Israel: "*I* ... will draw forth *my* sword." Yet, when this judgment came, none of the Israelites saw God's presence; instead, they saw his agent—the marauding army of Babylon.

This judgment of Jerusalem is in the distant past as Jesus gives the Olivet Discourse, but he uses the same lightning image to describe God's future (to him) and final judgment of Jerusalem: the *parousia* (presence) of the Son of Man would attend the judgment of the temple and it would be like lightning. Yet the Jews would not see his presence directly, but they would see him *indirectly* through his agent—the Roman army.

Isaiah's Prophecy of the Second Temple's Destruction. Isaiah wrote a passage of interest to our discovery of a prophetic model. He began by saying, "Woe to Ariel, to Ariel, the city where David dwelt!" (Isa 29:1). John Gill says this woe about Jerusalem is a prophecy of the same "great tribulation" of which Jesus is speaking in the Olivet Discourse: "This chapter contains a prophecy concerning the temple's destruction and city of Jerusalem by the Romans."[6]

This seems possible because several elements of this prophecy match Jesus' prophecy in the Olivet Discourse and the historical record of what happened when the temple fell. These details include the facts that: (1) an army would surround Jerusalem (Isa 29:3; cp. Luke 21:20); (2) Jerusalem would fall to the ground (Isa 29:4; cp. Matt 24:1–2); (3) destruction would come in an instant (Isa 29:5), like lightning with thunder following (Isa 29:6; cp. Matt 24:27); (4) fire would devour Jerusalem (Isa 29:6; cp. the "scorched earth" tactics of the Romans[7]); (5) Israel would be in deep sleep (Isa 29:10; cp. Rom 11:8); (6) Israel was drawing near to God with their mouths, but not their hearts (Isa 29:13; cp. Matt 15:7–9); (7) the wisdom of their wise men would perish (Isa 29:14; cp. 1 Cor 1:19–24); and (8) Israel, like a clay pot from the hand of God, would argue with its maker (Isa 29:16; cp. Rom 9:19–21). Most of these individual elements were true of Israel at other times, but that *all* these characteristics describe that nation in the generation preceding the temple's fall suggests Gill is right.

I want to make the same points as before: God would be present when this judgment happened—"*I* will camp against thee ... and *I* will raise forts against thee" (Isa 29:3). Yet the inhabitants of Jerusalem would not see God with their naked eyes; they would see his agents instead—the Roman armies (Gill would say). God used thunder—the result of lightning—as a figure of speech to emphasize his presence and the severity of the coming judgment; this does not mean Ariel would hear a literal thunderclap. Jesus uses this same cluster of images in the Olivet Discourse to describe the coming judgment on the temple; and he uses them just as Isaiah had done.

The Song of Moses. Earlier, I used the Song of Moses[8] to help explain why Jesus referred to the "great tribulation" as the "days of vengeance"; now it will help me explain his lightning-sign. God used lightning imagery in the music he wrote to accompany his future judgment of Israel: "I sharpen *my flashing sword* and my hand takes hold on judgment, I will take *vengeance* on my adversaries and will repay those who hate me" (Deut 32:41 ESV). Here, "'my flashing sword' is in Hebrew 'the *lightning* of my sword.'"[9] God was saying, "I will sharpen my dagger *like lightning*"[10] against apostate Israel.

The Song of Moses was describing the same judgment Jesus is now describing in the Olivet Discourse. I have made the case for this already, but here is one more piece of evidence: before Moses gave the Song, he said, "Yet the LORD hath not given you an heart to perceive, and eyes to see, and ears to hear, unto this day" (Deut 29:4). He was not talking about Israel's perception of literal (i.e., physical) events through seeing and hearing; he meant they could not discern the true significance of God's redemptive acts in the Exodus. Moses said their lack of discernment would continue after his death: "I know that after my death ye will utterly corrupt yourselves ... and evil will befall you in *the latter days*;

because ye will do evil in the sight of the LORD, to provoke him to anger through the work of your hands" (Deut 31:29). In the Olivet Discourse, Jesus is echoing Moses and his Song: Israel's "latter days" had arrived, the end of the Mosaic age was at hand (Matt 24:1–3; cp. Deut 31:29). He had already said that Israel still had the sight problem Moses identified: "They seeing see not.... Their eyes they have closed" (Matt 13:11, 15; cp. Deut 29:4). Moses and Jesus both foretold the lightning-like vengeance-judgment that would fall on the temple because of this blindness (Matt 24:27; cp. Deut 32:41).

Neither Moses nor Jesus meant the Jews would see literal lightning or God's presence (i.e., his *parousia*) with their natural eyes when the temple fell, but that they would see him use his lightning-sword—the Roman armies—to destroy the temple. They would "see" the *parousia* (presence) of the Son of Man in the historical events that unfolded around them. Most of them would remain blind until death.

Kernel of Literal Truth. I mentioned earlier that prophetic images like this often have a kernel of *literal* truth within them. Tacitus, the Roman historian, confirms this is true of Jesus' lightning imagery in his description of the temple's destruction:

> In the sky appeared a vision of armies in conflict, of glittering armour. *A sudden lightning flash* from the clouds lit up the temple. The doors of the holy place abruptly opened, a superhuman voice was heard to declare that the gods were leaving it, and in the same instant came the rushing tumult of their departure. Few people placed a sinister interpretation upon this. The majority were convinced that the ancient scriptures of their priests alluded to the present as the very time when the Orient would triumph and from Judaea would go forth men destined to rule the world.[11]

The literal lightning (or whatever it was) on this occasion was not the fulfillment of Jesus' sign; his imagery described the judgment-presence of the Son of Man during the temple's fall. But the literal lightning that accompanied that event made the sign even more impressive.

Summary. Before giving the Olivet Discourse, Jesus had already used lightning to describe the coming of the kingdom of God: "The kingdom of God cometh not with observation.... For as the lightning, that lighteneth out of the one part under heaven, shineth unto the other part under heaven; *so shall also the Son of man be* in his day" (Luke 17:20, 24). David Brown says,

> When the whole polity of the Jews, civil and ecclesiastical alike, was broken up at once, and its continuance rendered impossible by the destruction of Jerusalem, it became as manifest to all *as the lightning of heaven* that the kingdom of God had ceased to exist in its old, and had entered on a new and perfectly different form.[12]

The lightning, the Son of Man, and the kingdom of God were not coming "with signs to be observed" (Luke 17:20 NASB), but they *were* coming. The disciples understood Jesus' meaning: a few weeks after the Olivet Discourse, Stephen preached that "Jesus of Nazareth shall destroy this place, and shall change the customs which Moses delivered us" (Acts 6:14).

In the Olivet Discourse, Jesus is using lightning imagery just as the prophets had done before him: to signify God's presence—now, the presence (*parousia*) of Christ—when he would execute his vengeance-judgment on Jerusalem and the temple.

Vultures

The middle couplet in our chiasm of Jesus' immediate signs reveals the traumatic *results* of events surrounding the temple's fall: (B.) "Wherever the corpse is, there the vultures will gather" (Matt 24:28 ESV) and (B.') "Then shall all the tribes of the earth[13] mourn" (Matt 24:30b). The "lightning" of Jesus' judgment against the temple would produce many literal corpses that would attract real vultures; they would gather for a grand feast. The dead bodies in Israel, and especially in Jerusalem, would provide carrion enough for their feasting.

This curse of fowls consuming the flesh of the dead was an ancient prophetic image of divine judgment against Israel. The prophet Ahijah used it to describe God's coming judgment against the house of Jeroboam, king of Israel and the enemy of God: "Him that dieth in the field *shall the fowls of the air eat*" (1 Kgs 14:11). Hosea, probably speaking about the coming of the Assyrian king and his armies against Israel, said, "Set the trumpet to your lips! *One like a vulture* is over the house of the LORD, because they have transgressed my covenant and rebelled against my law" (Hos 8:1 ESV). Jeremiah used this image to describe Jerusalem's judgment: "Thus saith the Lord; Behold, I will give this city into the hand of the king of Babylon, and he shall burn it with fire.... I will even give them into the hand of their enemies, and into the hand of them that seek their life: and their dead bodies shall be for meat *unto the fowls of the heaven*, and to the beasts of the earth" (Jer 34:2, 20). The Scriptures contain several other examples, but these are enough to show that vultures devouring flesh was a common way for the prophets to describe the aftermath of God's judgment against Israel by invading foreign armies.

As with the lightning figure, Jesus had used the image of vultures feasting before. In the passage where he had said "the kingdom of God cometh not with observation," Jesus also said,

> So will it be on the day when the Son of Man is revealed. On that day, let the one who is on the housetop, with his goods in the house, not come down to take them away, and likewise let the one who is in the field not turn back.... I tell you, in that night there will be two in one bed. One will be taken and the other left. There will be two women grinding together. One will be taken and the other left." And they said to him, "Where, Lord?" He said to them, "*Where the corpse is, there the vultures will gather.*" (Luke 17:30–37 ESV)

As we saw earlier, elect Jews (i.e., Christians) would avoid destruction by obeying Jesus' command to flee when they saw Jerusalem surrounded by the Roman armies (cf. Luke 21:20–21). As a result, they were *left* to serve God in the messianic age after the temple fell. Those who ignored Jesus' instructions were *taken* to destruction and became vulture food.

This vulture-figure has a *large* kernel of physical reality, one that comprises almost the entire seed. Dead bodies being "meat unto the fowls of the heaven" (Jer 34:20) represented the decimation of a city or nation under God's judgment. In the Olivet Discourse, Jesus is using this sign to show God would give Israel over to destruction: many literal vultures would feed on a host of dead human bodies. Josephus, who witnessed the devastation caused by the Roman armies before the temple fell, describes the kernel of this symbol:

> One would have thought that the hill itself, on which the temple stood, was seething hot, as full of fire on every part of it, that the blood was larger in quantity than the fire, and those that were slain more in number than those that slew them; for the ground did nowhere appear visible, for the dead bodies that lay on it; but the soldiers went over heaps of these bodies, as they ran upon such as fled from them.[14]

This eyewitness account shows the appropriateness of Jesus' vulture-sign; he is using an ancient prophetic image to describe the temple's fall.

Cosmic Collapse

The internal couplet of signs in our chiasm depicts the temple's destruction: (C.) the universe would collapse and (C.') the sign of the Son of man would appear in heaven (Matt 24:29–30). These form the climax of Jesus' sign list for the temple's fall; his crescendo for the Song of Moses. Their position in our chiasm draws attention to their centrality: one shows the end of the Mosaic age, and the other shows the continuation of the messianic age. In this section, I will consider the cosmic-collapse sign:

> Immediately after the tribulation of those days shall the sun be darkened, and the moon shall not give her light, and the stars shall fall from heaven, and the powers of the heavens shall be shaken. (Matt 24:29)

Does this sign show Jesus has changed—without notice—his topic of discussion from the temple's destruction to the end of the created order? No. He is using ancient cosmic-collapse imagery to show the significance of the coming historical events. Ezra P. Gould makes an important observation about this imagery:

> This darkening and fall of the heavenly bodies is so common an accompaniment of O.T. prophecy, and its place is so definitely and certainly fixed there, as belonging to the Apocalyptic imagery of prophecy, and *not to the prediction of events*, that it presents no difficulty whatever, and does not even create a presumption in favor of the view that this is a prophecy of the final catastrophe [i.e., the end of the *kosmos*].... It is needless to minimize these words into eclipses, or earthquakes, or meteoric showers, or to magnify them into actual destruction of sun and moon and stars. They are not events, but only *imaginative portrayal of what it means for God to interfere in the history of nations*.[15]

David Brown also describes the cosmic-collapse sign Jesus uses:

> Nearly every expression will be found used of the Lord's coming in terrible national judgments, as of Babylon, &c.; and from Luke 21:28, 32, it seems undeniable that its *immediate* reference was to the destruction of Jerusalem.[16]

In another place, Brown provides a longer list of references: the prophets had used this imagery regarding God's judgment "of Babylon (Isa. 13:9–13); of Idumea (Isa. 34:1, 2, 4, 8–10); of Egypt (Ezek. 32:7, 8): compare also Ps. 18:7–15; Isa. 24:1, 17–19; Joel 2:10, 11, &c."[17] When the prophets used cosmic-collapse imagery to describe God's coming judgment of a city or nation, they were not foretelling the end of the physical universe.

These signs elevate the intensity of Jesus' imagery to the highest level. The previous images—lightning and vultures—described earthbound events; now, Jesus is describing a disintegrating universe. This disintegration would occur immediately after the "great tribulation" Jesus has just described—the temple's fall would then be the collapse of Israel's world.

I will use David Brown's list of examples to show how the prophets had used this imagery and add some other examples that pertain to our discovery of a prophetic model.

Babylon. Isaiah introduced his prophecy about Babylon's future destruction with these words: "The burden of Babylon, which Isaiah the son of Amoz did see" (Isa 13:1). I mentioned earlier that God had used Babylon as his lightning-sword to judge Israel. Here, Isaiah told of a time when God would judge Babylon; he used cosmic-collapse imagery to do so:

> The day of the LORD is at hand; it shall come as a destruction from the Almighty.... For the stars of heaven and the constellations thereof shall not give their light: the sun shall be darkened in his going forth, and the moon shall not cause her light to shine. (Isa 13:6, 10)

God destroyed Babylon two hundred years later (in 539 BC) by stirring up the Medes against them (cf. Isa 13:17). Babylon's universe disintegrated, so to speak, but the physical stars, sun, and moon continued to shine; the solar system remained intact for Copernicus to observe two thousand years later.

Isaiah's cosmic collapse was not a prophecy of an event—the disintegration of the physical *kosmos*; it was a figurative description of God interfering in the history of a wicked nation.

Idumea (Edom). Isaiah described God's coming wrath against Idumea (i.e., Edom) using the dramatic image of a decomposing universe:

> All the host of heaven shall be dissolved, and the heavens shall be rolled together as a scroll: and all their host shall fall down, as the leaf falleth off from the vine, and as a falling fig from the fig tree. For my sword shall be bathed in heaven: behold, it shall come down upon Idumea, and upon the people of my curse, to judgment. (Isa 34:4–5)

These images, and those that follow, create a striking picture of what God planned to do. The Scriptures do not describe the fulfillment of this prophecy, but we know that that nation no longer exists. As Joseph Addison Alexander says, "The whole is a magnificent prophetic picture, the fidelity of which, so far as it relates to ancient Edom, is notoriously attested by its desolation for a course of ages."[18]

This passage uses cosmic-collapse imagery with other images Jesus uses in the Olivet Discourse:

> For *my sword* shall be bathed in heaven: behold, it shall come down upon Idumea, and upon the people of my curse, to judgment.... The LORD hath a sacrifice in Bozrah, and a great slaughter in the land of Idumea....
> For it is the day of the LORD'S *vengeance*. (Isa 34:5–8)

The HCSB gives a marginal reading for the first clause based on the Dead Sea Scrolls: "My sword shall appear in the heavens." This sword is the same "lightning sword" we saw in Deuteronomy 32:41–42 and Ezekiel 21:2–3, 8–10; it is a symbol of power, devastation, and swift judgment. And Idumea's cosmic collapse would occur on the day God executed vengeance against her. These images—cosmic collapse, lightning, and the day of vengeance—occur in Isaiah's prophecy of Edom's destruction; they also occur in Jesus' prophecy of the temple's fall. Idumea's universe disintegrated; Israel's would, too. These prophecies have nothing to do with the end of the physical creation, but everything to do with God's judgment of a city or nation.

Egypt. God had a quarrel with Egypt, too; he revealed his plan for that nation through the prophet Ezekiel. He used several of the now-familiar images: vultures would feast on Egyptian carcasses (Ezek 32:4), God's lightning-sword would come upon them (Ezek 32:10), and all the light sources in Egypt's universe would go dark:

> And when I shall put thee out, I will cover the heaven, and make the stars thereof dark; I will cover the sun with a cloud, and the moon shall not give her light. All the bright lights of heaven will I make dark over thee, and set darkness upon thy land, saith the Lord GOD. (Ezek 32:7–8)

And, as before, these images describe God's use of an invading army to achieve his purposes. Ralph H. Alexander says, "Ezekiel delivered this funeral dirge for Egypt in March 585 B.C.... The slaughter of Egypt would occur at the hands of the Babylonians."[19] The Babylonians darkened Egypt's universe through death and destruction, and this happened without God destroying the physical heavens and earth. History and God's plan for the nations, including Egypt, continued unabated.

In the Olivet Discourse, Jesus is using the same images that Ezekiel used regarding Egypt; he is using them to describe the temple's fall. The physical heavenly luminaries would continue to shine after that event.

Israel. The prophets had used cosmic-collapse imagery to describe God's previous (to the disciples) judgment of Israel. Through Amos, God said, "I will send a fire upon Judah, and it shall devour the palaces of Jerusalem. Thus saith the LORD; For three transgressions of Israel, and for four, I will not turn away the punishment thereof" (Amos 2:5–6). Amos continues to describe this coming judgment against Israel (the northern kingdom) to the end of the book.

This lengthy passage contains several striking images to represent God's judgment, including the familiar lightning-sword (Amos 4:10; 7:9, 11, 17; 9:1, 4, 10). He also used the cosmic-collapse imagery that often accompanies the day of the Lord:

> Shall not the day of the LORD be darkness, and not light? even very dark, and no brightness in it? (Amos

5:20).... And it shall come to pass in that day, saith the Lord GOD, that I will cause the sun to go down at noon, and I will darken the earth in the clear day (Amos 8:9).... And the Lord GOD of hosts is he that toucheth the land, and it shall melt, and all that dwell therein shall mourn:[20] and it shall rise up wholly like a flood; and shall be drowned, as by the flood of Egypt (Amos 9:5).

The Assyrian armies fulfilled these predictions when they invaded Israel: the day of the Lord brought darkness, the sun went down at noon, and the land melted. As Douglas Stuart says, "God [had] revealed through Amos the end of the Northern Kingdom. The defeat and destruction wrought by the Assyrians in 722 was indeed devastating."[21] But the physical land of Israel did not melt in 722 BC; the Holy Spirit had inspired Amos to use the strongest figurative language available to convey the gravity of Israel's coming national disaster.

Psalm 97. John Gill describes the theme of Psalm 97: "It is of the same argument, and upon the same subject, as the preceding, *the coming and kingdom of Christ*; ... it respects his first coming into the world, when angels were called upon to worship him."[22] If so, here is what men would see as the Messiah established his kingdom:

> The LORD reigneth; let the earth rejoice; let the multitude of isles be glad thereof. Clouds and darkness are round about him: righteousness and judgment are the habitation of his throne. A fire goeth before him, and burneth up his enemies round about. His *lightnings* enlightened the world: the earth saw, and trembled. The hills melted like wax *at the presence of the LORD, at the presence of the Lord of the whole earth*. The heavens declare his righteousness, and all the people see his glory. Confounded be all they that serve graven images, that boast themselves of idols: worship him, all ye gods. (Ps 97:1–7)

This is a beautiful picture of the messianic age: the earth rejoices, the islands are glad, all the people see the Messiah's glory, and he puts those that worship idols to shame. But images of judgment similar to those Jesus is using in the Olivet Discourse are here, too: clouds surrounding the Messiah, a burning up of God's enemies, lightning, and hills melting—all in the *presence* of the Lord. The psalm did not mean for Israel to expect the literal hills to melt when the kingdom of God came; neither does Jesus mean for his disciples to think the literal stars would fall from the skies.

Conclusion. N. T. Wright makes an important point about cosmic-collapse imagery that commentators often overlook:

> As a literary genre, apocalyptic is a way of investing space-time events with their theological significance; it is actually a way of affirming, not denying, the vital importance of the present continuing space-time order, by denying that evil has the last word in it.[23]

This is an important observation because most interpreters associate this imagery with the end of the physical world. This is a mistake, for, as Wright says, God means for this imagery to affirm the *continuation* of the physical world under radically different conditions, not its annihilation.

The apostles knew history would continue after the "end of the age" associated with the temple's destruction. Just before speaking about the disintegration of the universe, Jesus had said there would never be a greater tribulation *after* the events of which he spoke; history must continue for the possibility of a future greater tribulation to exist. As I mentioned earlier, many passages speak of the end of the Mosaic age, but "there are none which speak of the end of the [*kosmos*]."[24]

Jesus did not mean for his cosmic-collapse imagery to convey the end of the created order; he—like the disciples in their question—was speaking about the judgment of Israel that would occur in his *parousia* (presence), a judgment that would destroy the temple and end the Mosaic age. This capstone sign was not about the end of the created order; it was about the end of the Mosaic age. History would continue during Jesus' *parousia*—the period of his reign as the messianic King. Cosmic-collapse imagery was the best tool available to convey the theological significance of the termination of the Mosaic age and the continuance of the messianic age.

The imagery of a collapsing cosmos had performed its "prophetic, historical, and symbolic"[25] role to describe God's judgment of Babylon, Idumea, Egypt, and the northern kingdom of Israel. In the Olivet Discourse, Jesus is using it to describe God's judgment of apostate Israel as the temple falls—the disintegration and collapse of their universe.

The Son of Man in Heaven

The collapse of Israel's universe meant God had a new creation in which his people would live—the kingdom of God. Jesus' next sign describes the new universe that would remain after the temple fell:

> And then shall appear the sign of the Son of man in heaven: and then shall all the tribes of the earth mourn, and they shall see the Son of man coming (Gk. *erchomai*) in the clouds of heaven with power and great glory. (Matt 24:30)

I will consider this sign by answering two questions of vital importance to our prophetic model: (1) What is "the sign of the Son of Man in heaven"? and (2) What does it mean to "see the Son of man coming"? I will postpone the intervening sign—"then shall all the tribes of the earth mourn"—until the next section.

The Sign of the Son Of Man in Heaven. This is the first time Jesus uses the word "sign" in direct response to the disciples' original question (Matt 24:3). Here is their sign question and his sign answer:

Q. "What will be the sign of *Your [parousia], and of the end of the age?*"[26]

A. "Then shall appear the sign of *the Son of man in heaven.*"[27]

Robert H. Gundry makes an important observation: "Here Matthew substitutes 'of the Son of man' for 'of your coming [*parousia*] and the end of the age.'... *The sign of Jesus' coming* [parousia] ... *and the sign of the Son of man ... are equivalent.*"²⁸ But this does not go far enough: Jesus equates the sign of *the entire triad* of events about which the disciples had asked—the temple's fall, the end of the (Mosaic) age, and Christ's *parousia* (his presence in the messianic age)—to the sign of the Son of Man in heaven. Said another way, the Son of Man in heaven is Jesus' ultimate answer to the disciples' question.

I will use an example Jesus gave earlier in his ministry to illustrate the concept of a person being a sign. Jesus had said that God would give only one sign to the Jews:

> Then certain of the scribes and of the Pharisees answered, saying, Master, we would see *a sign* from thee. But he answered and said unto them, An evil and adulterous generation seeketh after a sign; and there shall no sign be given to it, but *the sign of the prophet Jonas*: for as Jonas was three days and three nights in the whale's belly; so shall the Son of man be three days and three nights in the heart of the earth. The men of Nineveh shall rise in judgment with this generation, and shall condemn it: because they repented at the preaching of Jonas; and, behold, a greater than Jonas is here. (Matt 12:38–41)

The "sign of the prophet Jonas" was Jonas himself, his "resurrection" after three days in the fish's belly, his subsequent preaching to the Ninevites, and their response to it. The Jews of Jesus' generation should have learned the lesson this sign taught.

By analogy, the "sign of the Son of Man in heaven" *is* the Son of Man himself, his resurrection and enthronement, his subsequent preaching to Israel (through his disciples; cf. Matt 23:34–36), and Israel's response. Unlike the Ninevites, the Jews would not repent, making their destruction inevitable (cf. Matt 22:7): Jesus would bring "great tribulation," destroy Jerusalem, and cast the impressive stones of the temple to the ground. All of this would be "the sign of the Son of man in heaven."

In the first days of Jesus' life, an old and faithful servant of God had revealed this sign to Israel while standing, ironically, in the temple Jesus would later destroy:

> Then Simeon blessed them, and said to Mary His mother, "Behold, this Child is destined for the fall and rising (Gk. *anastasis*) of many in Israel, and *for a sign* which will be spoken against. (Luke 2:34 NKJV)

Now, in the last days of Jesus' life, this sign appears again like a bookend to Jesus' incarnation. As Jesus gives the Olivet Discourse, he joins Simeon in referring to himself as a sign, but now as a sign that would be *in heaven*. After his resurrection, ascension, and enthronement, Jesus would return in the clouds to destroy the temple and bring the "fall … of many in Israel" through his appointed agent (i.e., the Roman army). But Jesus was also a sign of the "rising again of many in Israel." Three days after giving the Olivet Discourse, Jesus would "give his life a ransom for many" (Mark 10:45) in Israel[29] to "resurrect" them and advance them "to a higher status (*anastasis*)."[30] The elect in Israel would escape the "great tribulation" and remain on earth to enjoy eternal life in the messianic-age kingdom.[31] In this way, Jesus would fulfill Simeon's prophecy given at the beginning of his life and his own at the end of his life. He would be "the sign of the Son of man in heaven."

Seeing the Son Of Man Coming. How does "the sign of the Son of man in heaven" relate to Jesus' statement that "they shall *see* the Son of man coming (Gk. *erchomai*) in the clouds of heaven with power and great glory" (Matt 24:30)? Proponents of the existing prophetic models often make three assumptions about this "seeing": (1) that the coming (Gk. *erchomai*) of Christ here is the same as his presence (Gk. *parousia*) in Matthew 24:27; (2) that this coming is a point-in-time event in our future; and (3) that this event will be visible to the natural eye. These assumptions then determine their interpretation of the rest of the Olivet Discourse.

RESPONSE: IMMEDIATE SIGNS

I have discussed the important differences between the two Greek words—*parousia* and *erchomai*—and the confusion caused by translating them both as "coming."[32] I have also addressed, in part, the timing assumption: Jesus is giving a sign of the temple's fall, not something in the disciples' distant future. (More about that is coming when Jesus answers the disciples' *when* question.)

But what about the visibility assumption? Jesus says the disciples would *see* the Son of Man. Does this mean they would look up and see Jesus in the clouds as the temple fell? I answer in the negative. Jesus does not mean he would appear in the sky, hovering long enough—for at least one twenty-four-hour period—for all the nations of the earth to see him. Neither does he mean people would see some portent in the sky, like the cross Emperor Constantine is reported to have seen.

I will provide four arguments for believing Jesus was speaking of a non-visible coming in this context. As I explain them, I will ignore the issues surrounding the first two assumptions above to concentrate on the single issue of the visibility of Christ's coming.

First, a visible presence of the Son of Man at the destruction of the Temple would *run counter to precedent without warning*. The Old Testament provides a significant number of examples of God's previous judgments against his enemies, including Jerusalem herself. God and his prophets had used the same prophetic images Jesus is using to describe these events—lightning, vultures, cosmic collapse, etc. The prophets had often emphasized the presence of God at these judgments, but the pre-incarnate Son of Man never appears visibly, though he does at other times. Even Old Testament prophecies of God's *future* judgments of Israel—some of which are of the same judgment that is the subject of Jesus' Olivet Discourse—contain no mention of a visible presence of a Divine Person.

Repeatedly, God had said humans would "see" him judge his enemies *indirectly*, through his agents, which were often invading armies. In the Exodus, Israel understood God's judgment of Egypt when they "saw" his lightning (Ps 77:18). The sinful people knew God's wrath against them when they "saw" him draw his sword (Ezek 21:3). They "saw" God encamp against them when the Roman armies came (Isa 29:3). When God judged Babylon, that nation "saw" the stars of heaven fall (Isa 13:10). But none of these were visible, direct sightings of God.

In the Olivet Discourse, Jesus does much to link his prophecy to those of the Old Testament: as David Brown said, nearly every expression Jesus uses is used in association with God's previous national judgments. I suggest that it is unlikely Jesus would deviate from Old Testament precedent by inserting a *visible* presence of Divinity without providing a clear sign that he was doing so. Previous examples suggest Jesus meant the Jews would "see" God's lightning, the collapse of their cosmos, and the presence of the Son of Man—not with their natural eyes, but *indirectly*, through the agents of judgment he would use.

Second, a visible coming of Christ in this context *would make Jesus violate the law of non-contradiction*. He had earlier said, "There be some standing here, which shall not taste of death, till they *see the Son of man coming (Gk.* erchomai*) in his kingdom*" (Matt 16:28). The assumed visibility of this coming creates the problem I mentioned at the beginning of this book: it makes Jesus a false prophet, for there is no record of a visible coming of the Son of Man in his kingdom within the lifetime of those who heard him speak. This problem expands when we dig a little deeper. The coming of Matthew 16:28 is identical to the coming Jesus mentions in the Olivet Discourse: "they shall *see the Son of man coming* (Gk. *erchomai*) in the clouds of heaven with power and great glory" (Matt 24:30).[33] If one is visible, both are visible. But Jesus also said: "The kingdom of God cometh (Gk. *erchomai*) *not with observation*: neither shall they say, Lo here! or, lo there!" (Luke 17:20–21). Insisting that, in the Olivet Discourse, Jesus is speaking of a *visible* coming causes him to violate what we now call the law of non-contradiction: he is saying his coming (in his kingdom) would be both observable and non-observable at the same time and in the same relationship.[34] Paul might say, may it never be!

A non-visible (to the natural eye) coming of the Son of Man accords with the precedent set by the Old Testament prophets. It also removes the conflict between Jesus' various statements about his coming. In contexts like Matthew 16:28 and 24:27, Jesus means people would see his coming (Gk. *erchomai*)—or his presence (Gk. *parousia*)—*indirectly*, through the events surrounding the temple's fall; he does not mean it would be *directly* visible to the natural eye.

Third, a visible coming of Christ in this context *would invalidate Jesus' final verbal witness to the Jewish leaders*. Two days after giving the Olivet Discourse, Jesus stood before Caiaphas the high priest to answer charges made against him related to the temple's destruction:

> At last two came forward and said, "This man said, 'I am able to destroy the temple of God, and to rebuild it in three days.'" And the high priest stood up and said, "Have you no answer to make? What is it that these men testify against you?" But Jesus remained silent. And the high priest said to him, "I adjure you by the living God, tell us if you are the Christ, the Son of God." Jesus said to him, "You have said so. But I tell you, *from now on you will see the Son of Man seated at the right hand of Power and coming (Gk.* erchomai) *on the clouds of heaven.*" (Matt 26:60–64 ESV)

It is important to our prophetic model for us to know *how* Caiaphas would "see" these things.

I will begin with the first thing Jesus said the high priest would see: "the Son of Man seated at the right hand of Power." The day after talking to Caiaphas, Jesus died on the cross; on the third day, he rose from the dead; after forty more days, he ascended to the Father. Caiaphas might have observed these things with his natural eyes, as the disciples did; but, at the ascension, "a cloud received him out of their sight" (Acts 1:9) and the disciples could not see—nor could Caiaphas, had he been there—what happened next. The prophet Daniel had "seen" it in a night vision five centuries earlier:

> I saw in the night visions, and, behold, one like the Son of man came *with the clouds of heaven*, and came to the

> Ancient of days, and they brought him near before him. And there was given him dominion, and glory, and a kingdom, that all people, nations, and languages, should serve him: his dominion is an everlasting dominion, which shall not pass away, and his kingdom that which shall not be destroyed. (Dan 7:13–14)

A cloud prevented men from seeing Jesus approach the Father to receive his kingdom; they could not see him with ocular sight as he "sat down on the right hand of the Majesty on high" (Heb 1:3). This event lay beyond the limits of natural vision.

So, Jesus did not mean Caiaphas would, with his eyes, see "the Son of Man seated at the right hand of Power." Yet he said Caiaphas would see him, and that he would do so *"from now on."*[35] God "would raise up Christ to sit on his throne" (Acts 2:30) within a few days, and from that point forward, Caiaphas would "see" Jesus sitting on his throne in heaven.

I suggest this statement means Caiaphas would see Jesus' enthronement the same indirect way Israel saw God lead them through the Red Sea (by the hands of Moses and Aaron) and the way they saw God's sword flash like lightning (by the sword of the king of Babylon). The high priest would "see" Jesus in heaven, not with his natural eyes, but through the agents Jesus would use to work his sovereign will in the events of history.

Jesus said Caiaphas would "see" the Son of Man doing *two* things: sitting in heaven and *coming in the clouds of heaven*. I can't imagine that Jesus meant he would see these two actions in different ways, one indirectly—as he *must* see Jesus sitting in heaven—and the other directly. Jesus meant Caiaphas would see both actions the same way—*indirectly*; he would see "the Son of Man coming in the clouds of heaven" through the agents—the Roman armies—whom he would send to destroy the temple. Caiaphas, with his natural eyes, could not see Christ sitting in heaven, neither could he see him that way "coming in the clouds of heaven"—he would see both indirectly.

Significantly, Jesus told Caiaphas the same things he had—two days earlier, in the Olivet Discourse—told the disciples:

> Olivet Discourse: "Then shall appear the sign of the Son of man in heaven ... and they shall see the Son of man coming in the clouds of heaven." (Matt 24:30)

> Before Caiaphas: "From now on you will see the Son of Man seated at the right hand of Power and coming on the clouds of heaven." (Matt 26:64 ESV)

In both instances, Jesus speaks of seeing two things: the Son of Man in heaven and the Son of Man coming in the clouds of heaven. Caiaphas would "see" both these things *indirectly*; the disciples would see them the same way. They would see "the Son of man in heaven" and "the Son of man coming in the clouds of heaven" (Matt 24:30) to destroy the temple, not with their the naked eyes, but *indirectly*, through the agents he would use.

Fourth, a visible coming of Christ in this context *would run counter to the Song of Moses*.[36] I have stressed this Song's importance to our understanding of the signs Jesus is giving in the Olivet Discourse. It said, "The LORD shall judge his people"; Jesus is saying the same thing. In the Song, after God judges his people, he gives a command: "*See* now that I, even I, am he, and there is no god with me" (Deut 32:39). Earl S. Kalland says,

> The word for "see" here means "understand" or "grasp this mentally." In the same way David, in speaking to Saul after he had cut off a corner of his robe, emphatically called on Saul to "see" (using the imperative of see twice, which the NIV translates, "See, my father, look") and then added, "understand and recognize," the word "recognize" being another translation of "see" in parallel with "understand" (1 Sam 24:11).[37]

Israel would "see" the solitariness of God indirectly, by his acts of vengeance: "I kill, and I make alive; I wound, and I heal: neither is there any that can deliver out of my hand" (Deut 32:39). In the Olivet Discourse, Jesus says the disciples will "see" things connected to the same day of God's vengeance: "The sign of the Son of man in heaven ... and ... the Son of man coming in the clouds of heaven" (Matt 24:30). The "seeing" here is the same as it was in the Song: it is understanding that the Son of Man would be present at the temple's fall, not in a manner visible, but present, nonetheless.

Conclusion. This understanding of the sign of the Son of Man in heaven and his coming accounts for the sharp contrast Jesus made between the false prophets and his disciples: just before the temple's fall, the false prophets would say, "Lo, here is Christ, or there" (Matt 24:23). The disciples, however, would *not* say, "Lo here! or, lo there!" (Luke 17:21). The false prophets would proclaim the visible bodily presence of a false christ; the disciples would *not* proclaim the physical presence of the true Christ, for they would "see" his *parousia* (presence) through the events happening around them.

This understanding of this sign also confirms that the disciples knew the temple's fall would mean the end of the Mosaic age and the necessary continuance of the new messianic age. In the Olivet Discourse and before Caiaphas, Jesus says the Son of Man would come in the clouds to destroy the temple and end the Mosaic age, and he would sit as King in heaven, ruling during the messianic age. This is a strong affirmation of the importance of the "continuing space-time order"[38]—the messianic age—*after* the temple fell. Table 10-1 (next page) summarizes this sign on the two occasions Jesus gave it.

This summary completes my analysis of the couplet at the heart of the chiasm of Jesus' immediate signs. These two signs demonstrate the theological significance of the historical events some of Jesus' disciples would witness. The temple's fall would end the Mosaic age and fully inaugurate the messianic age. From then on, men would see "the Son of Man seated at the right hand of power."

RESPONSE: IMMEDIATE SIGNS

Occasion	Continuing Messianic Age	End of the Mosaic Age
Olivet Discourse	Son of Man in Heaven	Son of Man coming (i.e. to Destroy the Temple)
Before Caiaphas	Son of Man seated at the Right Hand of Power	Son of Man ... coming (i.e. to Destroy the Temple)

Table 10-1. The Sign of the Coming of the Son of Man

Mourning Tribes

Jesus, having described the end of Israel's universe (v. 29) and the new messianic-age cosmic order (v. 30a, c), gives another sign associated with the temple's destruction:

> And then shall appear the sign of the Son of man in heaven: *and then shall all the tribes of the earth (Gk. gē) mourn*, and they shall see the Son of man coming in the clouds of heaven with power and great glory. (Matt 24:30)

This sign completes the middle couplet in our chiasm of the immediate signs in the Olivet Discourse. Paired with the vulture-sign in Matthew 24:28, it shows the historical suffering in Israel during the "great tribulation" before the temple's fall. Jesus is alluding to a passage in Zechariah where God says:

> I will pour upon the house of David, and upon the inhabitants of Jerusalem, the spirit of grace and of supplications: and they shall look upon me whom they have pierced, and *they shall mourn for him*, as one mourneth for his only son, and shall be in bitterness for him, as one that is in bitterness for his firstborn. In that day shall there be *a great mourning in Jerusalem*, as the mourning of Hadadrimmon in the valley of

Megiddon. And *the land shall mourn* ... All the families that remain, every family apart, and their wives apart. (Zech 12:10–14)

Commenting on Matthew 24:30b, Donald A. Hagner says, "This language is virtually the same as that of Zech 12:10–14 (where both the same verb as in Matthew, 'mourn,' and the phrase 'all the tribes,' as well as ... 'the land [of Israel],' occur)."[39]

Forty-eight hours after Jesus gives this sign, on the night of his betrayal, he will quote another part of this passage[40] in Zechariah: "Then saith Jesus unto them, All ye shall be offended because of me this night: for it is written, I will smite the shepherd, and the sheep of the flock shall be scattered abroad" (Matt 26:31; cp. Zech 13:7). This, and other elements in Zechariah, show the prophet was speaking about the last days of the Mosaic age, just as Jesus is doing in the Olivet Discourse.

This match between Zechariah and the Discourse helps us understand Jesus' mourning-tribes sign. First, it would be mourning by *the tribes of Israel in their land*, not a lament by the nations throughout the world as the current prophetic models suggest. The translations make this difficult to see; they speak of "all the tribes of the earth" (ESV), "all the peoples of the earth" (HCSB, NIV), or something similar. This is very misleading, for Jesus is speaking about armies that will surround *Jerusalem* (Luke 21:20) and destroy the temple. The Greek word Jesus uses (*gē*) can mean either "land" or "earth." We will do well to follow Milton Terry's advice:

> Some words have a variety of significations, and hence, whatever their primitive meaning, we are obliged to gather *from the context*, and from familiarity with the usage of the language, the particular sense which they bear in a given passage of Scripture.[41]

Zechariah helps us see that Jesus means the "land" of Israel in this context: "In that day shall there be a great mourning *in Jerusalem*.... And *the land* shall mourn" (Zech 12:11–12). John Gill makes another observation that supports this conclusion. Jesus is speaking about mourning in "the land of Judea; *for other lands, and countries, were not usually divided into tribes, as that was.*"[42]

R. T. France uses the context in Zechariah to amplify the fact that Jesus is limiting his mourning sign to the tribes of Israel:

> The allusion is to Zech 12:10–14: "they will look on the one they have pierced, and they will mourn for him." There the mourners are identified as "the house of David and the inhabitants of Jerusalem" (v. 10), who are then listed by families (the families of David, Nathan, Levi, Shimei, and others, vv. 12–14). That is why the phrase *pasai hai phylae tēs gēs must here refer to all the tribes of the land* (i.e., as in Zech 12, a specifically Jewish mourning), not "of the earth."[43]

Jesus' mourning-sign, according to Zechariah, is one that will affect the tribes of Israel in their land before the end of the Mosaic age.

There is a possibility that Zechariah associated the future mourning of Israel with the temple's fall. In his next-to-last vision, he says, "Open thy doors, O Lebanon, that the fire may devour thy cedars" (Zech 11:1). Kenneth L. Barker makes an interesting observation:

> In the Talmud the Jewish rabbis identified Lebanon here with *the second temple*, "which was built with cedars from Lebanon, towering aloft upon a strong summit— the spiritual glory and eminence of Jerusalem, as the Lebanon was of the whole country" (Baron, pp. 378–79, esp. n. 2, where the reference in the Talmud is given). 1 Kings 6:15–18 and 2 Chronicles 2:8–9 may support such an interpretation of "Lebanon."[44]

Zechariah then describes "the howling of [Israel's wicked] shepherds" (Zech 11:3). This would match Jesus' prophecy in the Olivet Discourse: he is discussing the fall of the second temple and the mourning in the land associated with it.

I must here forego a discussion of several other interesting aspects of Zechariah's visions. One of the most intriguing involves the nature of Israel's mourning: it sometimes appears to be a mourning of regret because of the temple's fall; at other times, it seems to be a mourning of repentance. Both are true: sorrow unto repentance and a cry of anguish were both in the land of Israel during Jesus' generation. For now, I will say that Israel's tribes mourned in the land during the "great tribulation" that brought the temple's fall, just as Jesus says in the Olivet Discourse.

Angelic Gathering

The final "immediate sign" associated with the temple's destruction creates a positive ending for Jesus' list:

> And he [the Son of Man] shall send his angels with a great sound of a trumpet, and they shall gather together his elect from the four winds, from one end of heaven to the other. (Matt 24:31)

This gathering-sign completes the outer couplet of our chiasm and is a welcome contrast to the earlier (threatening) atmospheric phenomenon. Here, instead of lightning flashing "out of the east ... unto the west," Jesus says he will send his angels "from one end of heaven to the other" (Matt 24:27, 31). Instead of vultures, falling stars, and mourning, the elect experience a gathering of cosmic proportions.

Sam Storms explains this sign:

> This text is primarily a description of Christ's ingathering of his people into the Church throughout the course of the present age following the judgment that befell national Israel in A.D. 70. The passage is a clear allusion to both Deuteronomy 30:4 and Zechariah 2:6. There we read: "If your outcasts are in the uttermost parts of heaven, from there the Lord your God will gather you, and from there he will take you" (Deut. 30:4); "Up! Up! Flee from the land of the north, declares the Lord. For I have spread you

abroad as the four winds of the heavens, declares the Lord" (Zech. 2:6).[45]

This view of Jesus' last sign fits well in the inmillennial prophetic model we have discovered. I want to reinforce Storms' view by adding to his list of Old Testament passages that refer to this gathering.

I will begin by discussing the angels (Gk. *angelos*) Jesus would send. The Greek word means "messenger, envoy, … one that announces or tells." These angels, in many cases, are not heavenly beings; in Greek literature, an angel could be, for example, a bird, a poet, or a beacon.[46] A key passage supports Storms' application of this word to men who preach the gospel; it is the passage from which Jesus took his mourning-tribes sign, Zechariah 12:8–14. There, the Lord said he would, in the last days of the Mosaic age, "defend the inhabitants of Jerusalem; and he that is feeble among them at that day shall be as David; and the house of David shall be as God, *as the angel* of the LORD before them" (Zech 12:8). This use of "angel" agrees with something Paul said to the Galatians during the interim between the Olivet Discourse and the temple's fall: "you received me as *an angel of God*" (Gal 4:14 NKJV). As such, he labored "for the elect's sakes, that they may also obtain the salvation which is in Christ Jesus with eternal glory" (2 Tim 2:10); he gathered the elect to Christ. Such considerations led George L. Murray to say,

> Christ's ministers and messengers were therefore the *angelous* or *angels* commissioned to gather His elect from the four winds of heavens by the preaching of the gospel. This worldwide mission, which really began with the destruction of Jerusalem, removed the shackles of Judaism and formally brought to an end the old dispensation. The blowing of the great trumpets is also a figurative expression. The metaphor abounds in Scripture in connection with such important pronouncements as the day of Jubilee and other similar occasions. The messengers of Christ were now to go forth in His

name, heralding the day of Jubilee for as many as should believe the Gospel.[47]

In the Olivet Discourse, Jesus means that, in the messianic age, his *preaching disciples* would serve as the *angels* of God to gather his elect.

Jesus' preceding sign—mourning tribes in the land—came from a single Old Testament passage in Zechariah. In contrast, his gathering sign is a prominent theme *in every section of the Old Testament*: the law, the writings, and the prophets all predicted God would gather his people during the messianic age. I will give examples from each to show Storms and Murray are right to apply Jesus' gathering-sign to the messianic age and ministers of the gospel.

Gathering in the Law. Near the end of his life, Jacob sent a message to his sons—the incipient nation of Israel: "Gather yourselves together, that I may tell you that which shall befall you in the last days" (Gen 49:1). Perhaps with a bit of irony, he wanted them to *gather* so he could tell them about another *gathering* in Israel's "last days":

> The sceptre shall not depart from Judah, nor a lawgiver from between his feet, until Shiloh come;[48] and unto him shall *the gathering of the people* be. (Gen 49:10)

Four hundred years later, God used Moses to establish the tabernacle as the gathering spot for Israel:

> The LORD spoke to Moses, saying, "Make two silver trumpets.... for summoning the congregation.... And when both are blown, *all the congregation shall gather themselves* to you at the entrance of the tent of meeting." (Num 10:1–3 ESV)

Later in Israel's history, God established the Davidic line of kings: "The men of Judah came, and there they anointed David king over the house of Judah" (2 Sam 2:4). According to Jacob's prophecy, this royal line would not cease until Israel's "last days."

And that is where we are in our discovery process: Jesus is giving the Olivet Discourse at "the end of the [Mosaic] age" (Matt 24:3), during

Israel's "last days." As a sign of that end, he says he will *gather* his elect to himself after the temple's fall (Matt 24:30b), which is just what Jacob had said would happen.

Gathering in the Writings. John Gill says Psalm 50 refers "to the times of the Gospel dispensation; for it treats of the calling of the Gentiles, of the abrogation of legal sacrifices, and of the controversy the Lord would have with the Jews for retaining them, and rejecting pure, spiritual, and evangelical worship."[49] He says "the perfection of beauty" (v. 2) is Christ, the incarnate Son of God who, the psalmist says, will come. When he does,

> A fire shall devour before him.... He shall call to the heavens from above, and to the earth, that he may judge his people. (Ps 50:3–4)

According to Gill, this would be "the fire of divine wrath coming upon the Jews to the uttermost; and even it may be literally understood of the fire that consumed their city and temple, as was predicted, Zech. 11:1; Matt. 22:7."[50]

After this judgment of Israel, the Messiah would say, "*Gather my saints together unto me*; those that have made a covenant with me by sacrifice" (Ps 50:5). Gill says, "These words are spoken by Christ to the heavens and the earth; that is, to the angels, *the ministers of the Gospel*, to gather in, by the ministry of the word, his elect ones among the Gentiles; see Matt. 24:30."[51]

The psalmist placed the gathering of God's saints in the same place Jesus puts it in the Olivet Discourse: after the Messiah's ministry in the flesh and after his judgment of his Mosaic-age people in the "great tribulation," the time in which their temple would fall.

Gathering in the Prophets. The Prophets are a rich treasure chest of passages that foretell the messianic-age gathering. All of them conform to the scheme Storms and Murray (and inmillennialism) suggest. I will provide representative passages with a few comments.

Isaiah had foretold the resurrection of Christ and what it would mean: "Thy dead men shall live, together with my dead body shall they arise. Awake and sing, ye that dwell in dust: for thy dew is as the dew of herbs, and the earth shall cast out the dead" (Isa 26:19). Then, in that day, God would "cause them that come of Jacob to take root: Israel shall blossom and bud, and fill the face of the world with fruit" (Isa 27:6). Israel—whom the New Testament defines as those having faith in Christ (e.g., Rom 4:11–16; Gal 3:7)—would blossom, but there would be a purging of "Israel after the flesh" (1 Cor 10:18):

> Yet the defenced city shall be desolate, and the habitation forsaken, and left like a wilderness: there shall the calf feed, and there shall he lie down, and consume the branches thereof. When the boughs thereof are withered, they shall be broken off: the women come, and set them on fire: for it is a people of no understanding: therefore he that made them will not have mercy on them, and he that formed them will shew them no favour. (Isa 27:10–11)

After this judgment of his Mosaic-age people, God would gather his messianic-age people:

> And it shall come to pass in that day, that the LORD shall beat off from the channel of the river unto the stream of Egypt, and *ye shall be gathered one by one*, O ye children of Israel. And it shall come to pass in that day, that *the great trumpet shall be blown*, and they shall come which were ready to perish in the land of Assyria, and the outcasts in the land of Egypt, and shall worship the LORD in the holy mount at Jerusalem. (Isa 27:12–13)

This would be a gathering of individuals, one at a time, when the great trumpet would sound.

Jesus' gathering-sign in the Olivet Discourse matches this well. Through Jesus' resurrection and the outpouring of the Holy Spirit, God brought life to the elect in Israel. But the "great tribulation" followed in which God broke off Israel's withered branches. Then he continued gathering his people individually, "one by one." The New Testament explains the symbolism: "Jerusalem" means the "Jerusalem which is above," not the Jerusalem on earth that was in bondage (Gal 4:25–26), and Christ's heralds use the gospel of the kingdom as their trumpet to gather the elect (2 Thess 2:14).

In another passage, Isaiah foretold the coming of John the Baptist (Isa 40:3–4), then said that "the glory of the LORD shall be revealed, and all flesh shall see it together: for the mouth of the LORD hath spoken it" (Isa 40:5). By this he meant, Gill says, "Christ himself, who is the brightness of his Father's glory, and his own glory, as the glory of the only-begotten of the Father."[52] Then, says Isaiah,

> He shall feed his flock like a shepherd: *he shall gather the lambs* with his arm, and carry them in his bosom, and shall gently lead those that are with young. (Isa 40:11)

The Shepherd's gathering of his people would result from what John and Jesus announced—the coming of the kingdom of God (Matt 3:1; 4:17).

Isaiah saw the messianic-age gathering as one element in a group of wonderful developments: the Messiah would establish his rule over kings (Isa 41:2); establish justice among the Gentiles (Isa 42:1–3); and "magnify the law, and make it honourable" (Isa 42:21). The gathering, however, would only come *after* God judged Israel:

> Who gave Jacob for a spoil, and Israel to the robbers? did not the LORD, he against whom we have sinned? for they would not walk in his ways, neither were they obedient unto his law. Therefore he hath poured upon him the fury of his anger, and the strength of battle: and it hath set him on fire round about, yet he knew not; and it burned him, yet he laid it not to heart. (Isa 42:24–25)

John Gill makes this observation on Isaiah 42:24:

> [God] was justly provoked to it by the sins of the Jews, which were the meritorious and procuring causes of it; yet the Roman army could not have taken their city and

plundered it had it not been the will of God, who for their sins delivered it up to them; even Titus, the Heathen emperor, himself saw the hand of God in it, and acknowledged it; "God favouring us (says he) we have made war; it is God that drew the Jews out of those fortresses; for what could human hands and machines do against such towers?"[53]

God would preserve the faithful in Israel through this judgment, however:

> When thou passest through the waters, I will be with thee; and through the rivers, they shall not overflow thee: when thou walkest through the fire, thou shalt not be burned; neither shall the flame kindle upon thee. (Isa 43:2)

Then, God says, he would gather his people:

> Fear not: for I am with thee: I will bring thy seed *from the east, and gather thee from the west.* (Isa 43:5)

I can't imagine how Jesus could have matched his gathering-sign to Isaiah's prophecy better: he had established the kingdom of God; he was foretelling God's judgment of Israel in the "great tribulation"; and, after the temple fell, he would "gather together his elect from the four winds, from one end of heaven to the other" (Matt 24:31). The Olivet Discourse matches Isaiah's prophecy of messianic-age gathering.

Isaiah has several other prophecies of this gathering sign. I will list several of them here without comment:

> And he will lift up an ensign to the nations from far, and will hiss unto them from the end of the earth: and, behold, *they shall come* with speed swiftly. (Isa 5:26)

> And he shall set up an ensign for the nations, and shall assemble the outcasts of Israel, and *gather together* the dispersed of Judah from the four corners of the earth. (Isa 11:12)

And the ransomed of the LORD *shall return, and come* to Zion with songs and everlasting joy upon their heads: they shall obtain joy and gladness, and sorrow and sighing shall flee away. (Isa 35:10)

I have blotted out, as a thick cloud, thy transgressions, and, as a cloud, thy sins: *return unto me*; for I have redeemed thee. (Isa 44:22)

Assemble yourselves and come; draw near together, ye that are escaped of the nations.... Look unto me, and be ye saved, all the ends of the earth: for I am God, and there is none else. (Isa 45:20, 22)

Though Israel *be not gathered*, yet shall I be glorious in the eyes of the LORD, and my God shall be my strength. And he said, It is a light thing that thou shouldest be my servant to raise up the tribes of Jacob, and to restore the preserved of Israel: I will also give thee for a light to the Gentiles, that thou mayest be my salvation unto the end of the earth.... Behold, these *shall come* from far: and, lo, these from the north and from the west; and these from the land of Sinim.... Lift up thine eyes round about, and behold: all these *gather themselves together*, and come to thee. As I live, saith the LORD, thou shalt surely clothe thee with them all, as with an ornament, and bind them on thee, as a bride doeth. (Isa 49:5–6, 12, 18)

Therefore the redeemed of the LORD *shall return, and come* with singing unto Zion; and everlasting joy shall be upon their head: they shall obtain gladness and joy; and sorrow and mourning shall flee away. (Isa 51:11)

> For the LORD hath called thee as a woman forsaken and grieved in spirit, and a wife of youth, when thou wast refused, saith thy God. For a small moment have I forsaken thee; but with great mercies *will I gather thee*. (Isa 54:6–7)
>
> Behold, thou shalt call a nation that thou knowest not, and nations that knew not thee shall *run unto thee* because of the LORD thy God, and for the Holy One of Israel; for he hath glorified thee. (Isa 55:5)
>
> Even them will I bring to my holy mountain, and make them joyful in my house of prayer: their burnt offerings and their sacrifices shall be accepted upon mine altar; for mine house shall be called an house of prayer for all people. The Lord GOD *which gathereth* the outcasts of Israel saith, Yet will I *gather others* to him, beside those that are *gathered* unto him. (Isa 56:7–8)

The prophet Jeremiah also predicted the messianic-age gathering, placing it in a context that agrees with Jesus in the Olivet Discourse:
> Hear the word of the LORD, O ye nations, and declare it in the isles afar off, and say, He that scattered Israel *will gather him*, and keep him, as a shepherd doth his flock. (Jer 31:10)

The gathering would occur in association with Herod's murder of the innocents:
> Thus saith the LORD; A voice was heard in Ramah, lamentation, and bitter weeping; Rahel weeping for her children refused to be comforted for her children, because they were not. (Jer 31:15; cp. Matt 2:18)

It would occur when God created "a new thing in the earth," which Gill takes to be the incarnation of Christ,[54] and which I extend to include the new-creation people he represents (Jer 31:22; cp. 2 Cor 5:17; Gal 6:5). Jeremiah's future gathering prophecy pertained to the new covenant (Jer 31:31–34; cp. Heb 8:6–13; 10:15–18).

Summary of Jesus' Gathering Sign. The disciples understood Jesus' gathering-sign because their Scriptures had emphasized the messianic-age gathering to an extraordinary degree, often associating it with God's judgment of Israel. Also, they had heard John the Baptist refer to it:

> John answered, saying unto them all, I indeed baptize you with water; but one mightier than I cometh, the latchet of whose shoes I am not worthy to unloose: he shall baptize you with the Holy Ghost and with fire: whose fan is in his hand, and he will throughly purge his floor, and will *gather the wheat* into his garner; but the chaff he will burn with fire unquenchable. (Luke 3:16–17)

They had heard Jesus refer to it concerning the kingdom of God:

> If I with the finger of God cast out devils, no doubt *the kingdom of God* is come upon you. When a strong man armed keepeth his palace, his goods are in peace: but when a stronger than he shall come upon him, and overcome him, he taketh from him all his armour wherein he trusted, and divideth his spoils. He that is not with me is against me: and he that *gathereth not with me* scattereth. (Luke 11:20–23)

Jesus had taught them about his gathering role as the Shepherd:

> As the Father knoweth me, even so know I the Father: and I lay down my life for the sheep. And other sheep I have, which are not of this fold: *them also I must bring*, and they shall hear my voice; and there shall be one fold, and one shepherd. (John 10:15–16)

The disciples were aware of the fear that gripped the Jewish leaders because of Jesus' ministry and learned of an inadvertent prophecy Caiaphas, the high priest, made while suggesting a solution:

> And one of them, named Caiaphas, being the high priest that same year, said unto them, Ye know nothing at all, nor consider that it is expedient for us, that one man should die for the people, and that the whole nation perish not. And this spake he not of himself: but being high priest that year, he prophesied that Jesus should die for that nation; and not for that nation only, but that also he should *gather together in one* the children of God that were scattered abroad. (John 11:49–52)

On the day Jesus gave the gathering-sign in the Olivet Discourse, the disciples had heard Jesus speak of his gathering ministry in relation to the temple's destruction:

> O Jerusalem, Jerusalem, thou that killest the prophets, and stonest them which are sent unto thee, *how often would I have gathered thy children together*, even as a hen gathereth her chickens under her wings, and ye would not! Behold, *your house is left unto you desolate*. (Matt 23:37–38)

The disciples were prepared for Jesus to connect this gathering-sign to the temple's fall in the Olivet Discourse; they knew it would happen in the messianic age.

I have devoted much space to this gathering-sign because of the assumption many commentators make that it represents a point-in-time event in our future. They say God will send the angels from heaven to gather the elect in either the rapture or the resurrection. This approach severs this gathering from the temple's fall, the subject of Jesus' prophecy and the disciples' questions. There is *nothing* in the text that suggests we should make such a severance; there is no reason to separate the gathering of God's elect from the temple's fall at the end of the Mosaic age—except the assumptions built into the existing prophetic models. Instead, there are compelling reasons to leave this gathering-sign where Jesus (and the disciples) placed it. Thankfully, some commentators do so, among whom are the amillennialists Sam Storms and John L. Murray whom I mentioned earlier. I will end this section with the comments of

John Gill, a historic premillennialist, who also holds this view of Matthew 24:31:

> *And he shall send his angels*, &c.] Not the angels, *i.e.* ministering spirits, so called, not from their nature, but their office, as being sent forth by God and Christ; but men-angels, or messengers, the ministers and preachers of the Gospel, whom Christ would call, qualify, and send forth into all the world of the Gentiles, to preach his Gospel, and plant churches there still more, when that at Jerusalem was broken up and dissolved. These are called *angels*, because of their mission, and commission from Christ, to preach the Gospel; and because of their knowledge and understanding in spiritual things; and because of their zeal, diligence, and watchfulness. *With a great sound of a trumpet*, meaning the Gospel; see Isa. 27:13 so called in allusion either to the silver trumpets which Moses was ordered to make of one piece, and use them for the calling of the assembly, the journeying of the camps, blowing an alarm for war, and on their solemn and festival days, Numb. 10:1–10. The Gospel being rich and precious, all of a piece, useful for gathering souls to Christ, and to his churches; to direct saints in their journey to Canaan's land; to encourage them to fight the Lord's battles; and is a joyful sound, being a sound of love, grace, and mercy, peace, pardon, righteousness, life and salvation, by Christ: or else so called, in allusion to the trumpet blown in the year of *jubilee*; which proclaimed rest to the land, liberty to prisoners, a release of debts, and restoration of inheritances; as the Gospel publishes rest in Christ, liberty to the captives of sin, Satan, and the law, a payment of debts by Christ, and a release from them upon that, and a right and title to the heavenly inheritance. The Vulgate Latin reads it, *with a trumpet, and a great voice*; and so does Munster's Hebrew

Gospel; and so it was read in four of Beza's copies: *and they shall gather his elect from the four winds, from one end of heaven to the other*; that is, by the ministration of the Gospel; the spirit of God accompanying it with his power and grace, the ministers of the word should gather out of the world unto Christ, and to his churches, such persons as God had, before the foundation of the world, chosen in Christ, unto salvation, through sanctification of the spirit, and belief of the truth; wherever they are under the whole heavens, from one end to another; or in any part of the earth, though at the greatest distance; for in Mark 13:27 'tis said, *from the uttermost part of the earth, to the uttermost part of the heaven*. The Jews say, that "in the after-redemption (*i.e.* by the Messiah) all Israel shall be gathered together by the sound of a trumpet, from the four parts of the world."[55]

Conclusion

I will divide my conclusion into two parts, one regarding the immediate signs of the temple's fall, and the other regarding Jesus' overall sign list.

Immediate Signs. The signs Jesus gave that were immediately connected to the temple's fall are transitional: they occur at the point where the Mosaic age gives way to the messianic age. The chiastic arrangement in Figure 10-1 reinforces this point.

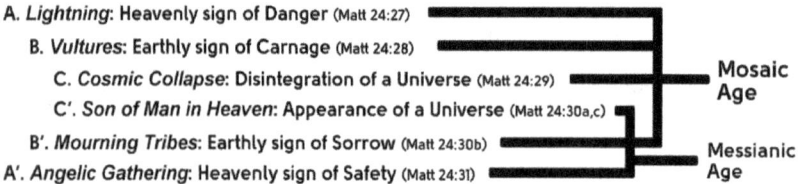

Figure 10-1. Interconnections of the Immediate Signs

I will also plot these signs on the traditional Jewish two-age view of history I am using to track the discovery of our prophetic model through the Olivet Discourse:

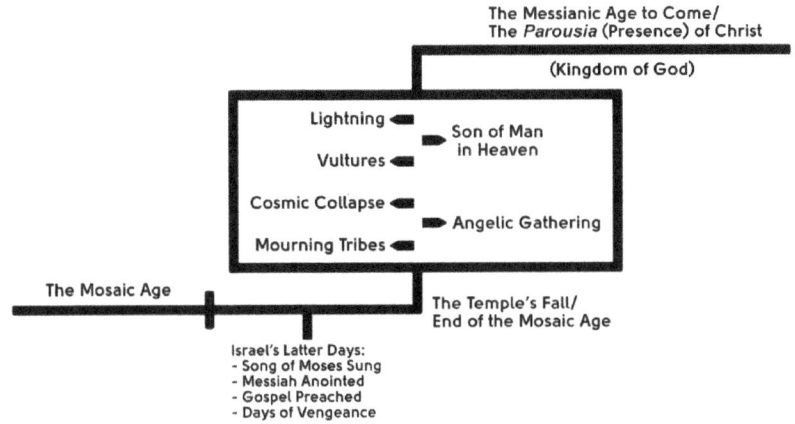

Figure 10-2. The Immediate Signs

All Signs. This is a critical point in our effort to discover an improved prophetic model. Jesus has now finished answering the disciples' request for a sign of the temple's fall, his *parousia* (presence), and the "end of the (Mosaic) age." Most commentators insist Jesus has changed subjects somewhere between Matthew 24:3 and here, interjecting topics related to the end of the *church* age that are far removed from the subject of his original prophecy. Inmillennialism says this view is a mistake; these signs pertain to the temple's fall, and they answer the disciples' question about that particular prophecy.

I can now update the diagram of our prophetic model. In Figure 10-3, on the next page, you will see all of the signs Jesus gave regarding the disciples' questions and his answers.

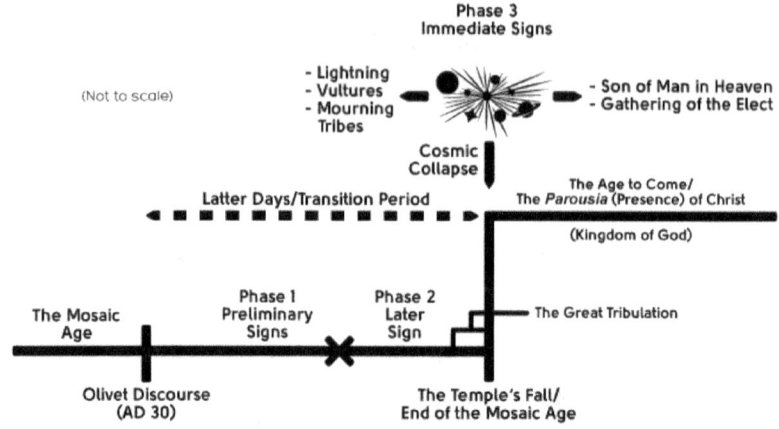

Figure 10-3. Inmillennialism through the Sign Answer

I will also add a key point to our list:

KEY POINT #9

The Scriptures refer to the period from the ministry of John the Baptist to the temple's destruction as Mosaic-age Israel's "last days," "latter days," et al. This was the "transition period" in which Jesus led his people out of the Mosaic and into the messianic age.

Notes

1 See my discussion of chiasms in Chapter 4.
2 The verb (Gk. *phanāsetai*) is passive.
3 I stress this point again because many writers interpret these as signs having a literal fulfillment. This does not correspond to the prophets' use of them.
4 See the discussion of *parousia* as "presence" in Chapter 7.
5 Bullinger, *Figures of Speech*, 732.
6 Gill, "Exposition," 5:163.
7 See the discussion of this tactic in the previous chapter.
8 See Appendix E for the entire Song of Moses.
9 Earl S. Kalland, "Deuteronomy," in *Deuteronomy–2 Samuel*, vol. 3 of *The Expositor's Bible Commentary*, ed. Frank E. Gaebelein (Grand Rapids: Zondervan, 1992), 215 (emphasis added). Cp. the ESV marginal note: "the lightning of my sword."
10 Rick Brannan et al., eds., *The Lexham English Septuagint* (Bellingham, WA: Lexham Press, 2012), Deut 32:41.
11 Tacitus, *The Histories*, ed. Betty Radice, trans. Kenneth Wellesley (New York: Penguin Books, 1998), 287–88 (5.13) (emphasis added).
12 Robert Jamieson, A. R. Fausset, and David Brown, *A Commentary, Critical, Experimental and Practical on the Old and New Testaments*, 3 vols. (n.d.; repr. Grand Rapids: Eerdmans, 1976), 3.1:300 (commentary on Luke 17:24) (emphasis added).
13 The location will become more precise when we consider the "tribes of the earth" (Matt 24:30) below; Jesus was speaking of the "tribes of the land."
14 Josephus, "The Works of Flavius Josephus," 1:452 (B.J. 6.275).
15 Gould, *Mark*, 250 (emphasis added).
16 Robert Jamieson, A. R. Fausset, and David Brown, *A Commentary, Critical and Explanatory, on the Old and New Testaments*, 2 vols. (Hartford, CT: S. S. Scranton, 1871), 2:122 (commentary on Luke 21:25–28). Brown still insisted that the ultimate fulfillment of this passage is in our future. The 1976 (reprint) edition of this commentary I cite elsewhere does not have Brown's reference to the destruction of Jerusalem.
17 Robert Jamieson, A. R. Fausset, and David Brown, *A Commentary, Critical, Experimental and Practical on the Old and New Testaments*, 3 vols. (n.d.; repr. Grand Rapids: Eerdmans, 1976), 3.1:194 (commentary on Mark 13:25) (emphasis added).
18 Alexander, *Isaiah*, 2:25.
19 Ralph H. Alexander, "Ezekiel," in *Isaiah–Ezekiel*, vol. 6 of *The Expositor's Bible Commentary*, ed. Frank E. Gaebelein (Grand Rapids: Zondervan, 1986), 901–2.

20 Cp. the "mourning-tribes" sign in Matt 24:30.
21 Stuart, *Hosea–Jonah*, 350.
22 Gill, "Exposition," 4:115 (emphasis added). I recognize that modern scholars hesitate to make such statements.
23 Wright, *The People of God*, 392.
24 Trench, *Synonyms of the New Testament*, 214 (emphasis added).
25 Ramm, *Protestant Biblical Interpretation*, 268.
26 Matt 24:3 NKJV.
27 Matt 24:30.
28 Robert H. Gundry, *Matthew: A Commentary on His Literary and Theological Art* (Grand Rapids: Eerdmans, 1982), 488. Gundry is a futurist; I am not implying he would agree with inmillennialism. His observation about the sign is valid regardless of the prophetic model one uses to interpret the Olivet Discourse.
29 I am speaking here about the "remnant according to the election of grace" in Israel (Rom 11:5). Christ ransomed his elect people among the Gentiles at the same time.
30 T. Friberg, B. Friberg, and N. F. Miller, *Analytical Lexicon of the Greek New Testament* (Grand Rapids: Baker, 2000), 52 (s.v. "ἀνάστασις"). In the New Testament, this Greek noun often means resurrection.
31 Cf. Luke 7:28.
32 See the section "*Parousia* vs. *Erchomai*; Presence vs. Coming" in Chapter 7.
33 The Greek phrases are almost identical for "the Son of man coming."
34 For a discussion of this law, see Joel McDurmon, *Biblical Logic: In Theory & Practice* (Powder Springs, GA: American Vision, 2009), 48.
35 Jesus used "the Greek phrase *ap' arti* (lit., 'from now')." [Carson, "Matthew," 555.]
36 See Appendix E for the entire Song of Moses and New Testament references to it.
37 Kalland, "Deuteronomy," 214.
38 Wright, *The People of God*, 392.
39 Hagner, *Matthew 14–28*, 714. The signs of inclusion are in the original. I have deleted Hagner's Greek words for the sake of readability.
40 "The Second Burden (12:1–14:21)." [Ralph L. Smith, *Micah–Malachi*, Word Biblical Commentary, ed. David A. Hubbard (Dallas: Word, 1984), 272.]
41 Milton S. Terry, *Biblical Hermeneutics: A Treatise on the Interpretation of the Old and New Testaments*, eds. George R. Crooks and John F. Hurst (New York: Eaton & Mains, 1890), 79. Emphasis added.
42 Gill, "Exposition," 7:294–95 (emphasis added).

43 R. T. France, *The Gospel of Matthew*, The New International Commentary on the New Testament, eds. Ned B. Stonehouse, F. F. Bruce, and Gordon D. Fee (Grand Rapids: William B. Eerdmans, 2007), 924–25 (emphasis added).

44 Kenneth L. Barker, "Zechariah," in *Daniel–Minor Prophets*, vol. 7 of *The Expositor's Bible Commentary: Daniel and the Minor Prophets*, ed. Frank E. Gaebelein (Grand Rapids: Zondervan, 1985), 674 (emphasis added).

45 Sam Storms, *Kingdom Come: The Amillennial Alternative* (Fearn, Scotland: Mentor, 2013), 197–98.

46 Henry George Liddell et al., eds., *A Greek-English Lexicon* (Oxford: Clarendon Press, 1996), s.v. "ἄγγελος." The definition and examples both come from this source.

47 George L. Murray, *Millennial Studies: A Search for Truth* (Grand Rapids: Baker, 1948), 125.

48 That is, "till the Messiah shall come." [Adam Clarke, *The Old and New Testaments With a Commentary and Critical Notes*, 6 vols. (Nashville: Abingdon, [1970?]), 1:267.]

49 Gill, "Exposition," 3:733.

50 Gill, "Exposition," 3:734.

51 Gill, "Exposition," 3:734 (emphasis added).

52 Gill, "Exposition," 5:222.

53 Gill, "Exposition," 5:244.

54 Gill, "Exposition," 5:576.

55 Gill, "Exposition," 7:295.

CHAPTER ELEVEN

Response: Time

THE UNITY, symmetry, and completeness of the Olivet Discourse make it a thing of beauty. Consider again, by glancing at our chiasm, the continuity and balance Jesus creates as he responds to the disciples' questions:

    A. *Exhortation*: observe!—the temple will fall (Matt 24:1–2)

        B. *When question*: what will be the time? (Matt 24:3a)

            C. *Sign question*: what will be the sign? (Matt 24:3b)

            C'. *Sign answer*: the signs of associated events, symbols (Matt 24:4–31)

        B'. *When answer*: *this* is the time (Matt 24:32–36)

    A'. *Exhortation*: observe! (Matt 24:37–25:46); watch! (Matt 24:42, 43; 25:13)

The bold print shows our current location.

Having brought his answer to the disciples' *sign* question to a dramatic climax, Jesus now gives his response to their *when* question. They had asked: "Tell us, when shall these things [about the temple's fall] be?" (Matt 24:3). Here is his answer:

> Now learn a parable of the fig tree; When his branch is yet tender, and putteth forth leaves, ye know that summer is nigh: so likewise ye, when ye shall see all these things, know that it is near, even at the doors.

> Verily I say unto you, This generation (Gk. *genea*) shall not pass, till all these things be fulfilled. Heaven and earth shall pass away, but my words shall not pass away. But of that day and hour knoweth no man, no, not the angels of heaven, but my Father only. (Matt 24:32–36)

Jesus' response to *when* the temple would fall is much shorter than his list of *signs*, yet he adorns it with a pattern of progression, too: regarding time, he moves from a longer (known) period, "this generation," to a shorter (unknown) time, the "day and hour," again bringing the focus of his answer to the temple's fall.

Our developing prophetic model, based on the Jewish two-age view of history, accommodated all the signs Jesus gave of the temple's fall; it will also assimilate his time statements. Before I show this, I want to review our outline of the Olivet Discourse again as another way for us to track our progress and to remind ourselves of Jesus' overall flow of thought. I will again show our current location in bold type:

I. Jesus prediction of the temple's destruction (Matt 24:1-2)

II. The disciples' two questions regarding *when* and the *sign* (Matt 24:3)

III. Jesus' response to the *sign* question (Matt 24:4–31)

    A. Phase 1: preliminary signs (Matt 24:4–14)—the beginning of birth pains (v. 8)

    B. Phase 2: later sign (Matt 24:15–26)—the period of "the end" (v. 14)

    C. Phase 3: immediate signs (Matt 24:27–31)—the end itself (v. 29)

IV. Jesus' response to the *when* question (Matt 24:32–36)

V. Jesus' exhortations to watchfulness (Matt 24:37–25:46)

Jesus divided his timing response regarding the temple's fall into three parts: (1) an introductory parable; (2) a statement of time certainty; and (3) a statement of time uncertainty.

A Stage-Setting Parable

Jesus begins his response to the disciples' *when* question with a parable that establishes the tone for the rest of his answer. He draws an analogy from the fruit-bearing of a fig tree:

> Now learn a parable of the fig tree; When his branch is yet tender, and putteth forth leaves, ye know that summer is nigh: so likewise ye, when ye shall see *all these things*, know that it is near, even at the doors. (Matt 24:32–33)

Jesus' words, "all these things," link his parable to his prophecy, the disciples' original question, and the signs he has just given (Matt 24:1–31). The signs would develop over a period like a fig tree develops fruit. As we saw, some signs would *not* mean the end of the Mosaic age was near; others would be the beginning of birth pains. As the time for the temple's fall would approach, the signs would intensify. Progress toward that climax would be like a fig tree sprouting new branches and leaves, showing the time of fruit is near; the progression of signs would show the disciples that the fall of the temple was imminent.

Jesus is emphasizing that the disciples would observe this progression toward the consummation: "When *ye* shall see all these things" (Matt 24:33). This lesson is for them, not some distant future generation, just as everything else in the Olivet Discourse has been: Jesus addressed his prophecy to *them* (Matt 24:2); warned *them* against deception (Matt 24:4); and said *they* would hear of wars and suffer affliction, hatred, and death (Matt 24:6, 9). After he finishes answering the disciples' *when* question (Matt 24:34–36), Jesus applies his sign and time answers to the disciples in a series of exhortations (Matt 24:37–25:46). The timing Jesus sets for the events under consideration demands the *disciples'* attention; it will have a significant bearing on the work he has given *them* to do.

Parables usually teach one primary lesson; this one—which serves as the introduction to Jesus' *when* answer—emphasizes that the events under consideration would occur in the disciples' near future. They would know when the fulfillment of Jesus' prophecy was "at the doors" (Matt 24:33) by observing the signs he has given. Jesus maintains this timing orientation throughout the rest of the Olivet Discourse. The improved prophetic model we are seeking must account for this fact.

A Time Statement of Certainty

Moving from parable to direct assertion, Jesus answers the disciples' request regarding *when* the temple would fall:

Q. "Tell us, when shall *these things* be?" (Matt 24:3).

A. "This generation (Gk. *genea*) shall not pass, till *all these things* be fulfilled" (Matt 24:34).

There is nothing ambiguous about what is happening here: (1) Jesus said the temple would fall (Matt 24:1–2); (2) the disciples asked when "these things"—i.e., things related to the temple's fall—would happen (Matt 24:3); and (3) Jesus answers their question—all these things would happen in "this generation."

Friedrich Buchsel observes the following facts about the word Jesus used for "generation": "In the NT [*genea*] is common in the Synoptics, rare in Paul, absent from [John], including [Revelation]. As a purely formal concept it is always qualified. It mostly denotes 'generation' in the sense of contemporaries."[1] He assigns this meaning to *genea* in the Olivet Discourse. D. A. Carson agrees with this meaning for *genea* in Matthew 24:34: "'this generation' ... can only with the greatest difficulty be made to mean anything other than the generation living when Jesus spoke."[2] This meaning makes Jesus' time statement here agree with one he had given earlier in his ministry: "There be some standing here, which shall not taste of death, till they see the Son of man coming in his kingdom" (Matt 16:28). All his signs would come to pass and the temple would fall in the disciples' generation; some of them would live to see it.

In the Olivet Discourse, Jesus forcefully affirms the truth of this time frame: "Heaven and earth shall pass away, but my words shall not pass away" (Matt 24:35). This statement of absolute certainty sustained the disciples in the interim before the temple's fall. As we have seen, they would preach the gospel as a witness to all nations (Matt 24:14), saying that "the end of all things is at hand" and that "the time is come that judgment must begin at the house of God" (1 Pet 4:7, 17). They would encounter last-days scoffers who would sneer: "Where is the promise of his coming (Gk. *parousia*)? for since the fathers fell asleep, all things continue as they were from the beginning of the creation" (2 Pet 3:4). But the disciples had Jesus' solemn word: the *signs* (including his *parousia*) and *time* of the temple's fall would come to pass just as he had said. This assurance sustained them in their last-days mission.

Josephus and other reliable historians of the first century show the fulfillment of Jesus' prophecy: the temple fell in AD 70, forty years after Jesus gave the Olivet Discourse. These historians also show the fulfillment of Jesus' signs observable to the natural eye (Matt 24:4–33): the Roman armies inflicted forty-two months of "great tribulation" on the Jews (Matt 24:21); they committed multiple abominations before making the house of God desolate (Matt 24:15; cp. Matt 23:36–38); a remnant of the Jews—followers of Jesus—fled Jerusalem and saved themselves as the Roman legions surrounded the city (Matt 24:16–17; cp. Luke 21:21); events within the walls of Jerusalem and certain military decisions shortened the duration of the war (Matt 24:22); many false prophets deluded the Jews with proclamations that God would deliver them from certain destruction (Matt 24:23–26), but, instead of delivering them, God took them to destruction (Matt 24:28); and, in the end, not one temple stone stood upon another (Matt 24:2). Nothing Jesus predicted in the Olivet Discourse failed to occur in his generation.

Jesus' "this generation" timestamp for "all these things" is an important element in the prophetic model we are discovering.

A Time Statement of Uncertainty

Jesus gave the disciples a definite answer to their *when* question—"this generation shall not pass, till all these things be fulfilled"—but he also stated that greater precision was impossible:

> But of that day (Gk. *hēmera*) and hour (Gk. *hōra*) knoweth no man, no, not the angels of heaven, but my Father only. (Matt 24:36)

As a man, Jesus did not know the precise time of the temple's destruction. The tension between knowing the outer limits for *when* ("this generation"), but not the precise time ("the day and hour") would produce a situation of urgency for the disciples. Their experience would resemble Noah's: he knew the flood would come in his lifetime, yet he did not know the precise time of its arrival (cf. Matt 24:37–39). He built the ark to prepare for the coming deluge within these time parameters, but the time uncertainty led the men of his generation to scoff at the coming judgment. In like manner, the disciples had to finish their task knowing Israel's judgment would come in their generation, but without knowing the precise day or hour. As I mentioned earlier, many of their contemporaries mocked when the judgment did not materialize for over three decades (cf. 2 Pet 3:4).[3]

Jesus had used parables to teach this lesson. In one, the disciples would be like servants waiting for their master to return from a wedding. They should work diligently because they knew their master would return within their lifetimes, but they did not know the precise time. Jesus explained this teaching to Peter:

> But and if that servant say in his heart, My lord delayeth his coming; and shall begin to beat the menservants and maidens, and to eat and drink, and to be drunken; the lord of that servant will come *in a day* (Gk. *hēmera*) when he looketh not for him, and at *an hour* (Gk. *hōra*) when he is not aware, and will cut him in sunder, and will appoint him his portion with the unbelievers. (Luke 12:45–46)[4]

The servants in the parable knew the *generation* in which their lord would return, but they did not know the *day* or *hour*.

The disciples later ministered from this perspective: they said that "the time is short" (1 Cor 7:29) and "the ends of the ages have come"

(1 Cor 10:11 NKJV); they spoke about "the age that is about to (Gk. *mellō*) come."⁵ And they used the terms "day" and "hour" to describe the approaching end of the age. For example, the writer of Hebrews told Christians to exhort one another, "and so much the more, as ye see the *day* (Gk. *hēmera*) approaching" (Heb 10:25). The apostle John, writing, perhaps, in AD 60–65,⁶ said, "Little children, it is the last *hour* (Gk. *hōra*); and as you have heard that the Antichrist is coming, even now many antichrists have come, by which we know that it is the last *hour* (Gk. *hōra*)" (1 John 2:18 NKJV). The apostle Paul placed these two time indicators together:

> Besides this you know the time, that the *hour* (Gk. *hōra*) has come for you to wake from sleep. For salvation is nearer to us now than when we first believed. The night is far gone; the *day* (Gk. *hēmera*) is at hand. (Rom 13:11–12 ESV)

The disciples *never* spoke of a coming *generation* in this uncertain way. The reason is obvious—they knew theirs was the generation that would witness "the end," but they, like Jesus, did not know the "day" and "hour." However, the signs Jesus had given—especially the one about false christs (Matt 24:24)—showed the precise time of the temple's fall was near.⁷

Jesus' two-part answer responds to the disciples' *when* question and maintains the simple beauty of the Olivet Discourse.

Unnecessary "Explanations"

> Catch us the foxes,
> The little foxes that spoil the vines,
> For our vines have tender grapes.
> — Song of Solomon 2:15 (NKJV)

There are little foxes that spoil the vine of an accurate prophetic model; they take the form of faulty assumptions that hide in the thick underbrush, ready to pounce on the tender grapes of truth as they emerge. I want to catch some of them before they spoil Jesus' answer to the disciples *when* question, before we have the chance to taste the wine of an accurate prophetic model.

The assumptions deep within the existing prophetic models spoil both the beauty and the apologetic value of Jesus' words. They cause commentators to misunderstand Jesus' signs and, as a result, to reject his time parameters. I have discussed several of these assumptions, but will list the most important ones here for ease of reference:

1. The coming (Gk. *erchomai*) of Christ is the same as the presence (Gk. *parousia*) of Christ: a point-in-time event in our future.
2. The coming/presence of Christ will be visible to the natural eye.
3. "The end of the age" means the end of the *church* age.
4. The cosmic-collapse imagery Jesus uses is literal and signifies the end of the physical world (Gk. *kosmos*) as we know it.

Some combination of these assumptions governs the interpretation of the Olivet Discourse in most modern commentaries and books on prophecy.

If these assumptions are true, Jesus' "this generation" timestamp creates a significant problem for one simple reason—these things did not happen in the disciples' lifetime. Conservative commentators wish to avoid making Jesus a false prophet, so they cast about to find some way to reconcile "all these things" with "this generation." This unnecessary problem, caused by assumptions in the existing prophetic models, produces bitter wine. In the most extreme cases, the conflict leads people to atheism, as it did for Bertrand Russell. His faulty assumptions about the coming/*parousia*, coupled with his correct understanding of Jesus' timestamps, led him to reject the Christian faith.[8]

Most Christians want to avoid Russell's conclusions, but their prophetic assumptions force them to become theological contortionists to do so. They cannot accept what H. A. W. Meyer admits: "[Jesus] had placed the *Parousia* and the setting up of the kingdom in the lifetime even of that generation."[9] So, they go to extraordinary lengths to maintain their prophetic presuppositions without accusing Jesus of error; they seek, as R. C. Sproul says, "to resolve this dilemma by separating the destruction of Jerusalem from the parousia of Jesus."[10]

I will describe the four most common tacks they take. First, some commentators say the word generation means *race*. Brock D. Hollett, for example, says it means the race of evil men in all generations.[11] William MacDonald agrees with Hollett's proposal, but, instead of the race of evil men, he says it means the *Jewish* race.[12] C. I. Scofield also held this position and gave his reasons:

> Gr. *genea*, the primary definition of which is, "race, kind, family, stock, breed." (So all lexicons.) That the word is used in this sense here is sure because none of "these things," i.e. the world-wide preaching of the kingdom, the great tribulation, the return of the Lord in visible glory, and the regathering of the elect, occurred at the destruction of Jerusalem by Titus, A.D. 70. The promise is, therefore, that the generation—nation, or family of Israel—will be preserved unto "these things"; a promise wonderfully fulfilled to this day.[13]

These commentators make the assumptions I listed above, then conclude *genea* must mean race.

It is true, the lexicons give race as a *non-temporal* meaning of *genea*. But those lexicons also give a *temporal* meaning: "the whole multitude of men living at the same time,"[14] or something similar. These commentators are applying the non-temporal meaning of *genea* in a context filled with time-related statements. The disciples had asked *when* the temple would fall (Matt 24:2–3). Jesus gave signs, some of which would indicate it was *not* chronologically near, and others that it was at hand. Some signs would mean that it was time for the disciples to flee Jerusalem (Luke 21:20–21), for *"then"* shall be great tribulation." *Days* would be shortened, and *immediately* after those days, the cosmos would collapse; *then*, the ultimate sign of the Son of Man in heaven would appear. No one, not even the Son, knew the *day* or the *hour* of the event under consideration. Jesus gave a parable involving a temporal event: *when* a fig tree puts out leaves, summer is *near*. This temporal perspective pervades every part of the Olivet Discourse. Earlier on the day he gave the Olivet Discourse,[15] Jesus had told the Jews their house would be left desolate in "this generation" (Matt 23:36). In this time-laden context, to choose the non-temporal meaning of *genea* over the temporal meaning is a severe mistake. To assert that "this generation" here is a term that "*transcends* the quantitative definition of a restricted, contemporary time period"[16] is an arbitrary and desperate attempt to achieve a laudable goal.

Scholars bear powerful testimony for the temporal meaning of *genea* in Matthew 24:34 like the one Louw and Nida provide:

> People living at the same time and belonging to the same reproductive age-class—'those of the same time, those of the same generation.'... 'the people of this generation will be punished' Lk 11:51. The expression 'the people of this generation' may also be expressed as 'the people living now' or 'the people of this time.'[17]

Craig S. Keener says the non-temporal meaning (i.e., race) is inappropriate:

> Though some wish to take "generation" (*genea*) as "race," Matt 23:35–36 leave no doubt that Jesus uses the term as normally (e.g., Jer 7:29) and as elsewhere in Matthew refers to the climactic "generation." Because Jesus' warning of judgment must precede A.D. 70, it is interesting that Jerusalem fell about forty years after Jesus' warning.[18]

Sam Storms makes a dramatic and important observation regarding the use of this word outside the Olivet Discourse:

> The word *genea* occurs twenty-seven times in the Gospels and never once means "race".... Every time the words "this generation" occur in the Gospels they

mean *Jesus' contemporaries*, i.e., the sum total of those living at the same time he did.[19]

Geerhardus Vos realizes that the natural meaning of *genea* creates difficulties for the existing prophetic models, but warns, "The solution should not be sought by understanding 'this generation' of the Jewish race or of the human race."[20] Edward E. Hindson agrees:

> While some have attempted to relate "generation" (Gr *genea*) to the race of the Jews, indicating the survival of their race until Christ's return, this seems somewhat stretched. Arndt and Gingrich prefer "age" or "period of time."[21]

The emphasis on time in the Olivet Discourse argues against "race"—whether of evil men, or the Jews—as Jesus' meaning. He is answering the disciples' *when* question.

Second, other commentators, seeking to avoid the implications of Jesus' statement, keep the usual meaning of *genea*—people living at the same time—but switch generations; they say Jesus is not talking about *his* generation, but about one in the distant future. For example, John MacArthur says:

> In the Olivet Discourse itself [Jesus] makes *no clear reference to the events of A.D. 70*. His entire reply is an extended answer to the more important question about the signs of His coming and the end of the age. *Virtually ignoring their initial question,* He said nothing whatsoever about *when* the destruction of Jerusalem would occur. That is because those events were not really germane to the end of the age. They were merely a foretaste of the greater judgment that would accompany His return, previews of what is to come ultimately.[22]

Louis A. Barbieri, Jr. agrees with this view: "The generation (*genea*) of people living in that future day will see the completion of all the events."[23]

These brothers ignore Jesus' near-demonstrative pronoun—*this*—and speak as though he had used the far-demonstrative—*that*—to mean a generation in the distant future. They accuse Jesus of ignoring his prophecy and the disciples' question about it; they make his Discourse a detached conversation irrelevant to what he had just prophesied and what the disciples had just asked. Their approach of making "this generation" mean "that generation" cannot be true in Mark and Luke, for those accounts of the Olivet Discourse do not speak of "the end of the age" or Christ's *parousia*. Did Jesus "virtually ignore" the disciples' question in those accounts, too? Of course not. The unity of the Olivet Discourse refutes the idea that Jesus jumps to a far-distant generation without indicating he was doing so. His prophecy was of the temple's fall, the disciples' *when* question was about the temple's fall, and Jesus' answer—in "this generation"—refers to the temple's fall.

Third, some commentators resort to the idea that prophecies can have multiple fulfillments. This allows them to say *something* happened in "this generation"—the temple fell in AD 70—but that was only the first fulfillment of Jesus' prophecy. For example, MacArthur says, "All prophecy … has *at least a double bearing*."[24] Robert H. Gundry says something similar: "Double fulfillment of biblical prophecy is a common phenomenon." He admits that this creates a problem because Jesus seems to say the disciples would see the temple fall. But, he says, "This difficulty is part of the ambiguity necessary to the phenomenon of double fulfillment, *which is to be accepted as fact* rather than objected to on literary grounds."[25] The blind acceptance of a dubious interpretive device is an outrageous price to pay for faulty beginning assumptions.

Milton Terry counters these claims of multiple fulfillments. He says there is "no double sense in prophecy," and the "theory of a double sense unsettles all sound interpretation."[26] J. Marcellus Kik says,

> Commentators have only added to the confusion of interpretation by indicating their "double meanings," "prophetic perspectives," and "partial and complete ful-

fillments." These intended solutions to the exegesis of difficult verses have in no way contributed to a right understanding of Jesus' prophetic discourse.[27]

I will make two observations from personal experience. First, no writer I have ever read has presented an obvious example of this supposed "common phenomenon"; some other interpretive device always provides a better explanation of their examples than dual fulfillment. Second, commentators that proclaim the merits of this proposed interpretive device never explain how to use it. For example, do *all* the signs Jesus gives in the Olivet Discourse have multiple fulfillments? Will the temple fall again? If not, how do we know which prophecies will happen again, and which ones will not? Are the ones that have multiple fulfillments limited to two, and how do we know? I suspect that commentators would never resort to unregulated corrective devices like this if their faulty assumptions did not require them to do so.

Fourth, the last unnecessary explanation of "this generation" I will mention is the slice-and-dice approach. It involves cutting some pieces out of the Olivet Discourse and applying them to the end of the church age while relating the remaining parts to the temple's fall in Jesus' generation. Some commentators are messy and make multiple cuts; others, like J. Marcellus Kik, make one clean break:

> The first thirty-four verses of Matthew 24, along with verse 35 in which Jesus confirms the certainty of his prophecies, deal with the destruction of Jerusalem and its temple.... With verse 36 Christ commences a new subject, namely, his second coming and the events preceding it. This verse may be termed the "transition text" of the chapter.[28]

This is a hard position to defend because, in other parallel passages, some events *after* Kik's transition text occur before those that precede it; his clean break between subjects does not exist in those passages.[29] Edward E. Stevens has a chart that makes this clear:[30]

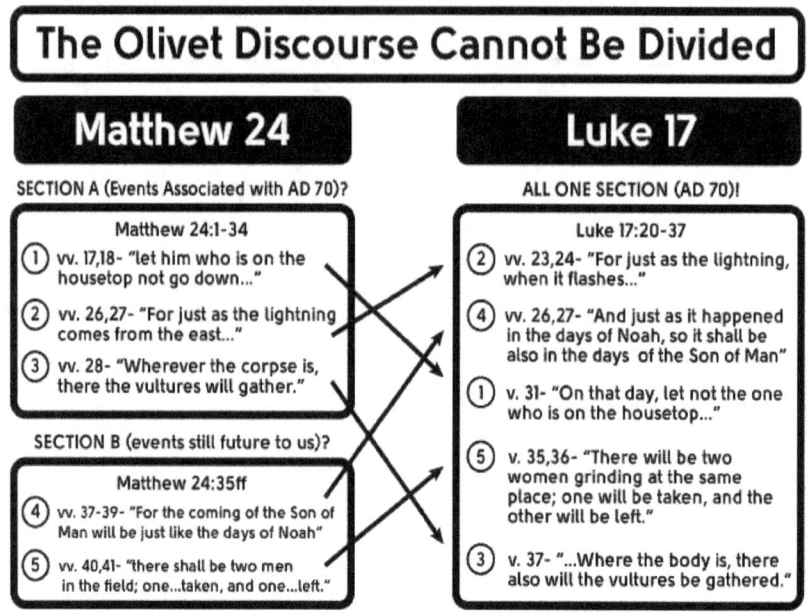

Figure 11-1. The Olivet Discourse Cannot be Divided

Kik's division of the Olivet Discourse would make the coming (Gk. *erchomai*) of Christ in Matt 24:30 different from the one in Matt 24:44; 25:31. It would require that the presence (Gk. *parousia*) of Christ in Matt 24:3, 27 differ from that of Matt 24:37, 39. The disciples would have had to understand all this with no explanation from Jesus. This is an untenable proposition.

Inmillennialism protects the tender grapes of truth in the Olivet Discourse from the faulty-assumption foxes. It replaces them with the following propositions, all of which we have already seen:

1. The coming (Gk. *erchomai*) of Christ is a point-in-time event within the lifetime of some of his disciples; the word *parousia* carries its fundamental meaning of presence and signifies a state of being—the presence of Christ with his churches during the messianic age.

2. The coming/presence of the Son of Man was/is not visible to the natural eyes of mankind; Caiaphas, for example, saw the Son of Man sitting in heaven and coming on the clouds of heaven indirectly, through the agents God used to destroy the temple (Matt 26:64).
3. "The end of the age" means the end of the *Mosaic* age—the age the temple symbolized.
4. Jesus' cosmic-collapse imagery is a figure the prophets had from ancient times used to signify God's judgment on a city or nation.

Jesus was not talking about the last days of the messianic (or church) age; he was speaking about the last days of the Mosaic age. This shift in perspective eliminates the need for "solutions" that make "this generation" mean "this race," "that generation," or "multiple generations"; and it removes the need to destroy the unified beauty of the Olivet Discourse. It allows us to look forward to sipping wine from the vineyard of the Olivet Discourse as we feast in other parts of God's inspired word.

Conclusion

God denounces men who pervert the timing of his judgments, especially those who refute near-at-hand judgment prophecies. Five hundred years before Jesus gave the Olivet Discourse, Ezekiel warned of a future (to him) judgment against the temple that would occur in his generation (Ezek 12:23–27). God said, "*The days are at hand.... The word that I shall speak shall come to pass; it shall be no more prolonged: for in your days*, O rebellious house, will I say the word, and will perform it." False prophets refused to believe God's timestamp and said, "The vision that he [Ezekiel] seeth is for many days to come, and he prophesieth of *the times that are far off.*" God said they were prophesying "out of their own hearts" and pronounced woes on them (Ezek 13:2f).

There is a lesson here for us: when Jesus says, "This generation shall not pass, till all these things be fulfilled," we should not say it was for "times that are far off" without thoroughly examining the assumptions and reasoning that cause us to do so. Jesus did not specify a precise time for the fulfillment of his prophecy—a day or an hour—but he restricted the fulfillment of "all these things" to his generation. His prophecy was about the temple's fall in the "last days" (Heb 1:2) of the Mosaic age.

I can now update the diagram of our prophetic model to show Jesus' "this generation" time frame and that the temple fell in AD 70:

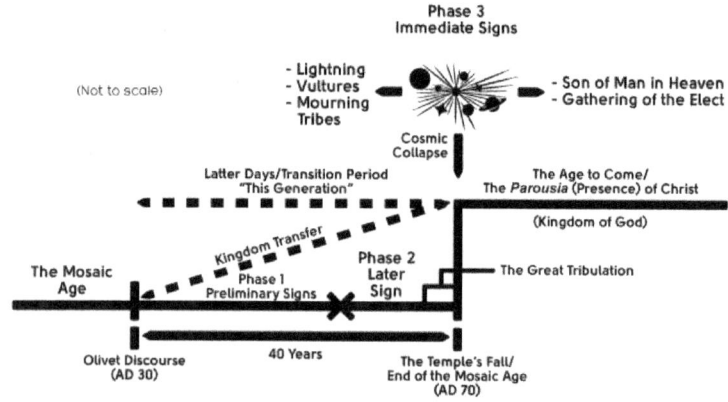

Figure 11-2. Inmillennialism through the Sign and When Answers

KEY POINT #10

Jesus said all the things of which he spoke in the Olivet Discourse would occur within his (temporal) "generation" without specifying the "day or hour" of their occurrence.

Notes

1 Friedrich Büchsel, "γενεά, κτλ," in *Theological Dictionary of the New Testament*, ed. Gerhard Kittel, trans. Geoffrey W. Bromiley (Grand Rapids: Eerdmans, 1964–76), 1:663.
2 Carson, "Matthew," 507.
3 Second Peter was written "to predominantly Jewish-Christian congregations in Asia Minor *c.* 61–2" per Robinson, *Redating the New Testament,* 198.
4 Jesus' teaching regarding readiness began in Luke 12:35.
5 Heb 6:5 in Wuest, *Expanded Translation,* 521.
6 Robinson, *Redating the New Testament,* 307.
7 Russell, *The Parousia,* 328–35.
8 See Chapter 2 for his reasoning.
9 Heinrich August Wilhelm Meyer, *Critical and Exegetical Hand-Book to the Gospels of Mark and Luke*, ed. William P. Dickson, trans. Robert Ernest Wallis and Matthew A. Riddle, 6th ed. (Winona Lake, IN: Alpha Publications, 1979), 470.
10 R. C. Sproul, introduction to *The Parousia: The New Testament Doctrine of Our Lord's Second Coming,* by J. Stuart Russell (1887; repr., Grand Rapids: Baker, 1999), ix.
11 Brock D. Hollett, *Debunking Preterism: How Over-Realized Eschatology Misses the "Not Yet" of Bible Prophecy* (Kearney, NE: Morris Publishing, 2018), 92–94.
12 MacDonald, *Believer's Bible Commentary,* 1296.
13 C. I. Scofield, ed., *The Scofield Reference Bible* (New York; London; Toronto; Melbourne; Bombay: Oxford University Press, 1917), 1034.
14 Thayer and Strong, *Thayer's Greek-English Lexicon,* 112 (s.v. "γενεά").
15 Tuesday of Passion Week per Robertson, *A Harmony,* 169–81.
16 Hollett, *Debunking Preterism,* 94.
17 Johannes P. Louw and Eugene Albert Nida, *Greek-English Lexicon of the New Testament: Based on Semantic Domains* (New York: United Bible Societies, 1996), 119.
18 Craig S. Keener, *The Gospel of Matthew: A Socio-Rhetorical Commentary* (Grand Rapids: Eerdmans, 2009), 589.
19 Storms, *Kingdom Come,* 235–36 (bold emphasis removed).
20 Vos, "Eschatology," 982.
21 Edward E. Hindson, "Matthew," in *KJV Bible Commentary*, eds. Edward E. Hindson and Woodrow Michael Kroll (Nashville: Thomas Nelson, 1994), 1949. See Danker et al., eds., *Greek-English Lexicon,* 191 (s.v. "γενεά").
22 MacArthur, *The Second Coming,* 80 (emphasis added).
23 Louis A. Barbieri, Jr., "Matthew," in *The Bible Knowledge Commentary: An Exposition of the Scriptures*, eds. J. F. Walvoord and R. B. Zuck (Wheaton, IL: Victor, 1985), 78.

24 MacArthur, *The Second Coming*, 229.
25 Gundry, *Matthew*, 491 (emphasis added).
26 Terry, *Biblical Hermeneutics*, 493.
27 Kik, *An Eschatology of Victory*, 59.
28 Kik, *An Eschatology of Victory*, 67.
29 I'm thinking of passages like Luke 17 and 1 Thess 4–5.
30 Edward E. Stevens, *What Happened in A.D. 70?* (Bradford, PA: Kingdom Publications, 1997), 18–19. Used with permission.

CHAPTER TWELVE

Exhortations

I HAVE used the following outline to track our progress through the Olivet Discourse; it shows we have arrived at its final major division:

I. Jesus prediction of the temple's destruction (Matt 24:1-2)

II. The disciples' two questions regarding *when* and the *sign* (Matt 24:3)

III. Jesus' response to the *sign* question (Matt 24:4–31)

    A. Phase 1: preliminary signs (Matt 24:4–14)—the beginning of birth pains (v. 8)

    B. Phase 2: later sign (Matt 24:15–26)—the period of "the end" (v. 14)

    C. Phase 3: immediate signs (Matt 24:27–31)—the end itself (v. 29)

IV. Jesus' response to the *when* question (Matt 24:32–36)

V. Jesus' exhortations to watchfulness (Matt 24:37–25:46)

I want to again present our chiasm of the entire Olivet Discourse for reasons that will soon be apparent:

    A. *Exhortation*: observe!—the temple will fall (Matt 24:1–2)

        B. *When question*: what will be the time? (Matt 24:3a)

            C. *Sign question*: what will be the sign? (Matt 24:3b)

            C'. *Sign answer*: the signs of associated events, symbols (Matt 24:4–31)

B'. *When answer: this* is the time (Matt 24:32–36)

A'. *Exhortation*: observe! (Matt 24:37–25:46); watch! (Matt 24:42, 43; 25:13)

This last section will add one important element to the inmillennial model—the final judgment. I will add it, understanding that another passage (1 Cor 15) will later provide additional details about this event. One of my principal goals here is to show that our prophetic model, though still incomplete, can help us understand key passages and avoid extreme, even heretical, positions.

At the end of the Olivet Discourse, Jesus applies his statement about the *day* and *hour* of the temple's fall to the disciples' situation. He gives five exhortations, each of which involves judgment. Matthew arranges these exhortations as another chiasm, and, based on John F. Hart's observation, this should not surprise us: "It is well known that Matthew brings order and precision to his Gospel. Chiastic structures in Matthew are quite common and are fully appropriate in light of his precision."[1] I will show the chiasm, make some introductory remarks about the exhortations as a group, and then discuss them individually in the following sections. Here are the *five judgments* that provide the basis for Jesus' exhortations:

A. Flood: event (distant past); all mankind—a creation judgment (Matt 24:37–44)

  B. Two-servants: parable (immediate); household—a covenantal judgment (Matt 24:45–51)

   C. Ten-virgins: parable (immediate); personal—a covenantal judgment (Matt 25:1–13)

  B'. Talents: parable (immediate); household—a covenantal judgment (Matt 25:14–30)

A.' Final: event (distant future); all mankind—a creation judgment (Matt 25:31–46)

This is the third chiasm I have listed for the Olivet Discourse; each one focuses our attention on Jesus' subject—the temple's fall. In the chiasm of the entire Discourse, the central elements are the signs of that event; in the chiasm of the immediate signs (see Chapter 10), the focus is on the collapse of the Mosaic-age cosmic order and the appearance of its messianic-age replacement as the temple falls. Now, at the end of the Olivet Discourse, Jesus' exhortation-chiasm again focuses attention on the central event: some individuals enter the messianic-age kingdom as the temple falls but others do not.

Two of Jesus' exhortations—the outermost couplet (A-A')—are narratives of historical events: judgments far removed from the destruction of the temple in AD 70. One judgment (the flood) is in the disciples' distant past, and the other (the final judgment) is in their distant future. I call these *creation* judgments because they are based on the fact that men are creatures accountable to their Creator. In both judgments, some persons have a special relationship with God (i.e., Noah's family and the sheep), but others do not (wicked men and the goats). Not everyone being judged is in a covenant-relationship with their Creator.

The middle three warnings appear as parables where judgment involves people who share a common identity: in two (B-B'), all those judged are servants in a household; in the other (C), all are virgins. But there are two *kinds* of persons in each category: faithful and evil servants; wise and foolish virgins. In two of these exhortations (B-B'), a man judges his servants for their performance while he is away. In the central parable (C), the bridegroom rewards the ten virgins according to their preparatory work as they waited for the wedding; he allows those who prepared well to enter the celebration, but he closes the door on the others. I will argue below that Jesus means for these categories—servants and virgins—to represent people in a covenant-relationship with God in the Mosaic age.

Judgment permeates each of these exhortations, even though none of them contain the word "judge." The Greek word-group used most often in the New Testament for "to judge" (Gk. *krinō* and its cognates) means to "separate, put asunder, distinguish."[2] In each of Jesus' exhortations, an authority figure separates and distinguishes one group of people from another—he judges them.

This idea of judgment was fresh in the disciples' minds because of something Jesus had said a few days before giving the Olivet Discourse:[3] "Verily I say unto you, That ye which have followed me, in the regeneration when the Son of man shall sit in the throne of his glory, ye also shall sit upon twelve thrones, judging (Gk. *krinō*) the twelve tribes of Israel" (Matt 19:28). This is very suggestive: by "the regeneration" Jesus means the approaching messianic age, for, in the eternal state, there will be no judgment of Israel. But, beginning in their generation, preaching the gospel of the kingdom would separate people in Israel; this "judgment" would have eternal consequences.

Jesus gives these judgment-exhortations in a critical historical setting. N. T. Wright provides a helpful description of it while discussing "some of the stories and riddles with which Jesus surrounded and interpreted his [final] journey to Jerusalem."[4] While commenting on the parable of the talents, Wright says,

> The other parables in chapter 25 are focused, not on the personal return of Jesus after a long interval in which the church is left behind, but on the great judgment which is coming very soon upon Jerusalem and her current leaders, and which signals the vindication of Jesus and his people as the true Israel. There is, of course, a time-lag to be undergone, but it is not the one normally imagined. It is not the gap between Jesus' going away and his personal return (the 'coming of the son of man' in the literalistic, non-Danielic sense); it is the time-lag, envisaged in Matthew 24, between the ministry of Jesus and the destruction of Jerusalem. This time-lag will be a period in which, in Jesus' absence, his followers will be open prey to the deceit of false Messiahs, and will face a period of great suffering before their vindication dawns.[5]

I will argue below that the three parables (B-C-B') each depict a division soon to occur *in Israel*. Through these parables, Jesus divides the nation into two subgroups: those who belong *only* to Israel after the flesh (1 Cor 10:18), and those who also are his disciples. The first group, as I will show, are God's Mosaic-age servants and virgins; the second group are his servants and virgins in an additional messianic-age sense—God will never cast *them* off. If we place these parables *after* the temple's fall, we jeopardize the doctrine of God's preservation of his saints, which Jesus teaches elsewhere (e.g., John 10:29). But the Scriptures teach that God would cast away some of his Mosaic-age servants and virgins. The generation in which Jesus lived created a unique situation where the old (Mosaic-age) and new (messianic-age) covenants were in existence at the same time. The parables Jesus gives cannot apply directly to any subsequent generation.

Flood Judgment

Jesus has just finished his responses to the disciples' *sign* and *when* questions regarding the temple's fall. That event would mark the end of the Mosaic age and the full transition to the messianic age; the old cosmos would collapse and a new one—with the Son of Man as King—would continue in its place. The people of God would inhabit a fresh new creation (cp. Matt 19:28; 2 Cor 5:17; Gal 6:15; et al.). God's judgment of Israel would accompany that new creation; in the Olivet Discourse Jesus has described it as a time of "great tribulation" (Matt 24:21), a time when God would judge his Mosaic-age people (cp. Deut 32:35; Heb 10:30).

This transition to a new creation would resemble, in several respects, the judgment-flood in Noah's day, and this forms the basis for Jesus' first exhortation (Matt 24:37–44). First, like Noah had proclaimed the soon-coming judgment to his peers, the disciples must preach Jesus' judgment-message to Israel (and the nations) in their generation. In Noah's day, people ignored his message; as a result, the judgment-flood "took them all away" to destruction. In like manner, most of the Jews would reject the gospel of the kingdom, so God would take them to destruction. Others—those who heeded the disciples' message—would be "left behind" after this judgment to enter the new kingdom age (cp. Luke 17:25–26).

Second, both judgments would come in the generation of men then living. This similarity reinforces the key points I made earlier about Jesus' answer to the disciples' *when* question. Jesus says, "Watch therefore: for ye know not what *hour* (Gk. *hōra*) your Lord doth come (Gk. *erchomai*).... Therefore be ye also ready: for in such an *hour* (Gk. *hōra*) as ye think not the Son of man cometh (Gk. *erchomai*)" (Matt 24:42, 44). The timing of the coming judgment here is the same as that he had given a few moments earlier—in "this generation," but at an unknown "day and hour" (cp. Matt 24:34, 36). Here, as earlier, Jesus places these time parameters on both "the presence (Gk. *parousia*) of the Son of Man" (Matt 24:37, 39 YLT) and "the coming (Gk. *erchomai*) of the Son of man" (Matt 24:42, 44). He has created an unbreakable connection between these two concepts—his point-in-time "coming" and his subsequent "presence" (cp. Matt 24:3, 27, 30), and he has placed both in his generation.

Third, the coming judgment of Israel would resemble the flood judgment in that the physical creation would continue, just as it had done in Noah's generation. The flood was a world-wide judgment that purged God's creation of sinners, but it was not an *absolute* purging; sin continued to plague God's handiwork. In like manner, God's judgment of Israel in Jesus' generation would purge sinners from the kingdom of God (e.g., 1 Cor 6:9–10), but it would not remove all effects of sin from his creation. The ultimate purging of sin would require another world-wide judgment—the *final* judgment.

But there is a significant difference between the flood-judgment of Noah's day and the judgment associated with the coming of the Son of Man in Jesus' generation. The flood judged men outside of a redemptive covenant relationship with God; the judgment in Jesus' generation would judge people in the Mosaic-age covenant. I will say more about this difference in the section on the final judgment.

Jesus' introduction of the flood judgment sets the stage for his three parables of the judgment in his generation; it also looks forward to the final judgment, creating a beautiful symmetry in his exhortations.

Two-Servants Judgment

Jesus' second exhortation (Matt 24:45–51) compares the disciples and their contemporaries to servants in a household. Both elements of this parable—the servants and the house—were familiar to the disciples. The Old Testament Scriptures frequently identified the nation of Israel as the *servants* of God. For example, when Nehemiah had asked God to bless his people to return from captivity to rebuild Jerusalem and its temple, he said,

> Let thine ear now be attentive, and thine eyes open, that thou mayest hear the prayer of thy servant, which I pray before thee now, day and night, for *the children of Israel thy servants*, and confess the sins of the children of Israel, which we have sinned against thee: both I and my father's house have sinned. (Neh 1:6)[6]

The Jews were the servants of God through the Mosaic-age covenant he had made with them. Solomon praised God for this: "O LORD God of Israel, there is no God like thee in the heaven, nor in the earth; which keepest *covenant*, and shewest mercy unto thy *servants*" (2 Chr 6:14). Jesus' exhortation is about a judgment of those who bear this covenant title—Israel comprised *servants* of God.

The disciples were also familiar with the other element in Jesus' exhortation—the household. The Old Testament used this figure in two ways: First, it referred to Israel herself as a house. For example, upon first seeing God's bread from heaven, *"The house of Israel* called the name thereof Manna" (Exod 16:31). Second, the Old Testament referred to the temple (or tabernacle) as the "house of God" (Matt 24:43). For example, God had said, "the first of the firstfruits of thy land thou shalt bring into *the house of the LORD thy God*" (Exod 23:19).[7]

The Jews were God's Mosaic-age house servants—they were responsible for the welfare of his house. Jesus' two-servant parable applies to them: *they alone* had served God as his servants. Jesus' use of this parable in a discourse about the destruction of the temple (Matt 24:1–3)—God's house, for which Israel was responsible—is fitting. Israel had defiled God's house and turned it into a den of thieves (Matt 21:13). Something similar had happened in the past: "All the leaders of the priests and the people [had] transgressed ... and defiled the house of the LORD" (2 Chr 36:14 NKJV). As a result, God had "brought against them the king of the Chaldeans, who killed their young men with the sword in the house of their sanctuary, and had no compassion on young man or virgin, on the aged or the weak; He gave them all into his hand" (2 Chr 36:17 NKJV). Jesus is saying a similar judgment would come on God's servants in his generation.

But this judgment would be more pivotal than any previous judgment: it would involve entrance into the messianic-age kingdom, the age of Christ's *parousia* (presence) with his people. That this is true appears from two similar parables Jesus had spoken a few hours before he gave the Olivet Discourse[8]—"The Parable of the Two Sons" (Matt 21:28–32) and "The Parable of the Wicked Vinedressers" (Matt 21:33–46). In them, Jesus' subject was the same as it is here: the judgment of the apostate Jews in his generation. Jesus told the Jews, "Tax collectors and prostitutes *are entering*[9] *the kingdom of God* before you!" (Matt 21:31 HCSB). He told them that God would take the kingdom from them and give it to another nation (Matt 21:43), meaning the "holy nation" of Christ's messianic-age people (cp. 1 Pet 2:9). The unbelieving Jews understood the parable: "And when the chief priests and Pharisees had heard his parables, they perceived that *he spake of them*" (Matt 21:45). *They*—the Mosaic-age servants of God—pronounced their own verdict: "He [the house master] will miserably destroy those wicked men, and will let out his vineyard unto other husbandmen, which shall render him the fruits in their seasons" (Matt 21:41). The judgment of which Jesus is speaking in the Olivet Discourse will complete the transfer of the kingdom of God from God's Mosaic-age wicked servants to his messianic-age faithful servants.

As for timing, nothing has changed from earlier in the Discourse: the lord of the wicked servant would "come in a day (Gk. *hēmera*) when he looketh not for him, and in an hour (Gk. *hōra*) that he is not aware of" (Matt 24:50). Jesus warned, "Therefore be ye also ready: for in such an hour (Gk. *hōra*) as ye think not the Son of man cometh (Gk. *erchomai*)" (Matt 24:44). These are the same "day and hour" of Matthew 24:36, the uncertain time of the temple's fall within Jesus' generation.

Consistent with everything we have seen in the Olivet Discourse, this cluster of events—kingdom entrance, kingdom transfer, and the judgment of God's Mosaic-age people—occurs at the coming of the Son of Man (Matt 24:44, 50). This coming is identical to the one Jesus has mentioned throughout the Olivet Discourse—"the Son of man coming (Gk. *erchomai*) in the clouds of heaven with power and great glory" (Matt 24:30); it would occur in his generation (Matt 24:34).

I will now give the inmillennial interpretation of this parable. Jesus, the Lord of God's house, was about to go "into a far country to receive for himself a kingdom, and to return" (Luke 19:12); he would ascend in clouds to the Ancient of Days to receive it (cp. Dan 7:13–14), then return "in the clouds of heaven with power and great glory," at which time the tribes of the land of Israel would mourn (Matt 24:30). At that time, he would "cut asunder" the wicked Jews—the evil servants in God's Mosaic-age house—and appoint them their place where "there shall be weeping and gnashing of teeth" (Matt 24:51). The faithful servants in Israel—those who obeyed Jesus—would become rulers over all the Lord's household goods during the messianic (kingdom) age. All this would happen in Jesus' generation (Matt 24:34).

This parable *cannot* apply to God's messianic-age servants because Jesus had said, "He who hears My word and believes in Him who sent Me has everlasting life, and *shall not come into judgment*, but has passed from death into life" (John 5:24 NKJV). The only way this parable could *ever* apply to God's future household servants is for him to reinstate the

Mosaic-age law, make his house comprise men who serve him through the sacrificial system it requires, construct a third temple in which those sacrifices would be offered, and then judge them for failing to obey that law. The exact scenario present in Jesus' generation would have to occur again. There is nothing in Scripture that suggests this is in God's plan—as Brock D. Hollett, a premillennialist, says, "the rebuilding of the temple after its destruction in AD 70 is *an inferred necessity*"[10] for some existing prophetic models, but there is nothing in the Bible about it.

Ten-Virgins Judgment

I have a vivid memory associated with Jesus' parable of the ten virgins (Matt 25:1–13). Another minister, whom I had never met, and I were scheduled to speak at a Bible conference in a distant city; we had chosen our topics without collaboration. I planned to do a four-lesson survey of Hebrews from an inmillennial[11] perspective. My first lesson would establish that "the last days" in Hebrews 1:2 means the end of the Mosaic age, not the end of history.

The other brother spoke first in the opening session of the conference. To my surprise, he announced he would preach through the Olivet Discourse over the next few days, and his strong dispensational perspective soon appeared. My wife, who knew my planned topic, leaned toward me and whispered, "This ought to be interesting."

Thankfully, the conference concluded without open eschatological conflict, and I enjoyed Christian fellowship with this dispensational brother. His love for Christ was obvious and refreshing. However, one thing he said shocked me: he taught that all ten virgins in Jesus' parable represented Christians! His argument went something like this: all the women were "virgins" with a purity that only saved people have; unbelievers, he said, cannot be "virgins" in God's sight. Further, all ten virgins had lamps that God had given them for light, and the oil that filled (or had filled) all ten lamps represented the Holy Spirit. Only Christians have the Spirit, so all ten virgins were saved individuals. By some reasoning process that escapes me at the moment, this brother said the ten virgins represent Jewish Christians that will live at the time Jesus establishes his future millennial kingdom. The virgins whose oil failed represent believing Jews who will go to heaven, but not enter the millennial kingdom age. Perhaps this brother had read, but misunderstood, J. Dwight Pentecost's quote from Schuyler English:

> The ten virgins represent the remnant of Israel.... The five wise virgins are the believing remnant, the foolish virgins the unbelieving, who only profess to be looking for Messiah's coming in power.[12]

I have often wondered how the disciples on the Mount of Olives could have known about this "believing remnant" in their distant future and what that knowledge would have meant for them and their ministries.

An inmillennialist would agree with my fellow conference speaker on one vital point—all ten virgins represent Israelites. In the Old Testament, God had often used the term "virgin" to refer to Israel in Mosaic-age covenant relationship with him. God's message to the king of Assyria was, "*The virgin the daughter of Zion* hath despised thee, and laughed thee to scorn; the daughter of Jerusalem hath shaken her head at thee" (2 Kgs 19:21). Because of Israel's sins, God said, "Therefore thus saith the LORD; Ask ye now among the heathen, who hath heard such things: *the virgin of Israel* hath done a very horrible thing" (Jer 18:13).

An inmillennialist would insist that Jesus uses this figure (i.e., virgins) to represent the Jews of his generation. All of God's Mosaic-age virgins possessed covenant lamps. Some of these lamps were sputtering and about to go out; the virgins who owned them failed to purchase new-covenant oil from the Great Supplier of covenant oil. They said, "Our lamps *are going out*" (ESV).[13] A. T. Robertson has this comment:

> When the five foolish virgins lit their lamps, they discovered the lack of oil. The sputtering, flickering, smoking wicks were a sad revelation. "And *perhaps* we are to understand that there is something in the coincidence of the lamps going out just as the Bridegroom

arrived. Mere outward religion is found to have no illuminating power" (Plummer).[14]

I would remove "perhaps" from Plummer's statement; this figure shows the fading away of the Mosaic-age covenant—it would end when the temple fell in the *parousia* (presence) of the Son of Man. Jesus is saying that Mosaic-age Jewish virgins must have new-covenant oil in their lamps to gain admittance to the kingdom wedding celebration.

Jeremiah had used the term *virgin* to refer to Israel in two ways. When God destroyed Jerusalem through the Babylonians, he said, "The ways of Zion do mourn, because none come to the solemn feasts: all her gates are desolate: her priests sigh, *her virgins are afflicted*, and she is in bitterness" and "*the virgins of Jerusalem* hang down their heads to the ground" (Lam 1:4; 2:10). These were God's virgins; he had judged them. But Jeremiah also spoke of Israel as she would exist in the messianic age: "Again I will build thee, and thou shalt be built, O *virgin of Israel*: thou shalt again be adorned with thy tabrets, and shalt go forth in the dances of them that make merry" (Jer 31:4). Jesus is using this same virgin imagery in the Olivet Discourse: God would judge some of Israel's virgins, and they would fail to enter the messianic-age kingdom because of their lack of preparation; others, possessing faith in Christ, would enter with joyous dancing. As N. T. Wright says, "The context of the whole passage is of course Jesus' announcement of the coming kingdom,"[15] which he compares to a wedding feast.

The timing and cause of this separation among God's Mosaic-age virgins are the same here as in the rest of the Olivet Discourse: Jesus says, "Watch therefore, for ye know neither the day (Gk. *hēmera*) nor the hour (Gk. *hōra*) wherein the Son of man cometh (Gk. *erchomai*)" (Matt 25:13). Jesus was coming in his kingdom in their generation (Matt 16:28; 24:34), but they would not know the specific time—the signs Jesus had given would show them when the last hour had come (e.g., 1 John 2:18).

I will repeat a point I made earlier: there is no other time in history that can accommodate this parable. When Jesus gave it, he and the disciples were living in the overlap of two ages—the Mosaic age and the messianic age. At that time, God had two kinds of covenant virgins: some were virgins in just the Mosaic-age covenant; others were also virgins in the messianic-age (everlasting) covenant. The Son of Man (i.e., the bridegroom) would shut the former out of his kingdom, but welcome the latter into the wedding feast. That division occurred in Jesus' generation; thereafter, he will *never* say, "I knew you not" to his new-covenant virgins. This assumes that this age-transition situation will never arise a second time—or multiple times—in our future.

The two-servants parable emphasized Israel's behavior during the time between the Olivet Discourse and the destruction of the Temple. This ten-virgins parable focuses on individuals entering the kingdom: "they that were ready went in" (Matt 25:10). This kingdom entrance serves as the centerpiece—the main focal point—of Matthew's chiasm of judgment exhortations. The following parable returns to the interim and maintains the symmetry of the passage.

Talents Judgment

The fourth exhortation is the parable of the talents (Matt 25:14–30). My comments will be brief because many of my observations about the previous two parables apply here, too. All those to whom the man left talents were servants in his house. As in the two-servants parable, these represent servants in God's Mosaic-age house. The man going into a far country represents Jesus going to receive his kingdom from the Ancient of Days after "the judgment was set, and the books were opened" (Dan 7:9–14).

Jesus says, "After a long time the lord of those servants cometh (Gk. *erchomai*), and reckoneth with them" (Matt 25:19). The return of the man represents the coming of the Son of Man, which Jesus said would happen in his generation. Most commentators assume the words "after a long time" (Matt 25:19) justify their belief that this is an event in our future. But, in the parable, the man returns within the lifetime of his servants, a time frame that fits Jesus' "this generation" limit (Matt 24:34). The prophets sometimes used "a long time" to refer to something almost beyond a human lifetime: Jeremiah told the exiled Jews in Babylon they would be there seventy years (Jer 29:10), but also said, "This captivity is long" (Jer 29:28). The seventy years were "long" regarding one human lifetime, but not regarding God's long-term redemptive plan. And so it is in Jesus' parable: the lord of the servants was away "a long time" concerning the activities under consideration, but this does not justify the assumption that many centuries would elapse before the thing signified—the return of the Son of Man—would occur. Jesus could not be clearer: the Son of Man would return in his generation.

The lord of the parable casts "the unprofitable servant into outer darkness: [where] there shall be weeping and gnashing of teeth" (Matt 25:30). Jesus had spoken this way when a Roman centurion exhibited faith in him:

> And I say unto you, That many shall come from the east and west, and shall sit down with Abraham, and Isaac, and Jacob, in the kingdom of heaven. But *the children of the kingdom shall be cast out into outer darkness: there shall be weeping and gnashing of teeth*. (Matt 8:11–12)

Gentiles, like the centurion, came "from the east and west" to take their place in the kingdom of heaven in Jesus' generation. The "children of the kingdom"—the servants who mismanaged God's assets in the Mosaic age—were cast out to weep and gnash their teeth before some of Jesus' hearers tasted death.

This parable, the last one Jesus gives in the Olivet Discourse, describes a division in God's Mosaic-age servants. Some would use God's blessings wisely and remain in God's household in the messianic age. Others would hide their blessings "in the earth" (Matt 25:25), remain unproductive, and perish. This parable is a warning about the judgment that would take place in the disciples' generation.

Final Judgment

The belief that the sheep-and-goats judgment (Matt 25:31–46) is the *final* judgment at the end of history has prevailed in the church since Jesus gave his exhortation based on it. In the last two centuries, however, two groups on opposite ends of the preterist-futurist continuum have abandoned this view. On the futurist end, some dispensationalists, like the engaging conference speaker I mentioned earlier, say Jesus is speaking of a judgment that will determine who enters the millennium, the thousand-literal-year reign of Christ that they think will follow the church age. John MacArthur, for example, describes this passage as "the sheep and goats judgment of the nations, in which believers will be separated from unbelievers (Matt. 25:31–33), for entrance into the millennial kingdom."[16] Readers who understand the inmillennial prophetic model as we have discovered it to this point will recognize the error in this view: it is incompatible with the fact that God established the kingdom of heaven, and his saints took possession of it (cp. Dan 7:18), in the "last days" of the Mosaic age.

On the far-left (preterist) side of the interpretive scale, some extreme preterists (sadly) restrict the sheep-and-goats judgment to the "last days" of the Mosaic age. J. Stuart Russell, for example, says, "The passage … belongs *wholly* to the subject of our Lord's discourse,—the judgment of Israel and the end of the [Jewish] age."[17] He sees this judgment as the separation of the Jews during the "great tribulation" that brought the temple's fall and thinks an unseen judgment sent some of them to "everlasting punishment" and others to "life eternal."[18] This view has led many of Russell's followers to deny the physical resurrection of the body and the final judgment, important parts of the orthodox church's confession for two thousand years. The differences between inmillennialism and this view may not be clear, so I will devote several pages to refuting Russell's arguments.

You may recall that, in the Preface, I described the soul-turmoil Russell's book caused me when I first read it. His interpretation of the sheep-and-goats judgment passage was one of the most disturbing things I had ever read, and it almost destroyed my faith. So, I have an intense interest in showing that this passage is consistent with the rest of the Olivet Discourse and that the historic Christian faith is right when it teaches us to confess, "I believe ... he shall come to judge the quick and the dead" and "I believe ... in ... the resurrection of the body."[19] Inmillennialism allows me to do both.

Russell's Argument. Russell begins by acknowledging the difficulties he faces as he defends his position:

> It may be freely admitted that this parable, or parabolic description, has many points of difference from the preceding portion of our Lord's discourse. *It seems to stand separate and distinct from the rest*, without the connecting links which we have found in other sections. Still more, it seems to take a wider range than Jerusalem and Israel; it reads like the judgment, not of a nation, but of all nations; not of a city or a country, but of a world; not a passing crisis, but a final consummation.[20]

He is right about all this except his assertion that this passage is a *parable*. I suspect Russell wanted to connect this judgment to the three parables Jesus has just given, all of which pertain to Israel. But this is *not* a parable, as S. M. Merrill shows:

> It neither begins nor ends as a parable. It is not announced as a parable, is not constructed like a parable, and will not bear interpretation like a parable. The only thing in it or about it that suggests the idea of a parable is the allusion to the shepherd dividing the sheep from the goats. This, however, does not make it a parable. It is simply a simile or a comparison, and that of a single point.[21]

A parable is "a placing beside, a comparison, a similitude, an illustration of one subject by another."[22] Jesus is not speaking metaphorically; he is describing what the Son of Man will do at this judgment without using some imaginary figure to represent him.

As I mentioned earlier, Jesus bases his first exhortation on an ancient historical event—the flood. In his next three exhortations, Jesus uses parables in which a fictional figure represents the Son of Man: a lord of a house, a bridegroom, and a man traveling to a far country. That Jesus returns to a non-parabolic manner of speaking suggests his last exhortation is, like his first one, based on a historical event. This weakens Russell's overall argument and strengthens the case against him—this exhortation stands "separate and distinct from the rest" because it is not a parable.

Russell enumerates five arguments against the idea that this is the final judgment of all mankind. I will address these individual arguments in the order he presents them.

Connecting Links. As his first argument, Russell says the traditional view of the sheep-and-goats judgment assumes it is "without connecting links" to the rest of the Olivet Discourse. But, he says, this connection "is apparent in the Greek, where we find the particle δὲ [*de*], the force of which is to indicate transition and connection,—transition to a new illustration, and connection with the foregoing context."[23] Some translations show the connecting word Russell mentions: "But (Gk. *de*) when the Son of Man comes (Gk. *erchomai*) in His glory...." (Matt 25:31 NASB).

Inmillennialism agrees with Russell here; this exhortation is the capstone of the Olivet Discourse. And our prophetic model gives an interpretation that makes it a more satisfying conclusion than the interpretation Russell proposes.

The Coming of the Son of Man in Matt 25:31. Second, Russell refers to the coming of the Son of Man in Matthew 25:31:

> This 'coming of the Son of man' has already been predicted by our Lord (Matt. 24:30, and parallel passages), and the time expressly defined, being included in the comprehensive declaration, 'Verily I say unto you, This generation shall not pass, till all these things be fulfilled' (Matt. 24:34).[24]

This statement causes major problems for other prophetic models, but, as I have shown, it is not a problem for inmillennialism: it sees the "coming (Gk. *erchomai*) of the Son of Man" as an event associated with the temple's fall in the disciples' generation.

A Comparison of Two Passages. Third, Russell stresses the similarity between Matthew 16:27–28 and Matthew 25:31–33; and this is where inmillennialism parts ways with him. After giving a list of elements that occur in both passages, he says, "We are fully warranted, therefore, in regarding the coming of the Son of man in Matt. 25 as *identical* with that referred to in Matt. 16."[25] This is almost, but not quite, true; and the dissimilarity separates inmillennialism from Russell's heretical view that denies the resurrection of the body.

I will open my counterarguments by comparing what the Son of Man does when he comes in each passage:

> "The Son of man shall come … then (Gk. *tote*) he shall reward.…" (Matt 16:27)

> "The Son of man shall come … then (Gk. *tote*) shall he sit.… " (Matt 25:31–32)

The coming of the Son of Man and the Greek adverb *tote*, here translated as "then," have the same meaning in both passages; but what does the Son of Man do "at that time"?[26] In the first, he *rewards*; but in the second, he *reigns*.

I have discussed these two actions before while arguing for an invisible coming of the Son of Man at the temple's fall. Two days after giving the Olivet Discourse, Jesus tells Caiaphas he will "see" them both. Here is the comparison I gave between Jesus' statement to the high priest and one he made in the Olivet Discourse:

> Olivet Discourse: "Then shall appear the sign of the Son of man in heaven … and they shall see the Son of man coming in the clouds of heaven with power and great glory." (Matt 24:30)

Before Caiaphas: "From now on you will see the Son of Man seated at the right hand of Power and coming on the clouds of heaven." (Matt 26:64 ESV)

In both places, Jesus says the men of his generation would "see" two things: (1) the Son of Man coming to destroy the temple; and (2) the Son of Man sitting "at the right hand of Power." The second of these would be "the sign of the Son of man in heaven"—his position of authority during the messianic age. Russell does not recognize the distinction between these two things in his comparison of Matthew 16:27–28 to Matthew 25:31–33.

At the risk of being redundant, I will provide an amplified version that shows both these elements in four key passages in Matthew, including the two Russell is comparing here. My amplifications are in brackets:

> For the Son of man shall come [in this generation] in the glory of his Father with his angels; and then [at that time] he shall reward *every man* according to his works [as he judges Israel]. Verily I say unto you, There be some standing here, which shall not taste of death, till they see the Son of man coming in his kingdom [in which he will sit on his throne]. (Matt 16:27–28)

> And then [in this generation] shall appear the sign of the Son of man in heaven [on his kingdom throne]: and then shall all the tribes of the [land of Israel] mourn, and they shall see the Son of man coming in the clouds of heaven with power and great glory [to judge Israel]. (Matt 24:30)

> When the Son of man shall come [in this generation] in his glory, and all the holy angels with him [to judge Israel], then [at that time] shall he sit upon the throne of his glory [in his kingdom]: And [at its end] before him shall be gathered *all nations*: and he shall separate them

one from another, as a shepherd divideth his sheep from the goats. (Matt 25:31–32)

From now on [after I ascend to the Ancient of Days to receive my kingdom] you will see the Son of Man seated at the right hand of Power [on his kingdom throne] *and* coming on the clouds of heaven [to judge Israel]. (Matt 26:64 ESV)

The coming of the Son of Man to judge Israel and his sitting on the throne of his kingdom are present (or implied) in each of these passages. The Son of Man's coming must occur in the disciples' generation, and his reign must follow that event. I will show that the term "every man" (Matt 16:27) applies to Israel below under Russell's fourth point.

My point here is that Russell cannot see that, in the two passages he is comparing (Matt 16:27–28 and Matt 25:31–32), Jesus does not handle these two elements the same way. In the first, he links his coming to his judgment of Israel, then mentions his messianic-age reign; in the second, he does not mention Israel's judgment but links his coming to his reign. And this is what he does before Caiaphas, except there he reverses the order, mentioning his reign first, then his coming. Jesus leaves the high priest (and us) to infer that the coming is to judge Israel. By this point in his ministry, Jesus has established the fact that the coming of the Son of Man in his generation would be for that purpose; he need not repeat this in every situation. Several passages show that the Jewish leaders understood his message.

In summary, the coming of the Son of Man to *reward* in Matthew 16:27–28 is not the same as the coming of the Son of Man to *reign* in Matthew 25:31–32, even though Jesus joins these two distinct ideas everywhere, either explicitly or implicitly. In his final exhortation in the Olivet Discourse, Jesus describes the *end* of his messianic-age reign. Russell is wrong when he asserts that these two passages are identical.

"Nations" means "Every Man." Fourth, Russell asks us "to give the phrase 'all the nations' a restricted signification, and to limit it to the nations of Palestine."[27] He does this after having just asked us to see "the coming of the Son of man in Matt. 25 as *identical* with that referred to in Matt. 16."[28] If these passages are identical, as Russell says, then the *objects* of the two judgments are the same: "all nations" in Matthew 25:32 is the same as "every man" in Matthew 16:27. I will show this is false by examining each argument Russell presents in its defense.

Russell begins by observing that we must sometimes understand universal propositions in a restricted sense. Nobody denies this principle, but Russell does not show why we should apply it *here*. Instead, he speaks of the "great probability" that "all the tribes (Gk. *phulē*) of the land" in Matthew 24:30 is the same as "all nations (Gk. *ethnos*)" in Matthew 25:32. Let me be blunt: the ultimate issue here is whether there is a bodily resurrection at the end of the messianic age or not, so I am not interested in "great probabilities"—is it true that "tribes" are the same as "nations," or not? Russell leaves us with just his assertion. I will go further: there are compelling reasons to believe the exact opposite is true—that Jesus uses "nations" (Gk. *ethnos*) in Matthew 25:32 in direct *contrast* to the "tribes" (Gk. *phulē*) in Matthew 24:30. My reason is simple: the New Testament *never* uses the plural of *ethnos* elsewhere to refer to just Israel; it always means the nations other than Israel (i.e., the "Gentiles"), all the nations including Israel, or something similar.

Russell's next reason for *ethnos* meaning "Israel," not "nations," in this context is that the disciples were, according to him, confused about the Great Commission.[29] He says, "The learned Professor Burton observes: 'It was not until fourteen years after our Lord's ascension that St. Paul travelled for the first time, and preached the gospel to the Gentiles.'"[30] This, says Russell, shows that the apostles did not understand Jesus to mean they should preach beyond Palestine when he said, "Go therefore and make disciples of *all the nations* (Gk. *ethnos*)" (Matt 28:19 NKJV). But, even if the apostles failed to understand the Great Commission (they didn't), this does not affect Jesus' meaning in the Olivet

Discourse. This imagined confusion does not prove Russell's point; it leaves us without *proof* that "nations" means something here that it never means elsewhere in the New Testament.

Russell next says that in both Matthew 16:27–28 and Matthew 25:31–33 "the judgment is represented as in some sense *universal*."[31] He is asking us to believe they are universal in the same sense. But this requires us to ignore significant differences in the terms Jesus uses. In the first passage, Jesus says, "The Son of Man ... will reward *each* (Gk. *hekastos*) according to his works" (Matt 16:27 NKJV). The Scriptures use this term, in most cases, regarding a subset of the human family. For example, Paul later uses it to mean the members of Christ's churches: "The manifestation of the Spirit is given to *every man* (Gk. *hekastos*) to profit withal" (1 Cor 12:7). A few moments before Jesus mentioned his judgment of the "nations," he used *hekastos* in a parable to designate *Israel*: "And unto one he gave five talents, to another two, and to another one; to *every man* (Gk. *hekastos*) according to his several ability" (Matt 25:15). In the four Gospels, this term *never* refers to anyone outside the geographic boundaries of the land of Israel.

So, Russell is asking us to believe that a term Jesus *never* uses for anyone outside Israel (i.e., *hekastos* in Matt 16:27) is identical to a term he *never* uses for Israel (i.e., the plural of *ethnos* in Matt 25:32). This is a request I must deny; the persons on trial are not the same in both passages—in the first, it is "every man" in Israel, but, in the second, it is "all the nations" of the earth.

Basis of Judgment. Fifth, Russell argues that the sheep-and-goats judgment is not the final judgment because of the basis upon which it proceeds. He says, "The destiny of the righteous and the wicked is made to turn on the treatment which they respectively offered to the suffering disciples of Christ."[32] Russell lists some problems he thinks this creates: it contradicts, he says, Paul's doctrine of justification by faith; it precludes the judgment of those who lived before Christ or those who have never heard of Christ; and it would be irrelevant for those who lived in Christian societies, for they would not be tempted to mistreat Christ's disciples as others have been. Therefore, Russell says, a judgment based on this standard "is manifestly inappropriate and inapplicable."[33] He says that the only way to make this a just judgment is to restrict it to Israel in Jesus' generation.

This argument is invalid; whatever problems Russell creates for such a judgment at the end of history, he also creates for a judgment at the end of the Mosaic age. He acknowledges that this judgment determines the eternal destiny of people:

> A more sure word of prophecy ... reveals 'the Son of man coming in his glory;' the King seated on the throne; the judgment set, and the books opened. It reveals the sheep and the goats separated the one from the other; the righteous entering into *everlasting life*; the wicked sent away into *everlasting punishment*.[34]

Was Paul's doctrine of justification by faith not valid for Israel in Jesus' generation? We know every individual whom God judged in the "great tribulation" had not heard of Jesus and interacted with his disciples, for Jesus said, "Ye shall not have gone over the cities of Israel, till the Son of man be come" (Matt 10:23). How could the Son of Man judge those who had not heard of him? Did Jesus, in his first-century coming, send people to their eternal destinies based on this "manifestly inappropriate and inapplicable"—as Russell calls it—standard? Russell does not solve his supposed problems by equating the judgment of "all nations" with the judgment of "all the tribes" of Israel at the end of the Mosaic age![35]

I will offer a few additional thoughts about the basis of the sheep-and-goats judgment. Men's treatment of Christ's disciples shows whether they have true faith. To persecute Jesus' followers is to persecute him. When Paul was abusing Christians, Jesus said to him, "Why persecutest thou *me*?" (Acts 9:4; cp. Acts 22:7–8; 26:14–15). And, a statement in Zechariah shows this relationship between God and his people existed before Christ came: "The LORD of Hosts says this: 'He has sent Me for His glory against the nations who are plundering you, for *anyone who touches you touches the pupil of His eye*'" (Zech 2:8 HCSB). The way men treat God's people shows whether they love God, so it will be just for God to proceed on this basis in the final judgment.

A judgment based on works—in this case, how men treat Christ's disciples—is not inconsistent with the doctrine of justification by faith. Paul said, "We are his workmanship, created in Christ Jesus unto good works, which God hath before ordained that we should walk in them" (Eph 2:10). Those who do good works—like ministering to Christ's servants—are God's sheep; those who do not are goats. As Paul said,

> God ... will render to every man according to his deeds: to them who by patient continuance in well doing seek for glory and honour and immortality, eternal life: but unto them that are contentious, and do not obey the truth, but obey unrighteousness, indignation and wrath, tribulation and anguish, upon every soul of man that doeth evil, of the Jew first, and also of the Gentile; but glory, honour, and peace, to every man that worketh good. (Rom 2:5–11)

James says God will judge us by the law of liberty, but also says, "Ye see then how that by works a man is justified, and not by faith only" (Jam 2:24).

I believe in the Five Solas of the Christian faith: we are saved by grace alone, through faith alone, in Christ alone, according to Scripture alone, and for God's glory alone. I understand Paul to mean that we will not be justified *because* of our good works, and James to mean we will not be justified *without* good works—both are true. In the Olivet Discourse, Jesus is saying that men's treatment of his disciples shows whether they will be justified or condemned in the final judgment.

Returning to the task at hand, I have finished with Russell's list of arguments, but will mention two more observations that militate against his view. First, Jesus said,

> I am the good shepherd, and know my sheep, and am known of mine. As the Father knoweth me, even so know I the Father: and I lay down my life for the sheep. And *other sheep I have, which are not of this fold*: them also I must bring, and they shall hear my voice; and there shall be one fold, and one shepherd. (John 10:14–16)

Caiaphas–the high priest who would see "the Son of man sitting on the right hand of power, and coming in the clouds of heaven" (Matt 26:64)–unwittingly helps us understand Jesus' meaning when he tells the Jews how to prevent the Romans from coming to take away their place and nation. He says, "One man [i.e. Jesus] should die for the people, and that the whole nation (Gk. *ethnos*, singular) perish not." But John adds this note: "And this spake he not of himself: but being high priest that year, he prophesied that Jesus should die for that nation; *and not for that nation only, but that also he should gather together in one the children of God that were scattered abroad*" (John 11:48–52). Jesus was about to die for his sheep in all nations, including those in Israel. Therefore, Russell is wrong to confine the judgment that makes the final division between his sheep and the goats to only Israel.

Second, I will again mention a point I made earlier: this judgment does not portray the sheep and goats as sharing a covenant relationship with God. It is like the first (flood) exhortation but different from the middle three exhortations. Jesus is elsewhere very clear about the goats being outside his covenant, as when he speaks to the apostate Jews:

> Ye believe not, *because ye are not of my sheep*, as I said unto you. *My sheep hear my voice*, and I know them, and they follow me: and *I give unto them eternal life*; and they shall never perish, neither shall any man pluck them out of my hand. (John 10:26–28)

The goats were never part of the eternal covenant God made with his sheep through Christ. This distinguishes this judgment from the three *parable*-judgments Jesus has just given. In them, those being judged were all servants or virgins; things true of Israelites in their Mosaic-age covenant relationship to God. The sheep-and-goats judgment is not like these three judgments; it is like the flood judgment where the greatest common denominator of those under judgment is that they are God's creatures. The sheep-and-goats judgment pertains to "all nations," not just to "all the tribes" of Israel, as Russell (and some other full preterists) would have us believe.

An Inmillennial Interpretation

I have not addressed one fact that undergirds all of Russell's arguments. He placed the sheep-and-goats judgment at the end of the Mosaic age because Jesus says, "This generation shall not pass, till *all these things* be fulfilled" (Matt 24:34). Russell, in a valiant effort to remain faithful to the words of Christ, places this judgment within this time frame.

But, as we have seen, Russell's view creates significant problems regarding the sheep-and-goats judgment, which I will summarize here for ease of reference:

1. It makes a historical event into a parable.
2. It fails to distinguish between the Son of Man coming in judgment against Israel and the Son of Man sitting in heaven; between him *rewarding* and him *reigning*.
3. It makes "all nations"—a term the Scriptures never use for Israel—identical to "every man" and "all the tribes" in that nation.
4. It fails to account for the fact that Jesus has sheep outside the nation of Israel.
5. It ignores the fact that this is a judgment of men as creatures, whereas the judgment of Israel in Jesus' generation was of a nation in covenant with God.
6. It leaves us with no final resolution to the problem of sin in God's creation.
7. It provides for no judgment for people living after AD 70.
8. It robs the church of the hope of the resurrection.

Is there a way to preserve Jesus' "this generation" timestamp, as Russell sought to do, yet avoid the above problems? Inmillennialism answers in the affirmative; there is a recognized principle that achieves both objectives. Commentators give this principle various names and descriptions. I will use the one Kenneth Gentry gives while speaking about John's vision of the Bride of Christ in Revelation:

> The picture he presents is … protensive: He looks at the *end results* of the present redemptive reality. This protensive view is common in Scripture, as when we read of "new wine" being found in the "cluster" (Isa. 65:8). Obviously *grapes* are found in clusters, not the end product of new wine. But the inherent quality of the grape to produce wine and its common usage for such allow the poet to see the developing wine through the original product. John is able to see in the historic, persecuted first-century church the beauty that is hers—because of her … future glory.[36]

Inmillennialism says Jesus is using this "protensive[37] view" to describe the "end product" of what was happening in his generation. Here, to use the imagery of Isaiah 65:8, the "cluster" is the coming of the Son of Man to destroy the temple; the "new wine" is the (implied) resurrection and final judgment of "all nations."

The Scriptures often present this protensive view in terms of "if-then" logic. The overall template is as follows:

> *If* [the "last days" events occur], *then* [the messianic age events will occur].

I will provide several examples of this pattern, where the "wine" of the messianic age vintage is joined to the "cluster" growing in the "last days" of the Mosaic age. In each, the "last days" *if* condition produces a *then* result in the resurrection and final judgment at the end of the messianic age. This allows for a direct comparison of these examples to what Jesus says regarding the sheep-and-goats judgment:

> *If* ["Christ was raised up from the dead"], *then* ["we shall also be in the likeness of his resurrection"] (Rom 6:4–5).
>
> *If* [God "raised up Jesus from the dead"], *then* [he "shall also quicken your mortal bodies"] (Rom 8:11).
>
> *If* ["Christ both died, and rose, and revived"], *then* ["we shall all stand before the judgment seat of Christ"] (Rom 14:9–12).
>
> *If* ["God . . . raised up the Lord"], *then* [he "will also raise up us"] (1 Cor 6:14).
>
> *If* ["Christ (is) risen from the dead"], *then* ["they that are Christ's" will rise] (1 Cor 15:20–23).
>
> *If* [God "raised up the Lord Jesus"], *then* [(he) "shall raise up us also by Jesus, and shall present us with you"] (2 Cor 4:14)
>
> *If* [God destroys the (Jewish) enemies], *then* [he will "change our vile body, that it may be fashioned like unto his glorious body] (Phil 3:19–21; cp. Phil 3:2–8)

This list shows that the protensive *if-then* view is common in Paul's writings. He often relates events in the "last days" of the Mosaic age to those at the end of the messianic age without describing the intervening period. I suggest he learned this pattern from the example set by Jesus, the other apostles, and the prophets.

I will provide two examples of the protensive view from the Old Testament. The first comes from Hosea:

> And the LORD said unto him, Call his name Jezreel; *for yet a little while*, and I will avenge the blood of Jezreel upon the house of Jehu, and will cause to cease the kingdom of the house of Israel.... Yet the number of the children of Israel shall be as the sand of the sea, which cannot be measured nor numbered; and it shall come to pass, that in the place where it was said unto them, Ye are not my people, there it shall be said unto them, Ye are the sons of the living God. (Hos 1:4, 10)

The Lord said he would judge Israel in the prophet's generation,[38] and then describes something that would happen over seven centuries later, without mentioning the intervening period. Paul verifies the fulfillment of this distant (to Hosea) prophecy in Romans 9:25–28. Hosea directly joins a judgment-event in his immediate future to an outcome in his distant future.

My second example from the Old Testament comes from the words of Moses to Israel just before they entered the promised land:

> When thou art come into the land which the LORD thy God giveth thee, thou shalt not learn to do after the abominations of those nations.... Thou shalt be perfect with the LORD thy God. For these nations, which thou shalt possess, hearkened unto observers of times, and unto diviners: but as for thee, the LORD thy God hath not suffered thee so to do. The LORD thy God will raise up unto thee a Prophet from the midst of thee, of thy brethren, like unto me; unto him ye shall hearken. (Deut 18:9, 14–15)

Moses brought a distant event—one that would occur at the end of the Mosaic age (i.e., the coming of Christ per Acts 3:22, 23; 7:37)—into immediate contact with an event in his generation—Israel's entrance into the land.

Jesus is taking this protensive view in the Olivet Discourse: he is bringing an event at the end of the messianic age—the final judgment—into immediate contact with an event in his generation, the coming of the Son of Man.

The protensive view is not a "corrective device" like the ones required in other prophetic models; it is not a "prophetic perspective" that says the prophets or apostles were ignorant of entire ages, or that can insert an age where it does not exist; nor is it a form of the ubiquitous "already-not-yet" view that can explain away uncomfortable time statements as needed. This view arises directly from the practice of inspired writers; and, as Gentry says, and the above examples show, it is common in Scripture. Whenever it occurs, the Scriptures give powerful evidence of its presence, as in the sheep-and-goats judgment.

KEY POINT #11

Jesus ended the Olivet Discourse in Matthew by describing the final judgment. This judgment is the necessary outcome of what God did in the "last days" of the Mosaic age; the kingdom of God requires the final judgment.

Conclusion

These exhortations reinforce the prophetic model we have discovered to this point. Israel, during the Mosaic age, contained God's covenant "servants" and "virgins," but, in the "last days" of that age, God would cast some of them out of his kingdom. This situation was unique to Jesus' generation, for, after the temple's fall, there will never be another time when God will cut some of his servants in two, or cast some of them into outer darkness, or shut some of his virgins out of the kingdom.

Here is a diagram that shows the judgments that provide the basis for Jesus' five exhortations at the end of his Olivet Discourse:

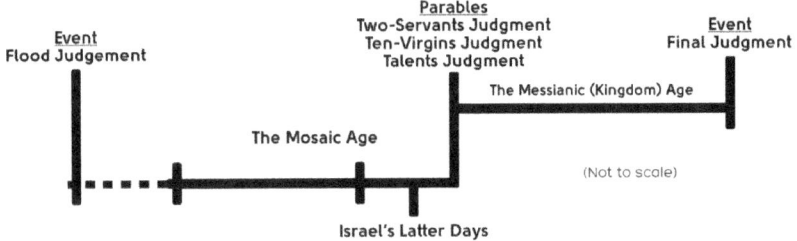

Figure 12-1. Five Exhortations in the Olivet Discourse

I regret that J. Stuart Russell rejected the sheep-and-goats judgment as the final judgment, but I want to acknowledge my debt to him and express my appreciation for the insights he gave me regarding prophetic timestamps. I join R. C. Sproul when he says, "I can never read the New Testament again the same way I read it before reading *The Parousia*."[39]

I have now discovered a simple prophetic model using the Olivet Discourse. A relatively small number of prophetic images were involved, and most of these have extensive Old Testament precedents. I have shown—through examining Jesus' five exhortations—the potential this model has for interpreting prophetic passages.

Inmillennialism challenges existing prophetic models the way Copernicus' model of the solar system challenged the prevailing models in the sixteenth century. It questions many previous assumptions about how things move in the prophetic solar system; perhaps, it says, many events we have assumed were in our future are in our past. But the inmillennial model is not quite complete and is, therefore, unable to sustain fully its challenges. It shows that the messianic age would follow the events Jesus describes in the Olivet Discourse, but provides few details about that age, the end of history, the resurrection, the ultimate resolution of the problem of evil, and other important issues. To correct these deficiencies, I will now turn to another significant prophetic passage that provides an overview of the messianic age.

Before I do, review the updated diagram of our model that shows the final judgment Jesus mentions at the end of the Olivet Discourse:

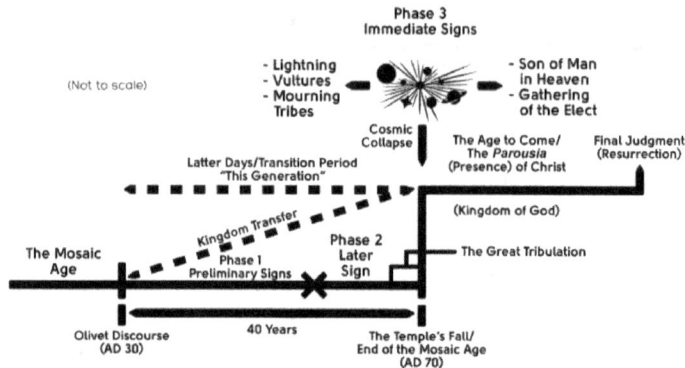

Figure 12-2. Inmillennialism through the Olivet Discourse

Notes

1 John F. Hart, "Should Pretribulationists Reconsider the Rapture in Matthew 24:36–44?," *JGES* 20 (2007): 53.
2 Liddell et al., eds., *Lexicon*, 996 (s.v. "κρίνω").
3 Robertson, *A Harmony*, 139, 144.
4 Wright, *Victory*, 632.
5 Wright, *Victory*, 636.
6 This title is found in many other Old Testament passages: Ps 136:22; Isa 41:8; 44:1, 21; 45:4; 49:3, 5; Jer 30:10; 46:27; Ezek 28:25; et al.
7 See also Exod 34:26; Deut 23:18; 26:13; et al.
8 Robertson, *A Harmony*, 160.
9 The verb is in the present tense.
10 Hollett, *Debunking Preterism*, 30.
11 This word did not exist at the time.
12 Pentecost, *Things to Come*, 283.
13 The verb is in the present tense.
14 Robertson, "Hebrews," 1:197. Just before this quote, Robertson has the following: "**Are going out** (σβεννυνται [*shennuntai*]). Present middle indicative of linear action, not punctiliar or aoristic."
15 Wright, *Victory*, 315.
16 John MacArthur, *1 & 2 Timothy: Encouragement for Church Leaders*, MacArthur Bible Studies (Nashville: W Publishing Group, 2001), 109. See also Charles Caldwell Ryrie, *Basic Theology: A Popular Systematic Guide to Understanding Biblical Truth* (Chicago: Moody, 1999), 577–78.
17 Russell, *The Parousia*, 102 (emphasis added).
18 Russell, *The Parousia*, 122.
19 From the Apostles' Creed as found in Philip Schaff, *The Creeds of Christendom With a History and Critical Notes*, 3 vols. (1931; repr., Grand Rapids: Baker, 1983), 1:21–22.
20 Russell, *The Parousia*, 102 (emphasis added).
21 S. M. Merrill, *The Second Coming of Christ Considered in Its Relation to the Millennium, the Resurrection, and the Judgment* (Cincinnati: Cranston & Stowe, 1879), 125–26.
22 William Smith, *Smith's Bible Dictionary* (Nashville: Thomas Nelson, 1986), s.v. "parable."
23 Russell, *The Parousia*, 102.
24 Russell, *The Parousia*, 103.
25 Russell, *The Parousia*, 104 (emphasis added).
26 Liddell et al., eds., *Lexicon*, 1808 (s.v. "τότε").
27 Russell, *The Parousia*, 106.

28 Russell, *The Parousia*, 104 (emphasis added).

29 I find it ironic that Russell takes this route since it is the same route futurist take; he and they charge the apostles with confusion to arrive at polar-opposite results.

30 Russell, *The Parousia*, 105.

31 Russell, *The Parousia*, 103–4.

32 Russell, *The Parousia*, 106.

33 Russell, *The Parousia*, 107.

34 Russell, *The Parousia*, 122 (emphasis added).

35 I could say the same for the dispensational "solution" of putting this judgment just before their literal thousand-year reign of Christ.

36 Gentry, *Revelation Made Easy*, 128 (emphasis in original).

37 Many dictionaries do not list "protensive." It means "having continuance in time" or "having lengthwise extent." [Philip Babcock Gove, ed., *Webster's Third New International Dictionary of the English Language, Unabridged* (Springfield, MA: G. & C. Merriam Co., 1981), s.v. "protensive."]

38 It happened in 722 BC.

39 Sproul, "Introduction to the Parousia," x.

CHAPTER THIRTEEN

Two Details from 1 Corinthians 15

OUR IMPROVED prophetic model is almost complete. In this chapter, I will add two key details from 1 Corinthians 15, a passage in which Paul provides a synopsis of the entire messianic age. My method will involve two steps. First, I will discuss the problem Paul is addressing and his solution to it. Second, I will show that Paul's solution provides the two elements that must become part of our prophetic model. Without them, Paul could not have used his chosen method to resolve the problem at Corinth. I will show how his reasoning affects our mission as modern-day Christians; along the way, I will show that Paul's assumed prophetic framework matches inmillennialism.

A Problem and Its Solution

In 1 Corinthians 15, Paul is addressing a problem in the church at Corinth. His resolution involves the kingdom, the gospel that proclaims that kingdom, and the Old Testament verse quoted most often in the New Testament.

The Problem. Some teachers in Corinth denied the resurrection, and Paul saw their denial as a rejection of the gospel he preached. Here is his reasoning:

> Now if Christ be preached that he rose from the dead,
> how say some among you that there is no resurrection

> (Gk. *anastasis*) of the dead? But if there be no resurrection of the dead, then is Christ not risen: and if Christ be not risen, then is our preaching vain, and your faith is also vain. Yea, and we are found false witnesses of God; because we have testified of God that he raised up Christ: whom he raised not up, if so be that the dead rise not. For if the dead rise not, then is not Christ raised: and if Christ be not raised, your faith is vain; ye are yet in your sins. Then they also which are fallen asleep in Christ are perished. If in this life only we have hope in Christ, we are of all men most miserable. (1 Cor 15:12–19)

For Paul, the resurrection is an essential part of the gospel of salvation through Christ.

The Scriptures use the concept of resurrection in two ways: (1) metaphorically to refer to a person or a corporate community passing from *spiritual* death to life, and (2) literally to mean a person or group passing from *physical* death to life.

The resurrection problem Paul is correcting in 1 Corinthians 15 is the denial of the *physical* resurrection. I say this for two reasons. First, the Corinthians were not denying the reality of a *spiritual* resurrection, for Paul addresses them as those who had received "the spirit which is of God" (1 Cor 2:12). His extended discussion of spiritual gifts (1 Cor 12–14) suggests they were overemphasizing the supernatural manifestations of their new spiritual life. They were not denying that God had raised them from the dead, or that they were "alive unto God through Jesus Christ our Lord" (cp. Rom 6:8–11). Instead, they were misusing the spiritual gifts God had given as part of their spiritual resurrection with Christ.

Second, that the resurrection in question was physical appears from the reasoning Paul uses to solve the problem. He says Christ is the *firstfruits* of this resurrection, so this must mean *physical* resurrection, for that is the only resurrection Christ ever experienced. In agriculture, the firstfruits guarantee a harvest *of the same crop*; here, the "crop" refers to dead humans who return to life with glorified bodies like Christ's. As Robert B. Strimple says, this firstfruits-harvest relationship shows that "Paul views the two resurrections not so much as two events but as two episodes of the same event."[1] The firstfruits and harvest could not be of different crops; this single, two-part resurrection affects *physical* bodies.

These considerations lead me to the same conclusion N. T. Wright reached regarding 1 Corinthians 15: "The overall structure and logic of the chapter thus confirms ... that this is intended by Paul as a long argument in favour of a future bodily resurrection."[2]

The Solution. Paul does not rely on anything new to prove the physical resurrection; instead, he argues that the gospel of the kingdom he has preached to the Corinthians *requires* it. Wright again helps us: "The substance of the chapter is about the final victory, but the start of the chapter, repeating the early gospel summary, explains how that comes about."[3] Paul's explanation will reveal the two new elements for our prophetic model that I mentioned earlier: both are necessary for him to make his case for a physical resurrection.

The Gospel of the Kingdom. Many Christians, if asked to define the gospel, would turn to the following verses in 1 Corinthians 15:

> Moreover, brethren, I declare unto you the gospel which I preached unto you, which also ye have received, and wherein ye stand; by which also ye are saved, if ye keep in memory what I preached unto you, unless ye have believed in vain. For I delivered unto you first of all that which I also received, how that Christ died for our sins according to the scriptures; and that he was buried, and that he rose again the third day according to the scriptures: and that he was seen of Cephas, then of the twelve: after that, he was seen of above five hundred brethren at once; of whom the

> greater part remain unto this present, but some are fallen asleep. (1 Cor 15:1–6)

But I say that this is *not* the gospel as Paul preached it.

Now, I understand that someone could take my last statement out of context and bring charges of heresy against me in the church to which I belong. But I will run that risk to make an important point: 1 Corinthians 15:1–6 is only *part* of the gospel Paul preached. He proclaimed the same gospel Jesus and his disciples preached before him: the gospel *of the kingdom of God* (cp. Matt 4:23; 9:35). In doing so, he was fulfilling a sign Jesus said would precede the temple's fall: "This *gospel of the kingdom* shall be preached in all the world for a witness unto all nations; and then shall the end [of the Mosaic age] come" (Matt 24:14). To cite the above passage as a stand-alone definition of the gospel is to stop short of Paul's full message, for we must go further in 1 Corinthians 15 to see the *kingdom* part of his gospel.

Paul could not have made his argument for the resurrection had his gospel not proclaimed the kingdom of God. Before showing why this is true, I will emphasize two points. First, I want to stress that the kingdom was the central thrust of Paul's message by examining his preaching around the time he wrote 1 Corinthians 15 in AD 57.[4] A few years before he wrote this chapter, Paul visited Ephesus for the first time: "he went into the synagogue, and spake boldly for the space of three months, disputing and persuading *the things concerning the kingdom of God*" (Acts 19:8). After writing to the Corinthians, when he was at Ephesus for the last time, Paul said, "I know that ye all, among whom I have gone *preaching the kingdom of God*, shall see my face no more" (Acts 20:25). A few years later, while a prisoner in Rome (AD 61–63), Paul requested to speak with the chief Jews of that city:

> And when they had appointed him a day, there came many to him into his lodging; to whom he *expounded and testified the kingdom of God*, persuading them concerning Jesus, both out of the law of Moses, and out of the prophets, from morning till evening. (Acts 28:23)

These examples show that the gospel that "turned the world upside down" (Acts 17:6) proclaimed *the kingdom of God*.

Second, I want to emphasize that Paul preached this kingdom-oriented gospel from the perspective Jesus established in the Olivet Discourse. Earlier in First Corinthians, Paul says, "Ye come behind in no gift; waiting for *the coming (*Gk. **apokalupsis***) of our Lord Jesus Christ*: who shall also confirm you unto *the end*, that ye may be blameless in the day of our Lord Jesus Christ" (1 Cor 1:7–8). Paul also says,

> We do speak wisdom among those who are mature; a wisdom, however, not of *this age* (Gk. *aiōn*) nor of the rulers of *this age* (Gk. *aiōn*), who are passing away; but we speak God's wisdom in a mystery, the hidden wisdom which God predestined before the ages to our glory; the wisdom which none of the rulers of *this age* (Gk. *aiōn*) has understood; for if they had understood it they would not have crucified the Lord of glory. (1 Cor 2:6–8 NASB)

Paul reminds the Corinthians that God had established a new temple—the church—in which men were now worshipping:

> Know ye not that *ye are the temple of God*, and that the Spirit of God dwelleth in you? If any man defile the temple of God, him shall God destroy; for *the temple of God is holy, which temple ye are*. (1 Cor 3:16–17)

Paul says that the Lord will come in his kingdom and the Corinthians will reign with him (1 Cor 4:5, 8). That kingdom, says Paul, "is not in word, but in power" (1 Cor 4:20); it is one the unrighteous cannot inherit (1 Cor 6:9).

These statements agree with the inmillennial model we observed in Jesus' Olivet Discourse: (1) the coming of the Lord would occur in Paul's generation; (2) the Lord's coming would cause the Mosaic age and its rulers to pass away; and (3) the temple at Jerusalem would fall, but God's new temple (i.e., the church) would remain. These things were necessary to establish the kingdom of God.

Paul's *timing* for "the end" of "this age" also matches what Jesus said in the Olivet Discourse. He tells the Corinthians that "the appointed time *has grown very short....* The present form of this world is passing away" (1 Cor 7:29, 31 ESV). He also says, "the end of the ages has come" (1 Cor 10:11). These timestamps agree with the one Jesus established for the end of the Mosaic age: "This generation shall not pass, till all these things be fulfilled" (Matt 24:34). As Paul wrote 1 Corinthians 15, he was twenty-seven years closer to the temple's fall than when Jesus gave the Olivet Discourse—the time had grown very short. The apostle is aware, it seems, of Jesus' promise that some who had heard him would "not taste of death, till they see the Son of man coming in his kingdom" (Matt 16:28). He tells the Corinthians that the risen Savior "was seen of above five hundred brethren at once; of whom *the greater part remain unto this present*, but some are fallen asleep" (1 Cor 15:6); Jesus was not yet a false prophet, as he would be if everyone had died. This eschatological perspective governs Paul's reasoning in 1 Corinthians 15.

Now, let me return to the point I was making: the gospel of the kingdom Paul preached, and the perspective from which he preached it, *required* the bodily resurrection. And that is how he addresses the resurrection problem at Corinth, by drawing a necessary conclusion from his gospel message. Some commentators have understood this point. W. Harold Mare, for example, says, "In the beginning of his masterly discussion of the resurrection, Paul reminds the Corinthian Christians that *it is an integral part of the gospel he had preached* and they had received and believed."[5] But the question arises: what, in the gospel of the kingdom, makes the physical resurrection *necessary*?

A Victory Verse. God's agenda for Christ's kingdom makes the bodily resurrection essential. To show that agenda, the New Testament writers turn to one Old Testament passage more than any other. In it, King David said, "The LORD said unto my Lord, Sit thou at my right hand, until I make thine enemies thy footstool" (Ps 110:1). Paul uses this truth about the messianic kingdom in his defense of a physical resurrection:

> Then cometh the end, when he shall have delivered
> up the kingdom to God, even the Father; *when he shall*

have put down all rule and all authority and power. For he must reign, *till he hath put all enemies under his feet.* The last enemy that shall be destroyed is death. (1 Cor 15:24–26)

Paul's gospel of the kingdom uses Psalm 110:1 to link Christ's resurrection to that of all Christians: the messianic (kingdom) age is the time during which Christ reigns as he defeats *all* his enemies, therefore there must be a resurrection during that reign. The following syllogism shows his reasoning:

> Major premise: Christ will defeat *all* his enemies in the messianic age.
> Minor premise: physical death is an enemy of Christ and his people.
> Conclusion: therefore, Christ will defeat physical death in the messianic age.

This conclusion is correct if the premises are true. I suppose few will argue against the minor premise: most humans have witnessed and felt the sting of death (cp. 1 Cor 15:55–56) as it claimed someone they loved.

The vital point is this: Psalm 110:1 guarantees that the major premise is true. This verse, then, is a vital element in the kingdom's gospel. As I mentioned, Jesus and his apostles quote or allude to it more than any other Old Testament passage. Christopher Beetham says,

> David Hay has compiled a list showing that Psalm 110:1 is quoted or alluded to twenty-three times in the NT. Hay writes that five of these are quotations, leaving eighteen allusions. *This frequency of citation crowns Psalm 110:1 as the most oft-referenced OT text in the NT.*[6]

In his book on the apostles' preaching (Gk. *kerygma*), C. H. Dodd mentions the central role Psalm 110:1 plays in the New Testament:

> Wherever we read of Christ being at the right hand of God, or of hostile powers being subjected to Him, the ultimate reference is to this passage. In view of the

place which [Ps 110:1] holds in the New Testament, we may safely put it down as *one of the fundamental texts* of the primitive *kerygma*.[7]

N. T. Wright believes "Psalm 110 ... might have a claim to be the best-known 'messianic' text among first-century readers."[8] No other passage captures the essence of the New Testament more clearly and succinctly than Psalm 110:1. This quintessential message of the gospel of the kingdom declares the victory of Christ over all his enemies during the messianic age, including physical death.

Paul uses this optimistic prophecy of the messianic age kingdom to refute the non-resurrection error in Corinth.

Kingdom Optimism

I have already shown how Paul's gospel of the kingdom fits within the inmillennial prophetic model we discovered in the Olivet Discourse. It describes the coming of the Lord, the end of the Mosaic age, the temple's replacement, and the "very short" time until "the end of the ages" the same way the Lord had. But I have not mentioned another matching element, and it distinguishes inmillennialism from other prophetic models—the *parousia* (presence) of Christ.

In the Olivet Discourse, Jesus and his disciples connected this word to the temple's fall and the end of the Mosaic age in their generation. According to our almost-complete prophetic model, they used it to describe Christ's presence with his churches during the messianic (kingdom) age. Now, Paul says, the physical resurrection will also occur "in his presence (Gk. *parousia*)" (1 Cor 15:23 YLT); it will bring a glorious culmination to Christ's kingdom-reign. Christ's *parousia* (presence) with his people began in the "last days" of the Mosaic age and will continue to the day of the resurrection. As I have stressed, *parousia* does not represent a point-in-time event in our future, as other prophetic models assume; it is a state of being, equivalent to the messianic (kingdom) age.

We could have inferred, perhaps, from the Olivet Discourse that the resurrection would occur in the *parousia* of Christ. We might have concluded that the final judgment at the end of the messianic age (cp. Matt 25:31–46) would require it. But we could not have discerned the new element Paul is adding—kingdom optimism based on Psalm 110:1, an optimism that *requires* the physical resurrection. Nor could we have discerned that, during his *parousia* (presence) with his churches, God had decreed that he defeat *all* his enemies, including physical death. For that, we needed to learn of the role Psalm 110:1 plays in the kingdom's history.

Kingdom Optimism in other Old Testament Passages. Paul's use of Psalm 110:1 in 1 Corinthians 15 is suggestive because even though it is the most-often quoted Old Testament passage, it is just one of many descriptions of the messianic (kingdom) age. I will use a few of them to show God's plan for the kingdom over which Christ now reigns. God means for Christ's reign, in which he is putting all enemies under his feet, to achieve the following results:

1. *To become a universal reign.*

> And the LORD shall be *king over all the earth*: in that day shall there be one LORD, and his name one. (Zech 14:9)

> And it shall come to pass in the last days, that the mountain of the LORD'S house shall be established in the top of the mountains, and shall be exalted above the hills; and *all nations shall flow unto it*. And many people shall go and say, Come ye, and let us go up to the mountain of the LORD, to the house of the God of Jacob; and he will teach us of his ways, and we will walk in his paths: for out of Zion shall go forth the law, and the word of the LORD from Jerusalem. (Isa 2:2–3)

2. *To defeat all other gods.*

> The LORD is the true God, he is the living God, and an everlasting king: at his wrath the earth shall tremble, and the nations shall not be able to abide his indignation. Thus shall ye say unto them, *The gods that have not*

made the heavens and the earth, even they shall perish from the earth, and from under these heavens. (Jer 10:10–11)

The LORD will be terrible unto them: for *he will famish all the gods of the earth*; and men shall worship him, every one from his place, even *all the isles of the heathen.* (Zeph 2:11)

3. *To gather all nations.*

And he will lift up an ensign to *the nations* from far, and will hiss unto them from the end of the earth: and, behold, they *shall come with speed swiftly.* (Isa 5:26)

Thus saith the Lord GOD, Behold, I will lift up mine hand to the Gentiles, and set up my standard to the people: and they shall bring thy sons in their arms, and thy daughters shall be carried upon their shoulders. And *kings shall be thy nursing fathers, and their queens thy nursing mothers: they shall bow down to thee with their face toward the earth, and lick up the dust of thy feet*; and thou shalt know that I am the LORD: for they shall not be ashamed that wait for me. (Isa 49:22–23)

O LORD, my strength, and my fortress, and my refuge in the day of affliction, *the Gentiles shall come unto thee from the ends of the earth*, and shall say, Surely our fathers have inherited lies, vanity, and things wherein there is no profit. (Jer 16:19)

See Hosea 1:7–11.

4. *To convert all nations so they serve and worship God.*

All the ends of the world shall remember and turn unto the LORD: and *all the kindreds of the nations shall worship before thee.* (Ps 22:27)

All the earth shall worship thee, and shall sing unto thee; they shall sing to thy name. (Ps 66:4)

In his days shall the righteous flourish; and abundance of peace so long as the moon endureth. He shall have dominion also from sea to sea, and from the river unto the ends of the earth. They that dwell in the wilderness shall bow before him; and his enemies shall lick the dust. The kings of Tarshish and of the isles shall bring presents: the kings of Sheba and Seba shall offer gifts. Yea, *all kings shall fall down before him: all nations shall serve him.... All nations shall call him blessed....* Let the whole earth be filled with his glory. (Ps 72:7–11, 17, 19)

Therefore thy gates shall be open continually; they shall not be shut day nor night; *that men may bring unto thee the forces of the Gentiles, and that their kings may be brought. For the nation and kingdom that will not serve thee shall perish; yea, those nations shall be utterly wasted.* (Isa 60:11–12)

See also Psalm 67:1–7; Psalm 86:8–9; Jeremiah 3:17; Zechariah 2:11; 8:22; 9:9–11; 14:16; Malachi 1:11.

5. *To create a prevailing peace.*

Many nations shall come, and say, Come, and let us go up to the mountain of the LORD, and to the house of the God of Jacob; and he will teach us of his ways, and we will walk in his paths: for the law shall go forth of Zion, and the word of the LORD from Jerusalem. And he shall judge among many people, and rebuke strong nations afar off; and *they shall beat their swords into plowshares, and their spears into pruninghooks: nation shall not lift up a sword against nation, neither shall they learn war any more.* (Mic 4:2–3)

6. *To produce a glory-filled earth.*

> The LORD said ... as truly as I live, *all the earth shall be filled with the glory of the LORD.* (Num 14:20–21)

> They shall not hurt nor destroy in all my holy mountain: for *the earth shall be full of the knowledge of the LORD, as the waters cover the sea.* (Isa 11:9)

See also Isaiah 27:6; 42:1–4; 54:1–5; Habakkuk 2:14.

I will close this section with a passage from Daniel that I used when discussing Jesus' sign of the Son of Man in heaven. It gives a succinct statement of Jesus' ascension, of the Father giving him the kingdom, of the saints' participation in it, and of the purpose of that kingdom:

> I saw in the night visions, and, behold, one like the Son of man came with the clouds of heaven, and came to the Ancient of days, and they brought him near before him. And there was given him dominion, and glory, and a kingdom, *that all people, nations, and languages, should serve him:* his dominion is an everlasting dominion, which shall not pass away, and his kingdom that which shall not be destroyed.... And the kingdom and dominion, and the greatness of the kingdom under the whole heaven, shall be given to the people of the saints of the most High, whose kingdom is an everlasting kingdom, and *all dominions shall serve and obey him.* (Dan 7:13–14, 27)

These passages show Israel's kingdom expectation as she waited for the Messiah. They corroborate Paul's use of Psalm 110:1 to argue for a physical resurrection—Christ must reign until he overcomes all his enemies, including death. As he overcomes more and more of his enemies, the world described in the above passages will appear.

Kingdom Optimism in the New Testament. When the apostles preached the gospel, they proclaimed that God, through Christ, was fulfilling the prophecies I listed in the previous section, and many more like them. Israel's kingdom expectations were coming true in Christ. Paul was preaching this gospel *of the kingdom* to the Corinthians, and it enabled him to do more than "get people saved." He could overcome a serious doctrinal error that robbed God's people of a comforting truth by drawing the logical conclusion to his optimistic message—Christ will reign until he has subdued all his enemies, including death.

This is the kingdom John the Baptist and Jesus preached at the start of their ministries (Matt 3:2; 4:17) and that Jesus promised to the poor in spirit (Matt 5:3). Jesus taught us to pray for this kingdom vision to come true:

> After this manner therefore pray ye: Our Father which art in heaven, Hallowed be thy name. *Thy kingdom come. Thy will be done in earth, as it is in heaven.* Give us this day our daily bread. And forgive us our debts, as we forgive our debtors. And lead us not into temptation, but deliver us from evil: for thine is the kingdom, and the power, and the glory, for ever. Amen. (Matt 6:9–13)

The Lord expects his followers to pray in faith, believing God will fulfill his kingdom promises to Christ during his present reign. The kingdom of God will produce glorious results during Christ's *parousia* (presence) with his churches in the messianic age. Christians should seek this kingdom above all else (Matt 6:33).

Jesus concealed his miracles from some people for a specific purpose:

> He warned them not to make Him known, so that what was spoken through the prophet Isaiah might be fulfilled: Here is My Servant whom I have chosen, My beloved in whom My soul delights; I will put My Spirit on Him, and He will *proclaim justice to the nations*. He will not argue or shout, and no one will hear His voice in the streets. He will not break a bruised reed, and He will not put out a smoldering wick, until He has led justice

to victory. *The nations will put their hope in His name.* (Matt 12:16–21 HCSB)

This is just what the prophets said would happen in the messianic age. To others, Jesus explained his miracles as evidence that he would rob Satan of his goods during the kingdom age:

> But if I cast out devils by the Spirit of God, then *the kingdom of God is come unto you.* Or else how can one enter into a strong man's house, *and spoil his goods*, except he first bind the strong man? and then he will spoil his house. (Matt 12:28–29)

In the Old Testament, God often delivered his people from human captors. Now that the kingdom of God has come, Jesus promises a greater deliverance. The "goods" held by the mighty man (Satan) are the children of God scattered among the nations; Jesus will now liberate them. In the kingdom of God, even the leaders of the nations—their kings and queens—who, in the Mosaic age, served Satan, will come to worship the Lord.

Jesus used another metaphor for the same purpose. He compared his kingdom's warfare to the attack of an army against a city:

> And I say also unto thee, That thou art Peter, and upon this rock I will build my church; and *the gates of hell shall not prevail against it.* And I will give unto thee the keys of the kingdom of heaven: and whatsoever thou shalt bind on earth shall be bound in heaven: and whatsoever thou shalt loose on earth shall be loosed in heaven. (Matt 16:18–19)

The "gates of hell" protect Satan's possessions within his city. These protective barriers cannot secure his "goods" against the onslaught of Christ's kingdom-church. The prophet Hosea helps us understand this imagery. Through him, God foretold that Ephraim could not withstand the Assyrian army: "The sword shall rage against their cities, *consume the bars of their gates*, and devour them" (Hos 11:6 ESV). Jesus says this is true of his church in the messianic (kingdom) age: the gates of hell's city cannot withstand the battering rams of God's attacking army.

Paul adopted this orientation; he wanted the churches to understand God's plan for the kingdom. I mentioned earlier that Paul preached the kingdom of God to the Ephesians on his first and last visits to their city. In his letter to them, he reinforces this message:

> On account of this … I constantly make mention of you in my prayers, that the God of our Lord Jesus Christ, the Father of the glory, might give to you a spirit of wisdom and revelation in the sphere of a full knowledge of Him, the eyes of your heart being in an enlightened state with a view to your knowing what is the hope of His calling, what is the wealth of the glory of His inheritance in the saints, and what is the superabounding greatness of His inherent power to us who are believing ones as measured by the operative energy of the manifested strength of His might, which might was operative in the Christ when He raised Him from among the dead and seated Him at His right hand in the heavenly places, over and above every government and authority and power and lordship and every name that is constantly being named, *not only in this age, but also in the one about to come (Gk. mellō). And all things He put in subjection under His feet, and Him He gave as Head over all things to the Church,* which is of such a nature as to be His body, the fulness of the One who constantly is filling all things with all things. (Eph 1:15–23 Wuest)[9]

The subjugation of "all things"—including gods, kings, and nations—in the age "about to come" (for Paul and his contemporaries) was an essential part of his message. He prayed that the churches would recognize their role in fulfilling God's Old Testament promises for the kingdom age.

Such is the kingdom-vision that the Lord and his apostles bequeathed to his churches. It is an *optimistic* vision: in our age, "The earth shall be full of the knowledge of the LORD, as the waters cover the sea" (Isa 11:9). Like Whitney's young guitarist that I mentioned in Chapter 2, this vision gives meaning to the present: we obey our King to turn the vision into reality, to his glory and praise.

This kingdom-optimism, and our part in it, must be part of our prophetic model. I know this will be difficult for many readers to accept. We have heard negative preaching about God's supposed plan for *this* age for so long that an optimistic message is strange to our ears. And to hear that God's churches have a role to play in achieving this vision is almost unheard of. Perhaps some readers may join Nicodemus in asking, "How can these things be?" (John 3:9). My answer, as to the vision, is: God has raised Christ to sit on his throne and promised that he would make all his enemies his footstool (Acts 2:30–36; cp. 1 Cor 15:24–26; Heb 1:3). The Messiah reigns in *this* age. We have seen that the Lord associated his coming in his kingdom, his *parousia*, and the start of the messianic age with the temple's fall in AD 70. If so, the glorious messianic-age prophecies for his reign *must* occur in this age.

I will show *how* this vision will come to pass in the next section.

Kingdom Gradualism

Besides kingdom optimism, Paul's citation of Psalm 110:1 also introduces the concept of *kingdom gradualism*. As we saw above, the complete subjugation of "all things" to Christ will occur in the resurrection at the end of the kingdom age. In the interim, between Christ's enthronement and his ultimate victory, he is making all his enemies his footstool. The writer of Hebrews describes this scenario: "Thou hast put all things in subjection under his feet. For in that he put all in subjection under him, he left nothing that is not put under him. *But now we see not yet all things put under him*" (Heb 2:8). The writer claims the promise of Psalm 110:1— Christ (the man who represents redeemed man) will reign until he defeats all his enemies—but a lot must happen before he defeats death, the last enemy. I will refer to the process of kingdom advance as *gradualism*. As Kenneth Gentry says, "This principle expects the developmental expansion of the kingdom over time"; it opposes the *catastrophism* required in some prophetic models to achieve God's purposes for the kingdom.[10]

In this section, I want to show that both the Old and New Testaments teach kingdom gradualism, and I want us to think through the role God means for us to play in it.

Gradualism in the Old Testament. As we have seen, the Old Testament contains many prophecies of the glory of the messianic age. They also show that the kingdom will begin small but grow throughout the messianic (kingdom) age until it reaches that glorious state.

A Growing Government. Isaiah prophesied that a miracle would one day come to pass: "The Lord himself shall give you a sign; Behold, a virgin shall conceive, and bear a son, and shall call his name Immanuel" (Isa 7:14). Later, Isaiah again spoke of this child:

> For unto us a child is born, unto us a son is given: and the government shall be upon his shoulder: and his name shall be called Wonderful, Counsellor, The mighty God, The everlasting Father, The Prince of Peace. *Of the increase* of his government and peace there shall be no end, upon the throne of David, and upon his kingdom, to order it, and to establish it with judgment and with justice from henceforth even for ever. The zeal of the LORD of hosts will perform this. (Isa 9:6–7)

This child is the Lord Jesus Christ (Matt 1:22–23), and this prophecy gives a key insight into the kingdom over which he reigns. It does not say the Messiah's government will never end—it says the *increase* of his government will never end. Christ's kingdom-victory will come through a gradual increase throughout the messianic age, not through a catastrophic intervention in history.

A Growing Mountain. In the book of Daniel, God gave Nebuchadnezzar, king of Babylon, a dream that revealed the timing for the kingdom's coming. This dream concerned "the latter days" (Dan 2:28), which, according to inmillennialism, means the "last days" of the Mosaic age. Daniel confirms this timing, for the king's dream was of a grand image, made of four kinds of metals that represented four successive empires: the Babylonian, the Medo-Persian, the Greek, and the Roman. Speaking of the Roman emperors, Daniel says, "*In the days of these kings* shall the God of heaven set up a kingdom, which shall never be destroyed: and the kingdom shall not be left to other people" (Dan 2:44a). The virgin birth occurred in the time of the second Roman emperor, Caesar Augustus (Luke 2:1), and the temple fell in the reign of Vespasian, the tenth emperor. The kingdom arrived during the days of the Roman kings as Daniel prophesied.

In agreement with Psalm 110:1, Daniel says this kingdom "shall break in pieces and consume all these kingdoms, and it shall stand for ever" (Dan 2:44b). But the thing of interest here is *how* this victory would occur. The kingdom would be like a stone that destroys all the other kingdoms:

> Then was the iron, the clay, the brass, the silver, and the gold, broken to pieces together, and became like the chaff of the summer threshingfloors; and the wind carried them away, that no place was found for them: and *the stone* [i.e., the kingdom of God] *that smote the image became a great mountain, and filled the whole earth.* (Dan 2:35)

Consistent with other kingdom prophecies, the Messianic kingdom here increases over time—a stone becomes a mountain—until it defeats all other kingdoms.

Daniel is describing kingdom gradualism.

A Ruler's Rod. In Psalm 2, God the Father speaks to God the Son concerning his future kingdom:

> I will declare the decree: the LORD hath said unto me, Thou art my Son; this day have I begotten thee. Ask of me, and I shall give thee the heathen for thine inheritance, and the uttermost parts of the earth for thy pos-

> session. *Thou shalt break them with a rod of iron; thou shalt dash them in pieces like a potter's vessel.* Be wise now therefore, O ye kings: be instructed, ye judges of the earth. Serve the LORD with fear, and rejoice with trembling. Kiss the Son, lest he be angry, and ye perish from the way, when his wrath is kindled but a little. Blessed are all they that put their trust in him. (Ps 2:7–12)

This is a picture of the Messiah subduing the nations and making them his footstool, to use the language of Psalm 110:1. It is a progressive conquest, for the kings of the nations can observe it and learn from God's judgments that they should submit joyfully to the Son, or perish for their refusal.

I will discuss typology in Chapter 14, but I want to make a brief comment about it here. Old Testament Scriptures like this one use military conquest to describe the Messiah's future reign, but, as Paul will say, "*The weapons of our warfare are not carnal* but mighty in God for pulling down strongholds, casting down arguments and every high thing that exalts itself against the knowledge of God, bringing every thought into captivity to the obedience of Christ" (2 Cor 10:4–5 NKJV). David is not saying the Son would bash the heathen with a literal rod of iron; the Spirit is using physical warfare to typologically represent spiritual conquest.

My principal point here is that this messianic conquest will be gradual: kings can learn from it and repent.

A Vision Verse. I will list the passage Paul uses in 1 Corinthians 15 to show kingdom gradualism and to reinforce the point I just made about typology. David says,

> The LORD said unto my Lord, Sit thou at my right hand, until I make thine enemies thy footstool. The LORD shall send the rod of thy strength out of Zion: rule thou in the midst of thine enemies. Thy people shall be willing in the day of thy power, in the beauties of holiness from the womb of the morning: thou hast

> the dew of thy youth. The LORD hath sworn, and will not repent, Thou art a priest for ever after the order of Melchizedek. The Lord at thy right hand shall strike through kings in the day of his wrath. He shall judge among the heathen, he shall fill the places with the dead bodies; he shall wound the heads over many countries. He shall drink of the brook in the way: therefore shall he lift up the head. (Ps 110:1–7)

The New Testament uses Psalm 110:1 many times to describe the messianic age, but the conquest it envisions is always through the gospel, as Paul shows in his defense of a physical resurrection. The typology here—"The Lord ... strike[ing] through kings in the day of his wrath"—symbolizes him using "the sword of the Spirit, which is the word of God" (Eph 6:17), to divide asunder soul and spirit (Heb 4:12). The ultimate physical punishment for those who reject this word will occur at the last judgment, after the resurrection (Matt 25:31–46).

The Path to Peace. Isaiah provides a glimpse of the messianic kingdom's progress in the world:

> And it shall come to pass in the last days, that the mountain of the LORD'S house shall be established in the top of the mountains, and shall be exalted above the hills; and *all nations shall flow unto it.* And many people shall go and say, Come ye, and let us go up to the mountain of the LORD, to the house of the God of Jacob; and he will teach us of his ways, and we will walk in his paths: for out of Zion shall go forth the law, and the word of the LORD from Jerusalem. And he shall judge among the nations, and shall rebuke many people: and they shall beat their swords into plowshares, and their spears into pruninghooks: nation shall not lift up sword against nation, neither shall they learn war any more. (Isa 2:2–4)

The prophet says God will establish the kingdom in "the last days" of the Mosaic age. It will increase as many people flow into it, inviting others to join them as they do so. They learn the Messiah's ways and how to walk in his paths, because the law—Paul will call it "the law of the Spirit of life in Christ Jesus (Rom 8:2)—will go forth from Jerusalem. The Lord will rebuke people, and they will go about converting their weapons into instruments of production; they will "learn" about physical warfare in reverse—how *not* to wage it. This describes a gradual process.

Gradualism in the New Testament. We have seen how the kingdom optimism of the Old Testament also characterizes the New; the same is true regarding kingdom gradualism. The kingdom is small, Jesus says, at its inception, but his comforting words are, "Fear not, little flock; for it is your Father's good pleasure to give you the kingdom" (Luke 12:31–32). The writer of Hebrews says, this little flock was "receiving a kingdom which cannot be moved" (Heb 12:28); it would grow until "the earth shall be full of the knowledge of the LORD, as the waters cover the sea" (Isa 11:9). Jesus and the apostles make several other statements regarding kingdom growth.

Mustard Seed. Jesus teaches gradualism in his kingdom parables. Consider his parable of the mustard seed:

> Another parable put he forth unto them, saying, The kingdom of heaven is like to a grain of mustard seed, which a man took, and sowed in his field: which indeed is the least of all seeds: but *when it is grown*, it is the greatest among herbs, and *becometh a tree*, so that the birds of the air come and lodge in the branches thereof.
> (Matt 13:31–32)

Modern commentators sometimes pervert the Lord's teaching here, as William MacDonald does when he says,

> The seed represents the humble beginning of the kingdom. At first the kingdom was kept relatively small and

pure as a result of persecution. But with the patronage and protection of the state, it suffered abnormal growth. Then the birds came and roosted in it.... The kingdom became a nesting place for Satan and his agents.[11]

Why would Jesus tell us to make seeking such a kingdom our top priority (cp. Matt 6:33)?

But Jesus is not teaching about a kingdom suffering abnormal growth; he is speaking of the growth of the kingdom foretold by the Old Testament prophets. A kingdom passage in Ezekiel may have been in his mind when he gave this parable:

> Thus saith the Lord GOD; I will also take of the highest branch of the high cedar, and will set it; I will crop off from the top of his young twigs a tender one, and will plant it upon an high mountain and eminent: in the mountain of the height of Israel will I plant it: and it shall bring forth boughs, and bear fruit, and be a goodly cedar: and *under it shall dwell all fowl of every wing; in the shadow of the branches thereof shall they dwell.* And all the trees of the field shall know that I the LORD have brought down the high tree, have exalted the low tree, have dried up the green tree, and have made the dry tree to flourish: I the LORD have spoken and have done it. (Ezek 17:22–24)

Kenneth L. Gentry sees the following relationships between this passage and Jesus' parable:

> The portrayal here is of a universal magnificence and exaltation of the kingdom of heaven, which will graciously provide shelter for all when it comes to full fruition. This seems to provide the specific backdrop of Christ's parable, which he adapted to mustard seed imagery. Both point to the dominance of Christ's kingdom: the twig is planted on a high mountain above all

the trees; the mustard seed becomes the largest plant in the garden. The Mustard Seed Parable speaks of the extension of the kingdom in the world.[12]

The parable shows that the kingdom of heaven begins small but grows to become great through a gradual process.

The Leaven. Jesus taught this lesson using another gradual process, the leavening of a lump of dough:

> Another parable spake he unto them; The kingdom of heaven is like unto leaven, which a woman took, and hid in three measures of meal, till the whole was leavened. (Matt 13:33)

The mustard seed *grows*, but the leaven *permeates*. What was once small becomes large; what was once insignificant comes to dominate its environment by penetrating its every part. This is Jesus' view of the kingdom.

I have a vivid memory associated with this parable. While working as an engineer with a power company, a large bakery we served lost power during the night. In the early morning hours, I was observing our linemen work to restore power when the manager of the bakery walked up. He asked me to step inside the building to see something. The sight was shocking; the bakers had just put yeast in their large vats of dough when the power went off. Over the next few hours, they had watched helplessly as the dough expanded, grew over the sides of the vats, and covered the floor. The manager was not happy about the interruption to his electrical service because it robbed him of his ability to control the yeast. But this episode showed the yeast's power to leaven and control the whole lump!

As with the mustard seed parable, some commentators make Jesus mean that an *evil* kingdom will leaven the world. This saddens me, and I doubt anyone would reach this conclusion if their prophetic model could accommodate the scriptural growth of God's kingdom in this messianic age. We should heed the prophet's warning: "Woe unto them that call evil good, and good evil; that put darkness for light, and light for darkness; that put bitter for sweet, and sweet for bitter!" (Isa 5:20). The kingdom of which Jesus is speaking in these parables is the kingdom *of God*. It will spread to fill (and transform) the whole earth (cp. Dan 2:35).

The Great Commission. How will this kingdom-growth happen? How will the nations come to the Messiah? The risen Christ—"the firstfruits of them that slept" (1 Cor 15:20)—commissioned his churches:

> Jesus came and spoke to them, saying, "All authority has been given to Me in heaven and on earth. Go therefore and *make disciples of all the nations*, baptizing them in the name of the Father and of the Son and of the Holy Spirit, teaching them to observe all things that I have commanded you; and lo, I am with you always, even to the end of the age." Amen. (Matt 28:18–20 NKJV)

Have the prophets declared that "all the kindreds of the nations shall worship before thee" (Ps 22:27)? Yes! And the resurrected Christ commands his disciples to "make disciples of all the nations" so they will do so.

This evangelization of the nations is more than the disciples' preaching to the nations as a witness before the temple fell (Matt 24:14); it is the *discipling* of the nations so "that all people, nations, and languages, should serve him … and all dominions shall serve and obey him" (Dan 7:14, 27).

By definition, this is kingdom gradualism. It is not the sudden imposition of Christ's rule by a dramatic intervention in history found in other prophetic models. Jesus taught his followers to preach and pray in faith, believing the kingdom of God will defeat all its enemies in the messianic age. This is how the nations will come to serve the Messiah.

Defeat of All Enemies. According to Beethan and Hay, Psalm 110:1 "is quoted or alluded to twenty-three times in the NT."[13] Each occurrence is a witness to the gradual increase in the kingdom's positive benefits for mankind. Peter, for example, referred to it immediately after the Father empowered his church by pouring out the Holy Spirit on the day of Pentecost:

> For David is not ascended into the heavens: but he saith himself, The LORD said unto my Lord, Sit thou on my right hand, until I make thy foes thy footstool. Therefore let all the house of Israel know assuredly, that God hath made that same Jesus, whom ye have crucified, both Lord and Christ. (Acts 2:34–36)

The messianic promise of victory is an integral part of the preaching that says, "The promise is unto you [i.e., Israel], and to your children, and to all that are afar off, even as many as the Lord our God shall call" (Acts 2:39). Through this message, the Lord adds "to the church daily such as should be saved" (Acts 2:47).

To preach the gospel of the kingdom of heaven as the apostles preached it requires that we include this element of optimistic kingdom gradualism.

Kingdom Warfare. I earlier mentioned that the Old Testament Scriptures sometimes used military conquest imagery to describe the Messiah's reign and that it was typological language. I now want to show that the Scripture I cited implies kingdom gradualism. The apostle Paul used a warfare metaphor to describe how the church carries out its mission:

> For though we walk in the flesh, we do not war after the flesh: (for the weapons of our warfare are not carnal, but mighty through God to the pulling down of strong holds;) *casting down imaginations, and every high thing that exalteth itself against the knowledge of God, and bringing into captivity every thought to the obedience of Christ.*
> (2 Cor 10:3–5)

The objectives here—pulling down strong holds, etc.—are the same as those in Psalm 110:1. This is the same conquest Paul mentioned in his response to the resurrection error in Corinth: Christ "must reign, till he hath put all enemies under his feet" (1 Cor 15:25). Christ empowers his people to subdue his enemies with the mighty spiritual weapons he provides. These weapons are not carnal, but they are mighty.

As we have seen, this warfare will continue until Christ defeats his last enemy; this is kingdom gradualism.

Conclusion

Paul's reasoning in 1 Corinthians 15 conforms to the inmillennial model we discovered in the Olivet Discourse and provides two important additions: kingdom optimism and kingdom gradualism. The following diagram shows the framework Paul uses in 1 Corinthians 15:

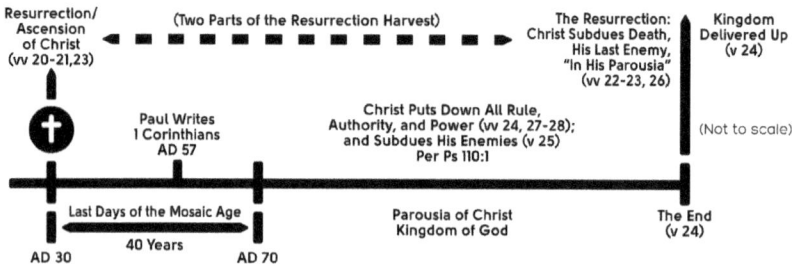

Figure 13-1. Paul's Reasoning in 1 Corinthians 15

Here, our prophetic model affects our daily lives. We see the vision God has given us for the kingdom to which we belong, and we must respond. This is equivalent to the young Kevin's view of his future virtuoso self in the illustration Whitney gave us in Chapter 2. We "practice" today so the kingdom will become what we know God means it to be.

This vision affects how we *understand* the gospel. Douglas Wilson makes an important point about the gospel vision built into Paul's message: "The gospel, as it was declared to Abraham, was that the heathen would all be converted. *That* is the gospel. *That* is what Abraham believed. *That* is what Abraham saw."[14] This understanding affects how we *preach* the gospel of the kingdom in obedience to Christ's

TWO DETAILS FROM 1 CORINTHIANS 15

Great Commission; for, as Köstenberger and O'Brien say, "Mission must be understood from an eschatological perspective."[15] Either inmillennialism or some other (perhaps less optimistic) view of the kingdom will dictate our understanding of what Jesus means for us (i.e., his churches) to accomplish.

I will now update the diagram of our now-complete prophetic model to show the kingdom optimism Paul assumes for the messianic age:

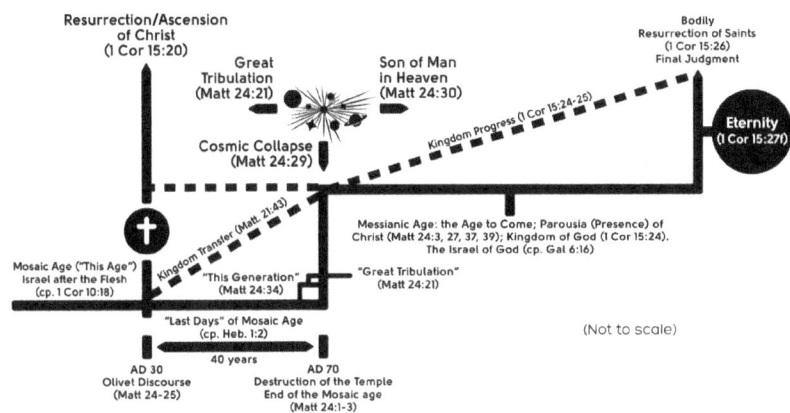

Figure 13-2. Inmillennialism through 1 Corinthians 15

KEY POINT #12

In 1 Corinthians 15, Paul links Christ's resurrection to the bodily resurrection of believers at the end of the messianic age. He uses Psalm 110:1 to do so, showing the importance of kingdom optimism and kingdom gradualism for our prophetic model.

Notes

1 Robert B. Strimple, "Hyper-Preterism on the Resurrection of the Body," in *When Shall These Things be?: A Reformed Response to Hyper-Preterism*, ed. Keith A. Mathison (Phillipsburg, NJ: P&R, 2004), 334.

2 N. T. Wright, *The Resurrection of the Son of GOD*, vol. 3 of *Christian Origins and the Question of GOD* (Minneapolis: Fortress Press, 2003), 314.

3 N. T. Wright, *The Day the Revolution Began: Reconsidering the Meaning of Jesus's Crucifixion* (San Francisco: HarperOne, 2016), 248.

4 I am using dates assigned by Frank J. Goodwin, *A Harmony of the Life of St. Paul* (Grand Rapids: Baker, 1977), 7–8.

5 W. Harold Mare, "1 Corinthians," in *Romans–Galatians*, vol. 10 of *The Expositor's Bible Commentary*, ed. Frank E. Gaebelein (Grand Rapids: Zondervan, 1976), 282 (emphasis added).

6 Christopher A. Beetham, *Echoes of Scripture in the Letter of Paul to the Colossians* (Leiden: Brill, 1980), 228 (emphasis added).

7 Dodd, *The Apostolic Preaching*, 15 (emphasis added).

8 Wright, *Paul*, 820.

9 Wuest, *Expanded Translation*, 449–50.

10 Gentry, *He Shall Have Dominion*, 257.

11 MacDonald, *Believer's Bible Commentary*, 1257.

12 Gentry, *He Shall Have Dominion*, 247.

13 Beetham, *Echoes*, 228 (emphasis added).

14 Douglas Wilson, *Heaven Misplaced: Christ's Kingdom on Earth* (Moscow, ID: Canon Press, 2008), 32.

15 Andreas J. Köstenberger and Peter Thomas O'Brien, *Salvation to the Ends of the Earth: A Biblical Theology of Mission* (Downers Grove, IL: InterVarsity, 2001), 250.

CHAPTER FOURTEEN

Confirmation through Typology

PAUL'S REASONING in 1 Corinthians 15 confirms our inmillennial model in another way: he introduces a typological truth. At the close of his argument for a physical resurrection, he reveals how certain type-antitype relationships connect the New Testament to the Old:

> It is written, "The first man Adam became a living being." The last Adam became a life-giving spirit. However, *the spiritual is not first, but the natural, and afterward the spiritual.* The first man was of the earth, made of dust; the second Man is the Lord from heaven. As was the man of dust, so also are those who are made of dust; and as is the heavenly Man, so also are those who are heavenly. And as we have borne the image of the man of dust, we shall also bear the image of the heavenly Man. (1 Cor 15:45–49 NKJV)

In Romans, Paul explicitly refers to Adam as a *type* of Christ: "Nevertheless death reigned from Adam to Moses, even over them that had not sinned after the similitude of Adam's transgression, who is the figure (Gk. *tupos*) of him that was to come" (Rom 5:14). And, in Galatians 4:21–31, he further emphasizes the "natural first, spiritual second" order in biblical typology. He says Abraham's two sons represented the old and new covenants. Ishmael, the son of Hagar, a bondwoman, represented the Mosaic-age covenant. His mother represented the Jerusalem on earth that, Paul says, is in bondage. Isaac, the son of Sarah, the free woman, represented the messianic-age covenant. His mother represented the free Jerusalem above. Paul says, "But as then he that was born after the flesh persecuted him that was born after the Spirit, even so it is now." Ishmael had persecuted Isaac like the apostate Jews were persecuting the Christians, but as Abraham had cast him out of his home, so God would soon cast the Jews out of their covenant relationship with him. The natural was about to end, but the spiritual, which had come second, would continue.

Before I show how Paul's typology confirms inmillennialism, I want to mention some points Wick Broomall makes about typology. He says, "A type is a shadow cast on the pages of OT history by a truth whose full embodiment or antitype is found in the NT revelation." He gives five characteristics of types: "(1) They are thoroughly rooted in history.... (2) They are prophetic in nature.... (3) They are definitely designed as an integral part of redemptive history.... (4) They are Christocentric.... (5) They are edificatory—having spiritual meaning for God's people in both dispensations." And he provides four safeguards for using them: "(1) One must distinguish between the type backed by NT authority and the type based on the speculation of the modern interpreter.... (2) One must distinguish between the type that definitely corroborates a doctrine and the type that has no relevance to a supposed doctrine.... (3) One must distinguish between what is essential in a type and what is peripheral in the same type.... (4) One must distinguish between the type that is completely fulfilled in the antitype and the type, though partly fulfilled, that still retains its typical significance for the future world."[1]

Typology can have another characteristic Broomall does not mention: the type and the antitype can relate inversely to one another. Paul uses this typological inversion to relate Adam and Christ as type and antitype. He says, "Therefore as by the offence of one [Adam] judgment came upon all men to *condemnation*; even so by the righteousness of one

[Christ] the free gift came upon all men unto *justification* of life" (Rom 5:18). Christ's typological fulfillment brought the *inverse* of what Adam had done. Typological inversion will play an important role in verifying our inmillennial prophetic model.

Paul's Exodus Typology

Earlier in his letter to the Corinthians, Paul introduced an important type—Israel's Exodus from Egypt under Moses. I will show how it validates the inmillennial model we have discovered in the Olivet Discourse and 1 Corinthians 15. He said:

> And I do not wish you to be ignorant, brethren, that all our fathers were under the cloud, and all passed through the sea, and all to Moses were baptized in the cloud, and in the sea; and all the same spiritual food did eat, and all the same spiritual drink did drink, for they were drinking of a spiritual rock following them, and the rock was the Christ; but in the most of them God was not well pleased, for they were strewn in the wilderness. And *those things became types (Gk.* tupos*) of us*, for our not passionately desiring evil things, as also these did desire. Neither become ye idolaters, as certain of them, as it hath been written, 'The people sat down to eat and to drink, and stood up to play;' neither may we commit whoredom, as certain of them did commit whoredom, and there fell in one day twenty-three thousand; neither may we tempt the Christ, as also certain of them did tempt, and by the serpents did perish; neither murmur ye, as also some of them did murmur, and did perish by the destroyer. And *all these things as types (Gk.* tupos*) did happen* to those persons, and they were written for our admonition, to whom the end of the ages did come, so that he who is thinking to stand—let him observe, lest he fall. (1 Cor 10:1–12 YLT)

As I mentioned earlier, this passage shows that Paul wrote from the time perspective built into inmillennialism: "the ends of the ages have come" (1 Cor 10:11 NKJV), he says, for him and the Corinthians. The Song of Moses[2] had prophesied that "the LORD shall judge his people" during their "latter days" (Deut 31:29; 32:36); now, Paul, like Jesus before him, is teaching that those days have arrived in his generation—God is about to judge his natural-born covenant people.

This passage satisfies all of Broomall's requirements for a type. More importantly, the apostle Paul explicitly affirms (twice) that Israel's Exodus was a type of what was happening in his generation. He mentions several specific elements of the Exodus that served as types: Israel passing through the Red Sea under the cloud; the people eating and drinking supernatural manna and water; their lusting, idolatry, and fornication in ungodly revelry; and God overthrowing the guilty in the wilderness. Paul says the water Israel drank represented "spiritual drink" and the rock from which it came represented Christ (1 Cor 10:4). Several of these examples use typological inversion—the Corinthians (and we) should do the *reverse* of what Israel did.

Expanding Paul's List

Broomall makes another important point: "It is not to be inferred, however, that no type is valid unless supported by specific NT authority."[3] For example, we could have inferred that the manna in the wilderness was a type of Christ, even if Paul had not listed it here, based on Jesus' words in John 6:22–40. Because of this, we can use other Scriptures to expand Paul's list of Exodus types. The types become a rich treasure house of images: the Passover, instituted the night before the Exodus, serves as a type of Christ's sacrifice. So Paul can teach the Corinthians that "Christ *our passover* is sacrificed for us" (1 Cor 5:7). Moses constructed the tabernacle during the Exodus; it was a type of "the true tabernacle, which the Lord pitched, and not man" and served as "the example and shadow of heavenly things" (Heb 8:2, 5). Moses himself was a type of Christ (Heb 3:5–6).

The Scriptures suggest that other Exodus events also serve as types by associating them with events that occurred in the "last days" of the Mosaic age. Israel's physical enslavement in Egypt was a picture of the spiritual slavery that bound God's covenant people (Acts 7:6–7; Rom 8:14–15). Therefore, Israel's redemption from Egypt through Moses prefigured the elect's redemption from sin through Christ (cp. Rom 6:17–18). Jesus paid a ransom—the "price for redeeming or liberating slaves"[4]—to rescue them from sin (e.g., Matt 20:28) like God had redeemed Israel from Egypt (e.g., Deut 7:8; Isa 43:3; 51:10). Jesus established the new covenant in his blood (e.g., Heb 13:20), the antitype of God establishing the Mosaic covenant (Heb 8:6–13). The "law of the Spirit of life" (Rom 8:2), the antitype, replaced the typical Mosaic law. In all these examples, the type-antitype relationship is clear, even though there is no "specific NT authority" that refers to them as types (Gk. *tupos*). The New Testament writers often avail themselves of this large reserve of Exodus types without explicitly saying they are doing so.

Key Exodus Types

I remember the theological thrill I had twenty years ago while reading Todd Dennis' article on typology.[5] As I mentioned earlier, I was struggling with some matters of eternal consequence, but Todd's insights taught me that God has gone to impressive lengths to show his prophetic plan through Exodus typology. He helped me believe that I could eventually gain a clearer understanding of hard passages like those Bertrand Russell used to justify his atheism. I hope that my presentation of this material here will be meaningful to others in the same way.

In my discussion of typology, I have sought to establish two facts: (1) Paul taught that the Exodus was a type of what God was doing in his generation, and (2) we can, with due caution, recognize other types for which we do not have specific New Testament authority. Now, I will select a subset of Exodus events and posit that they are types. I have already mentioned some of them but will list them again, with supporting Scriptures, for the sake of completeness. I will show the types in which I am most interested in *italics*.

Before the Exodus, Israel was in *physical bondage* from which they could not escape:

> The Egyptians made the children of Israel to serve with rigour: and they made their lives bitter with hard bondage, in morter, and in brick, and in all manner of service in the field: all their service, wherein they made them serve, was with rigour. (Exod 1:13–14)

God sent *Moses* to Egypt from a distant country to deliver his people from bondage: "Come now therefore, and I will send thee unto Pharaoh, that thou mayest bring forth my people the children of Israel out of Egypt (Exod 3:10)." Moses returned to Egypt, and performed *miracles* to show God had sent him. At God's appointed time, Moses instituted the *Passover* as the people prepared to leave their captivity. He said, "Thus shall ye eat it; with your loins girded, your shoes on your feet, and your staff in your hand; and ye shall eat it in haste: it is the LORD'S passover" (Exod 12:11). God told Moses how Israel would *cross the Red Sea* to freedom: "Lift thou up thy rod, and stretch out thine hand over the sea, and divide it: and the children of Israel shall go on dry ground through the midst of the sea" (Exod 14:16).

John Gill makes an interesting observation regarding *God giving the law*, the next major event after Israel crossed the Red Sea: "It [is] a generally received notion that the law was given 50 days after the passover."[6] The Scriptures allow this Jewish tradition of *fifty days* to be possible: Moses said the law was given "in the third month" after Israel left Egypt (Exod 19:1).

While Moses was on Mt. Sinai receiving the law, Israel committed several wicked acts, including idolatry and fornication. God punished them, "And there fell of the people that day about *three thousand men*" (Exod 32:28). Moses then led Israel to the border of the promised land, but Israel's unbelief kept them from entering. God announced his punishment: "But as for you, your carcases, they shall fall in this wilderness. And your children shall *wander in the wilderness forty years*, and bear your whoredoms, until your carcases be wasted in the wilderness" (Num 14:32–33).

God remained faithful to his people, sustaining them through a continuous display of *miracles* as he provided food, water, clothing, health, shelter, warmth, and protection. After forty years, Joshua, Moses' successor, led the people into Canaan. The ongoing *miracles stopped* when they crossed the Jordan River: "The manna ceased on the morrow after they had eaten of the old corn of the land; neither had the children of Israel manna any more; but they did eat of the fruit of the land of Canaan that year" (Josh 5:12). This does not mean God ceased to perform miracles, or that he stopped providing for his people; clearly, that was not the case. My point here is that the wilderness miracles—manna from heaven, for example—did not occur daily as they had done in the wilderness.

Israel's entrance into the promised land *completed their redemption* from Egyptian bondage: "And the LORD said unto Joshua, This day have I rolled away the reproach of Egypt from off you. Wherefore the name of the place is called Gilgal unto this day" (Josh 5:9). Had God failed to bring them into the land, their deliverance would have been incomplete; the surrounding nations would have judged God a failure (cp. Num 14:15–16).

I have one other important type from the Exodus, but will not mention it here for strategic reasons. The following chart shows the above selection of Exodus types:

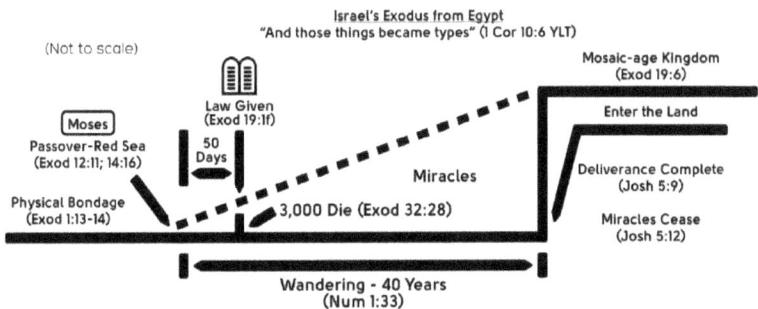

Figure 14-1. Exodus Types

As in previous diagrams, the elevated line represents Israel's new situation, that it was a remarkable improvement over their previous Egyptian bondage. Israel was now free to live as "a kingdom of priests, and an holy nation" in God's presence (Exod 19:6).

Exodus Antitypes

On the mount of transfiguration, Peter, James, and John watched as Jesus' appearance changed and his clothes became a dazzling white: "And behold, men, two of them, were talking with Him, who were of such a character as to be Moses and Elijah, who, having been caused to appear, surrounded with a heavenly brightness, were speaking of *His exodus* (Gk. *exodus*) which He was about to be (Gk. *mellō*) carrying into effect in Jerusalem" (Luke 9:30–31 Wuest).[7] The Exodus Jesus was about to accomplish would be infinitely more glorious than the one Moses had led. Let us meditate on this as we consider the New Testament' antitypes (or fulfillments) of the things I listed in the previous section. Many of these will use the typological inversion I mentioned earlier.

The people Jesus represented—the Israel of God (Gal 6:16)—were in *spiritual bondage*. Paul says Jesus "gave himself for us, that he might redeem us from all iniquity, and purify unto himself a peculiar people, zealous of good works" (Titus 2:14). He exhorted those whom Christ had freed to "stand fast therefore in the liberty wherewith Christ hath made us free, and be not entangled again with the yoke of bondage" (Gal 5:1). This *spiritual* redemption serves as the antitype of Moses' *physical* redemption.

When Christ came to earth from a far country (i.e., heaven), he validated his ministry through miracles as Moses had done. The apostle John selected some of them so we might believe in Christ (John 20:31). Whereas Moses' first miracle affecting the land of Egypt was to turn water into blood, John lists Jesus' first miracle as his turning water into wine (cp. Exod 4:9; John 2:11). The last miracle Moses performed was the *death* of the firstborn, but Jesus' last miracle was to raise Lazarus to *life* (cp. Exod 11:1f; John 11:43).

The night before his Exodus on the cross, Jesus instituted the Lord's Supper. The next day, "Christ our passover [was] sacrificed for us" (1 Cor 5:7). Through his death on the cross—his *Exodus*—our Lord Jesus Christ redeemed all that the Father had given him. To use the language of the earlier Exodus, nothing in *this* Israel remained in bondage: "not an hoof [was] left behind" (Exod 10:26). Through Jesus, this redefined Israel—i.e., those in Christ—crossed through the Red Sea of Christ's blood to freedom from sin and death.

But the transition from their Mosaic-age status to their messianic-age status for this Israel was just beginning. Fifty days after Jesus' death on the cross—while he was sitting on his throne of glory, after having received his kingdom (Dan 7:14)—he poured out the Holy Spirit on this Israel (Acts 2:33). Whereas three thousand had *died* at Mt. Sinai, God brought three thousand to *life* on the day of Pentecost—a glorious typological inversion (Acts 2:41). The law had brought death (Rom 7:10), but the Spirit produces life (Rom 8:2).

Instead of a punitive forty years of *wandering* in the wilderness, God blessed the church to *witness* to the nations by preaching the gospel of the kingdom for *forty years* before the temple fell (AD 30–70; Matt 24:14; cp. Dan 12:4).

Just as God sustained Israel after the flesh (1 Cor 10:18) through supernatural *miracles* during her forty years in the wilderness, so he provided the church with supernatural manifestations of the Spirit as she witnessed to the nations. He was "bearing them witness, both with signs and wonders, and with divers miracles, and gifts of the Holy Ghost, according to his own will" (Heb 2:4).

At the end of forty years, the church entered the messianic (kingdom) age (Matt 16:28) like Israel had entered her earthly kingdom (Exod 19:6). Just as redemption from Egypt was incomplete until "Israel after the flesh" arrived at Gilgal (Josh. 5:9), so, for the church, redemption was incomplete until the temple fell. For that reason, in the Olivet Discourse, Jesus said, "When these things begin to come to pass, then look up, and lift up your heads; for your *redemption* draweth nigh" (Luke

21:28). When the temple fell, *routine miraculous gifts in the church ceased* for "that which is perfect"—the messianic-age kingdom of God—had come (1 Cor 13:10).

The following diagram shows these Exodus types and their corresponding antitypes:

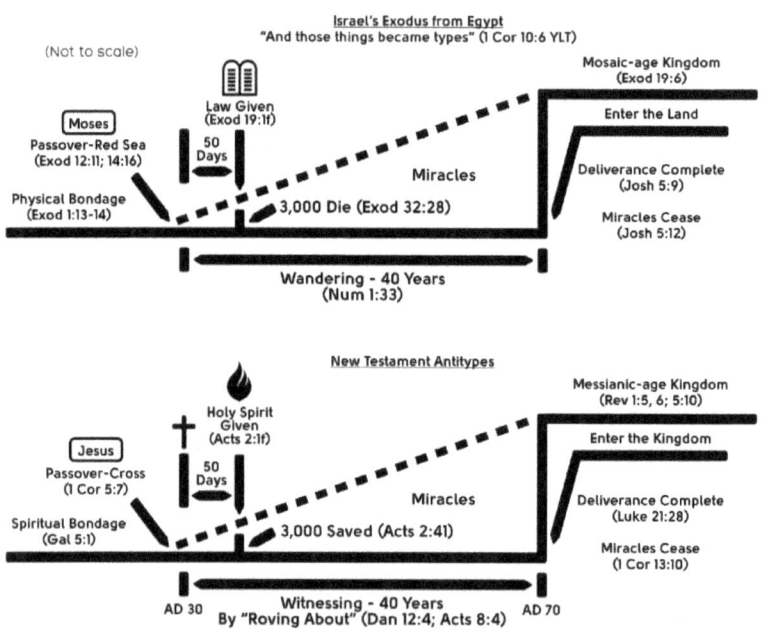

Figure 14-2. Exodus Types and Antitypes

The degree to which the antitypes in Jesus' generation match their Exodus types in Moses' generation is remarkable. That historical events in two generations separated by fifteen centuries correspond in this way cannot be accidental; it is an amazing display of God's sovereign power and wisdom. The Exodus events must have "had their ordination of God, and were designed by Him to foreshadow and prepare for the better things of the Gospel."[8] They are a beautiful confirmation of Paul's typological principle, that "the spiritual is not first, but the natural, and afterward the spiritual"; the *physical* types preceded their *spiritual* antitypes.

Inmillennialism and Exodus Types

The inmillennial prophetic model needs no "corrective devices" to accommodate these type-antitype relationships. The following (very busy) diagram shows that this is true:

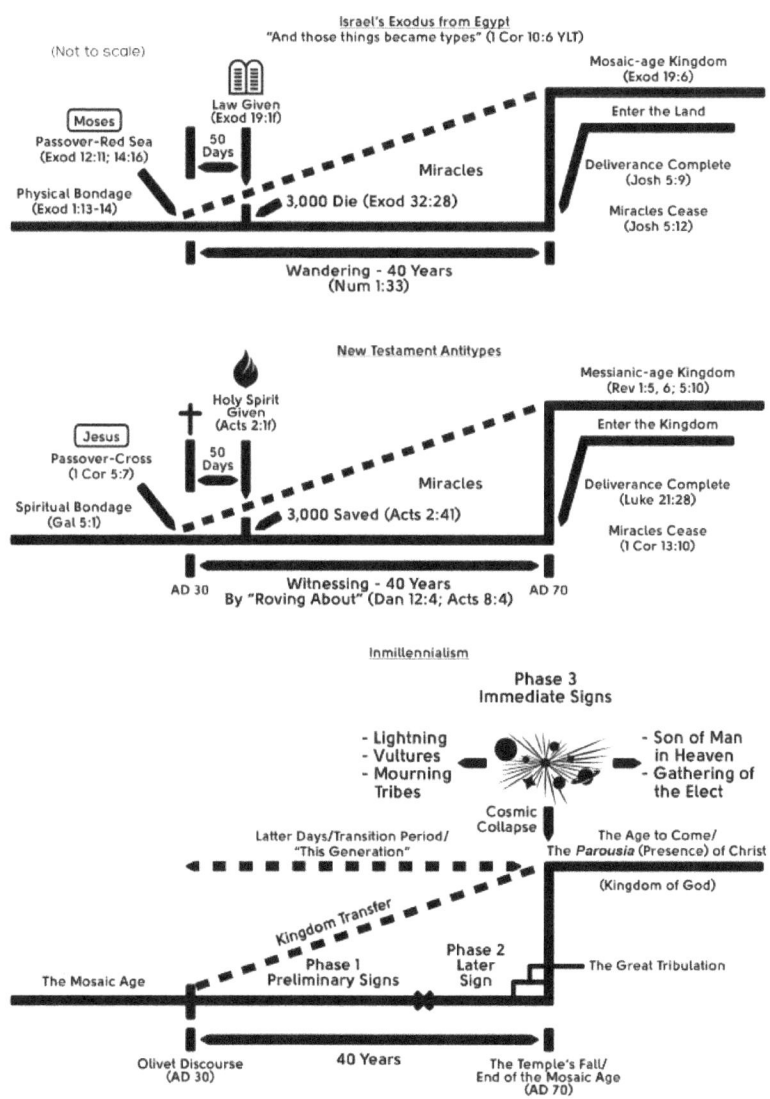

Figure 14-3. Exodus Types, Antitypes, and the Inmillennial Model

These diagrams reinforce Paul's overarching typological principle: "That was not first which is spiritual, but that which is natural; and afterward that which is spiritual" (1 Cor 15:46). Israel after the flesh (1 Cor 10:18) came first, Israel after the Spirit came second. Natural-born Jews inherited an earthly kingdom; Spirit-born Jews have now, through Christ, inherited the heavenly kingdom, for, from now on, "he is not a Jew, which is one outwardly; neither is that circumcision, which is outward in the flesh: but he is a Jew, which is one inwardly; and circumcision is that of the heart, in the spirit, and not in the letter; whose praise is not of men, but of God" (Rom 2:28–29).

Paul rejoiced to tell the Romans that, because of what Christ has done, "You are *not in the flesh but in the Spirit*, if indeed the Spirit of God dwells in you. Now if anyone does not have the Spirit of Christ, he is not His" (Rom 8:9 NKJV). God had elevated fleshly Israel's status during Moses' generation; in a far more glorious manner, he elevated the status of spiritual Israel in Jesus' generation. The true children of Abraham—those with faith in Christ—are now free to enjoy their inheritance. Now and forever, "The kingdom of God is not meat and drink [as it was in the Mosaic age] but righteousness, and peace, and joy in the Holy Ghost" (Rom 14:17).

Key Point #13

God meant for the Exodus of Israel after the flesh from Egypt to serve as a type. The antitype (or fulfillment) occurred in Jesus' generation: his Exodus on the cross freed spiritual Israel from bondage to sin. Many details in the two Exodus events correspond as type-antitype; our prophetic model must conform to those fulfillments.

Conclusion

I mentioned earlier that I was omitting one type-antitype combination. My reasons were partly practical—I could not get them on the chart!—and partly for a more noble purpose: I want it to culminate my typological argument. As I showed in the last chapter, a central part of the gospel of the kingdom is that Christ is reigning until he defeats all his enemies. This involves us in gospel warfare as we use our spiritual weapons to attack Satan's strongholds. This spiritual conflict matches the typology God built into Israel's history. At the start of their wilderness journey, God told Israel how he would bless them once they reached Canaan: "By little and little I will drive them out from before thee, until thou be increased, and inherit the land" (Exod 23:30). Almost forty years later, Moses reminded the people of how their victory would come: "And the LORD thy God will put out those nations before thee by little and little: thou mayest not consume them at once, lest the beasts of the field increase upon thee" (Deut 7:22). God had given Israel a wonderful prophetic model for their physical battles: their ultimate victory was certain and the path to that victory was clear—it was a vision of kingdom optimism and kingdom gradualism.

But the ten spies Moses sent into the land trusted more in what they saw with their eyes than they did in God's revealed will. They said,

> We came unto the land whither thou sentest us, and surely it floweth with milk and honey; and this is the fruit of it. Nevertheless the people be strong that dwell in the land, and the cities are walled, and very great.… We be not able to go up against the people; for they are stronger than we.… The land, through which we have gone to search it, is a land that eateth up the inhabitants thereof; and all the people that we saw in it are men of a great stature. And there we saw the giants, the sons of Anak, which come of the giants: and we were in our own sight as grasshoppers, and so we were in their sight. (Num 13:27–33)

They admitted the vision was glorious, the land was productive and desirable, but it could not be theirs for the opposition was too great.

The antitype is clear. Jesus has told us to make disciples *of all nations*, and that, through our Spirit-enabled obedience to his commands, we will succeed. But we often hear voices that sound eerily similar to those of the ten spies that brought an evil report to Moses and the people. These voices agree that the vision of all nations worshipping Christ is good and very desirable; we should pray for it, they say, even though it will never come to pass. But, according to their trusted prophetic models, this vision does not pertain to us—it is for a future age or the eternal state. The forces arrayed against us, they say, will grow stronger and stronger as our age progresses. At the end of our dispensation, it is doubtful that genuine faith will exist on the earth. Besides, they say, can we not read the newspapers? Things have never been this bad, and they are getting worse by the day. Surely, according to their prophetic models, we are living in the "last days" when evil will run rampant.

My dear reader, this is not the proper vision of the messianic-age kingdom. Inmillennialism declares that the negative passages in the New Testament refer either to the "last days" of the Mosaic age or to a temporary situation that exists only until the kingdom of God reverses it. For example, when Paul says, "Evil men and seducers shall wax worse and worse" (2 Tim 3:13), he is speaking about events "in the last days" (2 Tim 3:1) before the temple fell. He is not describing a permanent characteristic of the messianic age. The same is true for Jesus' narrow-gate metaphor: "Strive to enter through the narrow gate, for many, I say to you, will seek to enter and will not be able" (Luke 13:24 NKJV). As Douglas Wilson says, "When Jesus said that the way was narrow, and that only few would find it, He was speaking specifically about first century Judaism. From that body of people, only a remnant was saved, and then the Gentiles poured in."[9] Jesus describes this "pouring in" of the nations into the messianic-age kingdom:

> There will be weeping and gnashing of teeth, when you see Abraham and Isaac and Jacob and all the prophets in the kingdom of God, and yourselves thrust out. They will come from the east and the west, from the

north and the south, and sit down in the kingdom of God. (Luke 13:28–29)

The Scriptures nowhere describe the kingdom over which Jesus now reigns in negative terms. Nothing in the Bible suggests it will fail in its stated mission of filling the whole earth with the knowledge of the Lord, of bringing all nations, together with their rulers, into joyful service to our King.

This is God's vision for us and our churches. And this is the true value of inmillennialism. We need a prophetic model that conforms to the typology God embedded in Israel's Exodus, and one that encourages us to be antitypical Israel by subduing the nations of the world through our mighty spiritual weapons. The prophetic model we need should warn us of the need for a typological inversion in this matter. Israel of old took possession of their promised natural land as God had promised, but, in their latter end, God cast them out of their covenant relationship because of their unfaithfulness. God has revealed that, in the messianic age, his redefined Israel will prove faithful. The kingdom she now enjoys will grow to become a great mountain that destroys all other kingdoms.

Typology confirms the inmillennial prophetic model we have discovered in the Olivet Discourse and 1 Corinthians 15. And this model supports the vision God has given us for the age in which we live.

KEY POINT #14

The Exodus typology extends to Israel's conquest of Canaan. The antitype is the church's conquest of the nations by making disciples of them. The typical conquest was through physical weapons; the antitypical conquest is through spiritual warfare as the churches obey the Great Commission.

Notes

1 All these quotes are in Wick Broomall, "Type, Typology," in *Baker's Dictionary of Theology*, eds. Everett F. Harrison, Geoffrey W. Bromiley, and Carl F. H. Henry (Grand Rapids: Baker, 1975), 533–34.

2 See Appendix E for a list of New Testament passages that refer to the Song of Moses.

3 Broomall, "Type, Typology," 534.

4 Walter A. Elwell and Philip W. Comfort, *Tyndale Bible Dictionary* (Wheaton, IL: Tyndale House, 2001), 1111.

5 "The Forty Years in Biblical Typology," Todd Dennis, http://www.preteristarchive.com/Preterism/dennis-todd_p_40.html. Todd has blessed many through his ministry of making material related to prophecy available on his website. Some of it is hard to find elsewhere. Todd first wrote *The Forty Years in Biblical Typology* while holding a full preterist view of prophecy, but revised it after rejecting that position.

6 Gill, "Exposition," 1:421.

7 Wuest, *Expanded Translation*, 156.

8 Patrick Fairbairn, *Typology of Scripture* (1900; repr., Grand Rapids: Kregel, 1989), 1:46.

9 Wilson, *Heaven Misplaced*, 79.

CHAPTER FIFTEEN

Conclusion

AFTER I DECIDED to use Copernicus as a metaphor in this book, I discovered the following passage by Samuel Lee:

> Previous to the astronomic illumination given the world by Copernicus, there were theories explanatory of the phenomena of the heavens. Each theory had its advocates, and they were all alike in error. Of the all-comprehensive principle applicable to the case, and the recognition of which would solve all their difficulties, they were ignorant. We think the endless disputes in the department of religious truth are to be accounted for on a similar principle. The Bible contains a system of religious truth, but, like the facts in nature, the truths of the Bible are not presented in scientific arrangement; yet the latter as certainly as the former are in harmony with great and all-pervading principles. These principles must be understood, or the isolated facts will not be.... And we can no more hope for a consistent theological system, till these questions are correctly answered, than for a science of astronomy without the great Copernican fact.[1]

I believe Lee's observation is especially true regarding prophetic interpretation. The pre-Copernican models of the solar system required epicycles and equants to explain apparent but nonexistent retrograde planetary motion. Similarly, the existing prophetic models need corrective devices—dual fulfillment, elastic time, prophetic perspective, and others—to explain many prophetic passages that seem to defy explanation.

Copernicus made a simple but profound change: he recognized the sun as the center of the solar system instead of the earth, eliminating the need for astronomical corrective devices. The observations we have made in this book suggest we should make a similar move regarding the interpretation of prophecy: we should redefine the "last days" as the final period of the Mosaic age and recognize that Christ's *parousia* (presence) with his churches began then. The resulting model—inmillennialism—eliminates the need for several unregulated and unnecessary interpretive devices.

I know that the inmillennial model will produce a variety of reactions. My prayer is that many readers will embrace it and use it to advance God's kingdom. I ask those who understand what I have written but disagree to remember Mortimer Adler's advice. Please say one (or more) of the following to me: (1) "You are uninformed"; (2) "You are misinformed"; (3) "You are illogical—your reasoning is not cogent"; (4) "Your analysis is incomplete."[2] If you do, I promise, by God's grace, to listen with genuine interest to your reasons. I will attempt to remove the objection(s), if appropriate, in future editions of this book. To those who do *not* understand part (or all) of this book, please know that I will welcome your requests for clarification. To everyone, I request that you not reject inmillennialism simply because you are uncomfortable with the *consequences* of its conclusions.

I have presented the inmillennial model in church and conference settings. The follow-up question-and-answer times are always interesting! These experiences have caused me to test this prophetic model against many "proof texts" raised against it. I am thinking especially of passages that seem to require a visible coming of Christ (e.g., Acts 1:9–11), and those that appear to teach that the resurrection will occur at the moment of his coming (e.g., 1 Thess 4:15–17; 1 John 3:2). I am convinced that an unbiased person who examines such passages from an inmillennial perspective, at least as a thought experiment, will see how such passages fit into the overall scheme.[3] I am also convinced that any explanation of such passages that I might provide will be unacceptable to persons who will not attempt to understand the inmillennial framework. But Copernicus faced the same problem, didn't he?

Sometimes people have asked questions that none of the prophetic models can answer because God has not revealed the answers in Scripture. Some have asked, How will everything wind up? What will we be doing in the eternal state? Will the physical creation continue forever? Questions like these invite speculation, and I enjoy that as much as anyone. But I admit my inability to speak with authority on these topics.

That the inmillennial prophetic model does not show a visible coming of Christ may surprise some readers. I ask them to consider that the physical resurrection at the end of the messianic age requires a visible coming and/or going by Christ or his people. In the eternal state, they will, in their glorified bodies, enjoy visible and personal fellowship. Inmillennialism just says that most, perhaps all, of the passages that describe the Lord's coming are referring to something he did in the apostles' generation.

The eternal state will be the natural result of what God did through Christ in the "last days" of the Mosaic age. The kingdom he established then will grow to achieve dominion over all nations, as I showed in Chapter 13. This is the thousand-(symbolic)-year reign of Christ with his saints in Revelation 20:2–7. According to Revelation 20:7–10, Satan will attempt one final, but futile, rebellion at the end of the messianic age. After the resurrection (cp. Rev 20:11–15), Christ will deliver the successful kingdom to the Father. At that point, God will have purged his creation of all sin, and it will finally stop groaning for deliverance (cp. Rom 8:22–23). This does not mean the kingdom will end: the Father and Son will continue to reign, for "The LORD shall reign for ever" (Ps 146:10).

In my *opinion*, God will, through all eternity, reveal more and more of his glorious attributes to the saints as we praise him and his matchless grace.

I believe we should interpret prophetic passages in Scripture by using the inmillennial prophetic model. To use the astronomy metaphor one last time, I advocate using inmillennialism like astronomers used the Copernican model after he introduced it. For them, planetary movements became much more orderly; for us, prophetic passages will become much more understandable and applicable to our daily lives.

If the Lord wills, I plan to write a series of books that will use inmillennialism to interpret prophetic passages in individual books of the Bible. One of my principal objectives will be to answer the common questions people have when they first learn of this view. I want those who investigate this "system of religious truth" to see how it explains God's inspired word. And I pray that God will use it to "make disciples of all nations" as his word comes alive in the hearts of many.

Now, in closing, I want to tie up some loose ends. In Chapter 1, I provided a summary table that compared the existing prophetic models. I will now add inmillennialism and two questions (numbers 5 and 6) that highlight unique aspects of inmillennialism in Table 15-1 (next page).

I set out to discover an improved prophetic model from key New Testament passages that contain a minimum amount of figurative language. I chose the Olivet Discourse and 1 Corinthians 15 because of their length and influence on the rest of the New Testament. Figure 15-1 (next page), a repeat of Figure 13-2, shows the major elements of the model I discovered in those passages.

The inmillennial model should guide our interpretation of other prophetic passages, just as Copernicus' model directed astronomers as they expanded their knowledge of the solar system. It fulfills the VALUE acrostic I mentioned in Chapter 2. It defines God's *Vision* for the kingdom in which we now live. To achieve this vision, God has called us to pray for the kingdom, pursue the kingdom as our top priority, preach the kingdom, and participate in kingdom activities like serving one another, remem-

CONCLUSION

No.	Criteria	Amill.	Postmill.	Premill. (Hist.)	Premill. (Disp.)	Inmill.
1	Does fleshly Israel (1 Cor 10:18) now have a unique covenant?	No	No	No	Yes	No
2	Is the "thousand years" of Rev 20—the millennium—literal?	No	Yes/No (two forms)	Yes	Yes	No
3	Does the second coming (*parousia*) occur before or after the millennium?	After	After	Before	Before	Before (see no. 5)
4	Will the existing kingdom of God be triumphant *in history*?	No	Yes	No	No	Yes
5	Is the *parousia* of Christ coincident with the kingdom age?	No	No	No	No	Yes
6	Do the last days refer only to the final period of the Mosaic Age?	No	No	No	No	Yes

Table 15-1. Summary of Prophetic Models (including Inmillennialism)

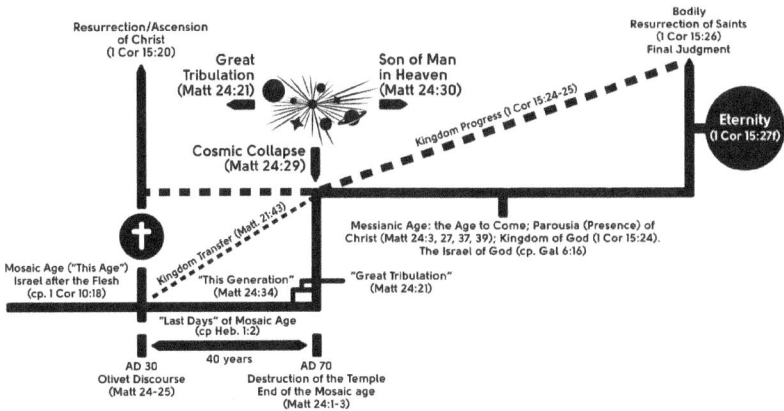

Figure 15-1. Inmillennialism: a Framework for Prophecy

bering the poor, being merciful, and other things he has commanded us to do. We do them knowing we are in Christ's presence (i.e., his *parousia*) as we wage such spiritual warfare to pull down enemy strongholds.

This model is a powerful *Apologetic* tool that allows us to refute charges that Jesus was a false prophet. It provides a rich interpretation of our *Legacy* by showing the culmination of Israel's history and the fulfillment of everything the prophets foretold. We can use this model to increase our *Understanding* of God's prophetic plan. And inmillennialism shows what God has for us to *Experience*: he has provided for us a spiritual "feast of fat things, a feast of wines on the lees, of fat things full of marrow, of wines on the lees well refined" (Isa 25:6) in his kingdom.

I say "Amen!" to the apostle Paul's prayer to God for you:

> That he would grant you, according to the riches of his glory, to be strengthened with might by his Spirit in the inner man; that Christ may dwell in your hearts by faith; that ye, being rooted and grounded in love, may be able to comprehend with all saints what is the breadth, and length, and depth, and height; and to know the love of Christ, which passeth knowledge, that ye might be filled with all the fulness of God. Now unto him that is able to do exceeding abundantly above all that we ask or think, according to the power that worketh in us, unto him be glory in the church by Christ Jesus throughout all ages, world without end. Amen. (Eph 3:16–21)

Notes

1 Samuel Lee, *The Bible Regained and the God of the Bible Ours; or, the System of Religious Truth in Outline* (Boston: Lee and Shepard, 1874), 13–14.
2 Adler and Doren, *How to Read a Book*, 156 (emphasis removed).
3 A few explanations will require a cursory knowledge of the original languages.

APPENDIX A

List of Key Points

The following list of key points shows the major observations that support the inmillennial prophetic model:

Key Point #1	55
Key Point #2	57
Key Point #3	60
Key Point #4	61
Key Point #5	68
Key Point #6	70
Key Point #7	81
Key Point #8	83
Key Point #9	180
Key Point #10	200
Key Point #11	232
Key Point #12	263
Key Point #13	276
Key Point #14	279

Key Point #1: The Olivet Discourse is a unit; a single subject controls it from beginning to end. This fact governs our interpretation of it.

Key Point #2: The subject of the Olivet Discourse is Jesus' prophecy of the temple's destruction and matters related to that event.

Key Point #3: The disciples ask two questions. Their *when* question relates to the subject of the Olivet Discourse—the temple's destruction and matters related to that event.

Key Point #4: The disciples' *sign* question relates to the subject of the Olivet Discourse—the temple's destruction and matters related to that event.

Key Point #5: Matthew recorded the disciples' *sign* question in the Olivet Discourse within a framework of age transition: the Mosaic age was giving way to the messianic age.

Key Point #6: In Matthew's account of the *sign* question, "the end of the age (Gk. *aiōn*)" means the end of the Mosaic age that would come when the temple fell.

Key Point #7: In Matthew's account of the *sign* question, "the *parousia* of Christ" means Christ's presence with his people in the messianic age; it does not refer to a point-in-time event in our future.

Key Point #8: Mark and Luke relate the *sign* question to the events surrounding the temple's fall; Matthew relates it to the *results*—the end of the Mosaic age and the start of the messianic age. The Scriptures refer to the new age as the kingdom of God, the kingdom of heaven, the age to come, the *parousia* of Christ, et al.

Key Point #9: The Scriptures refer to the period from the ministry of John the Baptist to the temple's destruction as Mosaic-age Israel's "last days," "latter days," et al. This was the "transition period" in which Jesus led his people out of the Mosaic and into the messianic age.

Key Point #10: Jesus said all the things of which he spoke in the Olivet Discourse would occur within his (temporal) "generation" without specifying the "day or hour" of their occurrence.

Key Point #11: Jesus ended the Olivet Discourse in Matthew by describing the final judgment. This judgment is the necessary outcome of what

God did in the "last days" of the Mosaic age; the kingdom of God requires the final judgment.

Key Point #12: In 1 Corinthians 15, Paul links Christ's resurrection to the bodily resurrection of believers at the end of the messianic age. He uses Psalm 110:1 to do so, showing the importance of kingdom optimism and kingdom gradualism for our prophetic model.

Key Point #13: God meant for the Exodus of Israel after the flesh from Egypt to serve as a type. The antitype (or fulfillment) occurred in Jesus' generation: his Exodus on the cross freed spiritual Israel from bondage to sin. Many details in the two Exodus events correspond as type-antitype; our prophetic model must conform to these fulfillments.

Key Point #14: The Exodus typology extends to Israel's conquest of Canaan. The antitype is the church's conquest of the nations by making disciples of them. The typical conquest was through physical weapons; the antitypical conquest is through *spiritual* warfare as the churches obey the Great Commission.

APPENDIX B

The Olivet Discourse: Matthew

Jesus' Prediction

¹ And Jesus went out, and departed from the temple: and his disciples came to *him*[1] for to shew him the buildings of the temple. ² And Jesus said unto them, See ye not all these things? verily I say unto you, There shall not be left here one stone upon another, that shall not be thrown down. (Matt 24:1–2)

The Disciples' Two Questions

³ And as he sat upon the mount of Olives, the disciples came unto him privately, saying, Tell us, when shall these things be? and what *shall be* the sign of thy coming, and of the end of the world? (Matt 24:3)

Jesus' Response to the Sign Question
Preliminary Signs—the Beginning of Birth Pains. ⁴ And Jesus answered and said unto them, Take heed that no man deceive you. ⁵ For many shall come in my name, saying, I am Christ; and shall deceive many. ⁶ And ye shall hear of wars and rumours of wars: see that ye be not troubled: for all *these things* must come to pass, but the end is not yet. ⁷ For nation shall rise against nation, and kingdom against kingdom: and there shall be famines, and pestilences, and earthquakes, in divers places. ⁸ All these *are* the beginning of sorrows. ⁹ Then shall they deliver you up to be afflicted, and shall kill you: and ye shall be hated of all nations for my name's sake. ¹⁰ And then shall many be offended, and shall betray one another, and shall hate one another. ¹¹ And many false prophets

---

1 The translators of the King James (Authorized) Version used italics to mark words not in the Greek manuscripts. All italics in this Appendix are in the original.

shall rise, and shall deceive many. ¹² And because iniquity shall abound, the love of many shall wax cold. ¹³ But he that shall endure unto the end, the same shall be saved. ¹⁴ And this gospel of the kingdom shall be preached in all the world for a witness unto all nations; and then shall the end come. (Matt 24:4–14)

Later Sign—the Period of "The End." ¹⁵ When ye therefore shall see the abomination of desolation, spoken of by Daniel the prophet, stand in the holy place, (whoso readeth, let him understand:) ¹⁶ then let them which be in Judaea flee into the mountains: ¹⁷ let him which is on the housetop not come down to take any thing out of his house: ¹⁸ neither let him which is in the field return back to take his clothes. ¹⁹ And woe unto them that are with child, and to them that give suck in those days! ²⁰ But pray ye that your flight be not in the winter, neither on the sabbath day: ²¹ for then shall be great tribulation, such as was not since the beginning of the world to this time, no, nor ever shall be. ²² And except those days should be shortened, there should no flesh be saved: but for the elect's sake those days shall be shortened. ²³ Then if any man shall say unto you, Lo, here *is* Christ, or there; believe *it* not. ²⁴ For there shall arise false Christs, and false prophets, and shall shew great signs and wonders; insomuch that, if *it were* possible, they shall deceive the very elect. ²⁵ Behold, I have told you before. ²⁶ Wherefore if they shall say unto you, Behold, he is in the desert; go not forth: behold, *he is* in the secret chambers; believe *it* not. (Matt 24:15–26)

Immediate Signs—the End Itself. ²⁷ For as the lightning cometh out of the east, and shineth even unto the west; so shall also the coming of the Son of man be. ²⁸ For wheresoever the carcase is, there will the eagles be gathered together. ²⁹ Immediately after the tribulation of those days shall the sun be darkened, and the moon shall not give her light, and the stars shall fall from heaven, and the powers of the heavens shall be shaken: ³⁰ and then shall appear the sign of the Son of man in heaven: and then shall all the tribes of the earth mourn, and they shall see the

Son of man coming in the clouds of heaven with power and great glory. ³¹ And he shall send his angels with a great sound of a trumpet, and they shall gather together his elect from the four winds, from one end of heaven to the other. (Matt 24:27–31)

Jesus' Response to the When Question

³² Now learn a parable of the fig tree; When his branch is yet tender, and putteth forth leaves, ye know that summer *is* nigh: ³³ so likewise ye, when ye shall see all these things, know that it is near, *even* at the doors. ³⁴ Verily I say unto you, This generation shall not pass, till all these things be fulfilled. ³⁵ Heaven and earth shall pass away, but my words shall not pass away. ³⁶ But of that day and hour knoweth no *man*, no, not the angels of heaven, but my Father only. (Matt 24:32–36)

Jesus' Exhortations to Watchfulness

The Flood Judgment. ³⁷ But as the days of Noe *were*, so shall also the coming of the Son of man be. ³⁸ For as in the days that were before the flood they were eating and drinking, marrying and giving in marriage, until the day that Noe entered into the ark, ³⁹ and knew not until the flood came, and took them all away; so shall also the coming of the Son of man be. ⁴⁰ Then shall two be in the field; the one shall be taken, and the other left. ⁴¹ Two *women shall be* grinding at the mill; the one shall be taken, and the other left. ⁴² Watch therefore: for ye know not what hour your Lord doth come. ⁴³ But know this, that if the goodman of the house had known in what watch the thief would come, he would have watched, and would not have suffered his house to be broken up. ⁴⁴ Therefore be ye also ready: for in such an hour as ye think not the Son of man cometh. (Matt 24: 37–44)

The Two-Servants Judgment. ⁴⁵ Who then is a faithful and wise servant, whom his lord hath made ruler over his household, to give them meat in due season? ⁴⁶ Blessed *is* that servant, whom his lord when he cometh shall find so doing. ⁴⁷ Verily I say unto you, That he shall make him ruler over all his goods. ⁴⁸ But and if that evil servant shall say in his heart, My lord delayeth his coming; ⁴⁹ and shall begin to smite *his* fellowservants, and to eat and drink with the drunken; ⁵⁰ the lord of that servant shall come in a day when he looketh not for *him*, and in an hour that he is not aware of, ⁵¹ and shall cut him asunder, and appoint *him* his portion with the hypocrites: there shall be weeping and gnashing of teeth. (Matt 24: 45–51)

The Ten-Virgins Judgment. ¹ Then shall the kingdom of heaven be likened unto ten virgins, which took their lamps, and went forth to meet the bridegroom. ² And five of them were wise, and five *were* foolish. ³ They that *were* foolish took their lamps, and took no oil with them: ⁴ but the wise took oil in their vessels with their lamps. ⁵ While the bridegroom tarried, they all slumbered and slept. ⁶ And at midnight there was a cry made, Behold, the bridegroom cometh; go ye out to meet him. ⁷ Then all those virgins arose, and trimmed their lamps. ⁸ And the foolish said unto the wise, Give us of your oil; for our lamps are gone out. ⁹ But the wise answered, saying, *Not so*; lest there be not enough for us and you: but go ye rather to them that sell, and buy for yourselves. ¹⁰ And while they went to buy, the bridegroom came; and they that were ready went in with him to the marriage: and the door was shut. ¹¹ Afterward came also the other virgins, saying, Lord, Lord, open to us. ¹² But he answered and said, Verily I say unto you, I know you not. ¹³ Watch therefore, for ye know neither the day nor the hour wherein the Son of man cometh. (Matt 25:1–13)

The Talents Judgment. ¹⁴ For *the kingdom of heaven is* as a man travelling into a far country, *who* called his own servants, and delivered unto them his goods. ¹⁵ And unto one he gave five talents, to another two, and to another one; to every man according to his several ability; and straightway took his journey. ¹⁶ Then he that had received the five talents went and traded with the same, and made *them* other five talents. ¹⁷ And likewise he that *had received* two, he also gained other two. ²⁸ But he that had received one went and digged in the earth, and hid his lord's money. ¹⁹ After a long time the lord of those servants cometh, and reckoneth with them. ²⁰ And so he that had received five talents came and brought other five talents, saying, Lord, thou deliveredst unto me five talents: behold, I have gained beside them five talents more. ²¹ His lord said unto him, Well done, *thou* good and faithful servant: thou hast been faithful over a few things, I will make thee ruler over many things: enter thou into the joy of thy lord. ²² He also that had received two talents came and said, Lord, thou deliveredst unto me two talents: behold, I have gained two other talents beside them. ²³ His lord said unto him, Well done, good and faithful servant; thou hast been faithful over a few things, I will make thee ruler over many things: enter thou into the joy of thy lord. ²⁴ Then he which had received the one talent came and said, Lord, I knew thee that thou art an hard man, reaping where thou hast not sown, and gathering where thou hast not strawed: ²⁵ and I was afraid, and went and hid thy talent in the earth: lo, *there* thou hast *that is* thine. ²⁶ His lord answered and said unto him, *Thou* wicked and slothful servant, thou knewest that I reap where I sowed not, and gather where I have not strawed: ²⁷ thou oughtest therefore to have put my money to the exchangers, and *then* at my coming I should have received mine own with usury. ²⁸ Take therefore the talent from him, and give *it* unto him which hath ten talents. ²⁹ For unto every one that hath shall be given, and he shall have abundance: but from him that hath not shall be taken away even that which he hath. ³⁰ And cast ye the unprofitable servant into outer darkness: there shall be weeping and gnashing of teeth. (Matt 25:14–30)

The Final Judgment. ³¹ When the Son of man shall come in his glory, and all the holy angels with him, then shall he sit upon the throne of his glory: ³² and before him shall be gathered all nations: and he shall separate them one from another, as a shepherd divideth *his* sheep from the goats: ³³ and he shall set the sheep on his right hand, but the goats on the left. 34 Then shall the King say unto them on his right hand, Come, ye blessed of my Father, inherit the kingdom prepared for you from the foundation of the world: 35 for I was an hungred, and ye gave me meat: I was thirsty, and ye gave me drink: I was a stranger, and ye took me in: 36naked, and ye clothed me: I was sick, and ye visited me: I was in prison, and ye came unto me. 37 Then shall the righteous answer him, saying, Lord, when saw we thee an hungred, and fed *thee*? or thirsty, and gave *thee* drink? 38 When saw we thee a stranger, and took *thee* in? or naked, and clothed *thee*? 39 Or when saw we thee sick, or in prison, and came unto thee? 40 And the King shall answer and say unto them, Verily I say unto you, Inasmuch as ye have done *it* unto one of the least of these my brethren, ye have done *it* unto me. 41 Then shall he say also unto them on the left hand, Depart from me, ye cursed, into everlasting fire, prepared for the devil and his angels: 42 for I was an hungred, and ye gave me no meat: I was thirsty, and ye gave me no drink: 43 I was a stranger, and ye took me not in: naked, and ye clothed me not: sick, and in prison, and ye visited me not. 44 Then shall they also answer him, saying, Lord, when saw we thee an hungred, or athirst, or a stranger, or naked, or sick, or in prison, and did not minister unto thee? 45 Then shall he answer them, saying, Verily I say unto you, Inasmuch as ye did *it* not to one of the least of these, ye did *it* not to me. 46 And these shall go away into everlasting punishment: but the righteous into life eternal. (Matt 25:31–46)

APPENDIX C

The Olivet Discourse: Mark

Jesus' Prediction

¹ And as he went out of the temple, one of his disciples saith unto him, Master, see what manner of stones and what buildings *are here*!¹ ² And Jesus answering said unto him, Seest thou these great buildings? there shall not be left one stone upon another, that shall not be thrown down. (Mark 13:1–2)

The Disciples' Two Questions

³ And as he sat upon the mount of Olives over against the temple, Peter and James and John and Andrew asked him privately, ⁴ Tell us, when shall these things be? and what *shall be* the sign when all these things shall be fulfilled? (Mark 13:3–4)

Jesus' Response to the Sign Question
Preliminary Signs—the Beginning of Birth Pains. ⁵ And Jesus answering them began to say, Take heed lest any *man* deceive you: ⁶ for many shall come in my name, saying, I am Christ; and shall deceive many. ⁷ And when ye shall hear of wars and rumours of wars, be ye not troubled: for *such things* must needs be; but the end *shall* not *be* yet. ⁸ For nation shall rise against nation, and kingdom against kingdom: and there shall be earthquakes in divers places, and there shall be famines and troubles: these are the beginnings of sorrows. ⁹ But take heed to yourselves: for they shall deliver you up to councils; and in the synagogues ye shall be beaten: and ye shall be brought before rulers and kings for my

---

1 The translators of the King James (Authorized) Version used italics to mark words not in the Greek manuscripts. All italics in this Appendix are in the original.

sake, for a testimony against them. ¹⁰ And the gospel must first be published among all nations. ¹¹ But when they shall lead *you*, and deliver you up, take no thought beforehand what ye shall speak, neither do ye premeditate: but whatsoever shall be given you in that hour, that speak ye: for it is not ye that speak, but the Holy Ghost. ¹² Now the brother shall betray the brother to death, and the father the son; and children shall rise up against *their* parents, and shall cause them to be put to death. ¹³ And ye shall be hated of all *men* for my name's sake: but he that shall endure unto the end, the same shall be saved. (Mark 13:5–13)

Later Sign—the Period of "The End." ¹⁴ But when ye shall see the abomination of desolation, spoken of by Daniel the prophet, standing where it ought not, (let him that readeth understand,) then let them that be in Judaea flee to the mountains: ¹⁵ and let him that is on the housetop not go down into the house, neither enter *therein*, to take any thing out of his house: ¹⁶ and let him that is in the field not turn back again for to take up his garment. ¹⁷ But woe to them that are with child, and to them that give suck in those days! ¹⁸ And pray ye that your flight be not in the winter. ¹⁹ For *in* those days shall be affliction, such as was not from the beginning of the creation which God created unto this time, neither shall be. ²⁰ And except that the Lord had shortened those days, no flesh should be saved: but for the elect's sake, whom he hath chosen, he hath shortened the days. ²¹ And then if any man shall say to you, Lo, here is Christ; or, lo, *he is* there; believe *him* not: ²² for false Christs and false prophets shall rise, and shall shew signs and wonders, to seduce, if *it were* possible, even the elect. ²³ But take ye heed: behold, I have foretold you all things. (Mark 13:14–23)

Immediate Signs—the End Itself. ²⁴ But in those days, after that tribulation, the sun shall be darkened, and the moon shall not give her light, ²⁵ and the stars of heaven shall fall, and the powers that are in heaven shall be shaken. ²⁶ And then shall they see the Son of man coming in the clouds with great power and glory. ²⁷ And then shall he send his angels, and shall gather together his elect from the four winds, from the uttermost part of the earth to the uttermost part of heaven. (Mark 13:24–27)

Jesus' Response to the When Question

[28] Now learn a parable of the fig tree; When her branch is yet tender, and putteth forth leaves, ye know that summer is near: [29] so ye in like manner, when ye shall see these things come to pass, know that it is nigh, *even* at the doors. [30] Verily I say unto you, that this generation shall not pass, till all these things be done. [31] Heaven and earth shall pass away: but my words shall not pass away. [32] But of that day and *that* hour knoweth no man, no, not the angels which are in heaven, neither the Son, but the Father. (Mark 13:28–32)

Jesus' Exhortations to Watchfulness

[33] Take ye heed, watch and pray: for ye know not when the time is. [34] *For the Son of man is* as a man taking a far journey, who left his house, and gave authority to his servants, and to every man his work, and commanded the porter to watch. [35] Watch ye therefore: for ye know not when the master of the house cometh, at even, or at midnight, or at the cockcrowing, or in the morning: [36] lest coming suddenly he find you sleeping. [37] And what I say unto you I say unto all, Watch. (Mark 13:33–37)

APPENDIX D

The Olivet Discourse: Luke

Jesus' Prediction

⁵ And as some spake of the temple, how it was adorned with goodly stones and gifts, he said, ⁶ *As for*[1] these things which ye behold, the days will come, in the which there shall not be left one stone upon another, that shall not be thrown down. (Luke 21:5–6)

The Disciples' Two Questions

⁷ And they asked him, saying, Master, but when shall these things be? and what sign *will there be* when these things shall come to pass? (Luke 21:7)

Jesus' Response to the Sign Question

Preliminary Signs—the Beginning of Birth Pains. ⁸ And he said, Take heed that ye be not deceived: for many shall come in my name, saying, I am *Christ*; and the time draweth near: go ye not therefore after them. ⁹ But when ye shall hear of wars and commotions, be not terrified: for these things must first come to pass; but the end *is* not by and by. ¹⁰ Then said he unto them, Nation shall rise against nation, and kingdom against kingdom: ¹¹ and great earthquakes shall be in divers places, and famines, and pestilences; and fearful sights and great signs shall there be from heaven. ¹² But before all these, they shall lay their hands on you, and persecute *you*, delivering *you* up to the synagogues, and into prisons, being brought before kings and rulers for my name's sake. ¹³ And it shall turn to you for a testimony. ¹⁴ Settle *it* therefore in your hearts, not to

---

1 The translators of the King James (Authorized) Version used italics to mark words not in the Greek manuscripts. All italics in this Appendix are in the original.

meditate before what ye shall answer: ¹⁵ for I will give you a mouth and wisdom, which all your adversaries shall not be able to gainsay nor resist. ¹⁶ And ye shall be betrayed both by parents, and brethren, and kinsfolks, and friends; and *some* of you shall they cause to be put to death. ¹⁷ And ye shall be hated of all *men* for my name's sake. ¹⁸ But there shall not an hair of your head perish. ¹⁹ In your patience possess ye your souls. (Luke 21:8–19)

Later Sign—the Period of "The End." ²⁰ And when ye shall see Jerusalem compassed with armies, then know that the desolation thereof is nigh. ²¹ Then let them which are in Judaea flee to the mountains; and let them which are in the midst of it depart out; and let not them that are in the countries enter thereinto. ²² For these be the days of vengeance, that all things which are written may be fulfilled. ²³ But woe unto them that are with child, and to them that give suck, in those days! for there shall be great distress in the land, and wrath upon this people. ²⁴ And they shall fall by the edge of the sword, and shall be led away captive into all nations: and Jerusalem shall be trodden down of the Gentiles, until the times of the Gentiles be fulfilled. (Luke 21:20–24)

Immediate Signs—the End Itself. ²⁵ And there shall be signs in the sun, and in the moon, and in the stars; and upon the earth distress of nations, with perplexity; the sea and the waves roaring; ²⁶ men's hearts failing them for fear, and for looking after those things which are coming on the earth: for the powers of heaven shall be shaken. ²⁷ And then shall they see the Son of man coming in a cloud with power and great glory. ²⁸ And when these things begin to come to pass, then look up, and lift up your heads; for your redemption draweth nigh. (Luke 21:25–28)

Jesus' Response to the When Question

²⁹ And he spake to them a parable; Behold the fig tree, and all the trees; ³⁰ when they now shoot forth, ye see and know of your own selves that summer is now nigh at hand. ³¹ So likewise ye, when ye see these things

come to pass, know ye that the kingdom of God is nigh at hand. ³² Verily I say unto you, This generation shall not pass away, till all be fulfilled. ³³ Heaven and earth shall pass away: but my words shall not pass away. (Luke 21:29–33)

Jesus' Exhortations to Watchfulness

³⁴ And take heed to yourselves, lest at any time your hearts be overcharged with surfeiting, and drunkenness, and cares of this life, and *so* that day come upon you unawares. ³⁵ For as a snare shall it come on all them that dwell on the face of the whole earth. ³⁶ Watch ye therefore, and pray always, that ye may be accounted worthy to escape all these things that shall come to pass, and to stand before the Son of man. (Luke 21:34–36)

APPENDIX E

The Song of Moses

The Song of Moses plays an important role in our prophetic model. I have collected relevant passages here for ease of reference.

Selections From Moses' Introduction

[16] And the LORD said unto Moses, Behold, thou shalt sleep with thy fathers; and this people will rise up, and go a whoring after the gods of the strangers of the land, whither they go to be among them, and will forsake me, and break my covenant which I have made with them.... [19] Now therefore write ye this song for you, and teach it the children of Israel: put it in their mouths, that *this song may be a witness*[1] for me against the children of Israel.... [21] And it shall come to pass, when many evils and troubles are befallen them, that *this song shall testify against them as a witness*.

[22] Moses therefore wrote this song the same day, and taught it the children of Israel.... [29] For I know that after my death ye will utterly corrupt yourselves, and turn aside from the way which I have commanded you; and evil will befall you *in the latter days*; because ye will do evil in the sight of the LORD, to provoke him to anger through the work of your hands. (Deut 31:16, 19, 21–22, 29)

The Song of Moses

[30] And Moses spake in the ears of all the congregation of Israel the words of this song, until they were ended. (Deut 31:30)

---

1 All italics in this Appendix are mine.

¹ Give ear, O ye heavens, and I will speak; and hear, O earth, the words of my mouth. ² My doctrine shall drop as the rain, my speech shall distil as the dew, as the small rain upon the tender herb, and as the showers upon the grass: ³ because I will publish the name of the LORD: ascribe ye greatness unto our God. ⁴ He is the Rock, his work is perfect: for all his ways are judgment: a God of truth and without iniquity, just and right is he. ⁵ They have corrupted themselves, their spot is not the spot of his children: they are a perverse and crooked generation. ⁶ Do ye thus requite the LORD, O foolish people and unwise? is not he thy father that hath bought thee? hath he not made thee, and established thee?

⁷ Remember the days of old, consider the years of many generations: ask thy father, and he will shew thee; thy elders, and they will tell thee. ⁸ When the most High divided to the nations their inheritance, when he separated the sons of Adam, he set the bounds of the people according to the number of the children of Israel. ⁹ For the LORD'S portion is his people; Jacob is the lot of his inheritance. ¹⁰ He found him in a desert land, and in the waste howling wilderness; he led him about, he instructed him, he kept him as the apple of his eye. ¹¹ As an eagle stirreth up her nest, fluttereth over her young, spreadeth abroad her wings, taketh them, beareth them on her wings: ¹² so the LORD alone did lead him, and there was no strange god with him. ¹³ He made him ride on the high places of the earth, that he might eat the increase of the fields; and he made him to suck honey out of the rock, and oil out of the flinty rock; ¹⁴ butter of kine, and milk of sheep, with fat of lambs, and rams of the breed of Bashan, and goats, with the fat of kidneys of wheat; and thou didst drink the pure blood of the grape.

¹⁵ But Jeshurun waxed fat, and kicked: thou art waxen fat, thou art grown thick, thou art covered with fatness; then he forsook God which made him, and lightly esteemed the Rock of his salvation. ¹⁶ They provoked him to jealousy with strange gods, with abominations provoked they him to anger. ¹⁷ They sacrificed unto devils, not to God; to gods

whom they knew not, to new gods that came newly up, whom your fathers feared not. [18] Of the Rock that begat thee thou art unmindful, and hast forgotten God that formed thee.

[19] And when the LORD saw it, he abhorred them, because of the provoking of his sons, and of his daughters. [20] And he said, I will hide my face from them, I will see what their end shall be: for they are a very froward generation, children in whom is no faith. [21] They have moved me to jealousy with that which is not God; they have provoked me to anger with their vanities: and I will move them to jealousy with those which are not a people; I will provoke them to anger with a foolish nation. [22] For a fire is kindled in mine anger, and shall burn unto the lowest hell, and shall consume the earth with her increase, and set on fire the foundations of the mountains. [23] I will heap mischiefs upon them; I will spend mine arrows upon them. [24] They shall be burnt with hunger, and devoured with burning heat, and with bitter destruction: I will also send the teeth of beasts upon them, with the poison of serpents of the dust. [25] The sword without, and terror within, shall destroy both the young man and the virgin, the suckling also with the man of gray hairs.

[26] I said, I would scatter them into corners, I would make the remembrance of them to cease from among men: [27] were it not that I feared the wrath of the enemy, lest their adversaries should behave themselves strangely, and lest they should say, Our hand is high, and the LORD hath not done all this. [28] For they are a nation void of counsel, neither is there any understanding in them. [29] O that they were wise, that they understood this, that they would consider their latter end! [30] How should one chase a thousand, and two put ten thousand to flight, except their Rock had sold them, and the LORD had shut them up? [31] For their rock is not as our Rock, even our enemies themselves being judges. [32] For their vine is of the vine of Sodom, and of the fields of Gomorrah: their grapes are grapes of gall, their clusters are bitter: [33] their wine is the poison of dragons, and the cruel venom of asps. [34] Is not this laid up in store with me, and sealed up among my treasures? [35] To

me belongeth vengeance, and recompence; their foot shall slide in due time: for the day of their calamity is at hand, and the things that shall come upon them make haste. 36 For the LORD shall judge his people, and repent himself for his servants, when he seeth that their power is gone, and there is none shut up, or left. 37 And he shall say, Where are their gods, their rock in whom they trusted, 38 which did eat the fat of their sacrifices, and drank the wine of their drink offerings? let them rise up and help you, and be your protection.

39 See now that I, even I, am he, and there is no god with me: I kill, and I make alive; I wound, and I heal: neither is there any that can deliver out of my hand. 40 For I lift up my hand to heaven, and say, I live for ever. 41 If I whet my glittering sword, and mine hand take hold on judgment; I will render vengeance to mine enemies, and will reward them that hate me. 42 I will make mine arrows drunk with blood, and my sword shall devour flesh; and that with the blood of the slain and of the captives, from the beginning of revenges upon the enemy. 43 Rejoice, O ye nations, with his people: for he will avenge the blood of his servants, and will render vengeance to his adversaries, and will be merciful unto his land, and to his people.

44 And Moses came and spake all the words of this song in the ears of the people, he, and Hoshea the son of Nun. 45 And Moses made an end of speaking all these words to all Israel. (Deut 32:1–45)

Singing the Song of Moses in the Last Days of the Mosaic Age

The following list contains selected quotations of and allusions to the Song of Moses in the New Testament. The Song is about Israel's "latter days" and God's judgment of her at that time. The New Testament writers wrote knowing that that judgment would come in their generation; Jesus had told them of it in the Olivet Discourse and in other similar passages.

Quotations

Song: "They have moved me to jealousy with that which is not God; they have provoked me to anger with their vanities: and *I will move them to jealousy with those which are not a people; I will provoke them to anger with a foolish nation."* (Deut 32:21)

Paul: "But I say, Did not Israel know? First Moses saith, *I will provoke you to jealousy by them that are no people, and by a foolish nation I will anger you.*" (Rom 10:19)

Note: Paul's quotation of the Song of Moses comes in his discussion of Israel's fall (Rom 11:12), as God was breaking off her dead branches (Rom 11:21). This context conforms to the announced purpose of the Song as God's witness in the "latter days."

Song: "I will make mine arrows drunk with blood, and my sword shall devour flesh; and that with the blood of the slain and of the captives, from the beginning of revenges upon the enemy. *Rejoice, O ye nations, with his people*: for he will avenge the blood of his servants, and will render vengeance to his adversaries, and will be merciful unto his land, and to his people." (Deut 32:42–43)

Paul: "Now I say that Jesus Christ was a minister of the circumcision for the truth of God, to confirm the promises made unto the fathers: and that the Gentiles might glorify God for his mercy; as it is written, For this cause I will confess to thee among the Gentiles, and sing unto thy name. And again he saith, *Rejoice, ye Gentiles, with his people*." (Rom 15:8–10; cp. Heb 1:6)

Note: God would judge Israel to bring salvation to the nations; so says the Song, and so says the apostle. Jesus said the same in the Olivet Discourse: he would gather his elect among the nations after Israel's "great tribulation" (Matt 24:21, 31).

Allusions

Song: "My doctrine shall drop as the rain, my speech shall distil as the dew, as the small rain upon the tender herb, and as the showers upon the grass." (Deut 32:2)

Paul: "I have planted, Apollos watered; but God gave the increase." (1 Cor 3:6)

Note: God's true doctrine "dropped as the rain" in Israel's last days. Paul delivered his churches to that doctrine (Rom 6:17 NKJV).

Song: "*He is the Rock.*" (Deut 32:4)
Peter and Christ: "And Simon Peter answered and said, *Thou art the Christ, the Son of the living God.* And Jesus answered and said unto him, Blessed art thou, Simon Barjona: for flesh and blood hath not revealed it unto thee, but my Father which is in heaven. And I say also unto thee, That thou art Peter, and *upon this rock I will build my church*; and the gates of hell shall not prevail against it." (Matt 16:16–18)
Paul: "And did all drink the same spiritual drink: for they drank of that spiritual Rock that followed them: and *that Rock was Christ.*" (1 Cor 10:4)
Note: Israel rejected the Rock during her last days; the church is built on that Rock.

Song: "His work is perfect: for all his ways are judgment: a God of truth and without iniquity, just and right is he." (Deut 32:4)
Jesus: "I am the way, the truth, and the life: no man cometh unto the Father, but by me." (John 14:6)
The saints: "Great and marvellous are thy works, Lord God Almighty; just and true are thy ways, thou King of saints." (Rev 15:3)
Note: *Jesus* is the God of truth and without iniquity. Israel rejected him, and his "ways of judgment" destroyed her in the apostles' generation (cp. Matt 10:6–7, 15, 23). Those Jews had "a terrifying expectation of judgment and the fury of a fire *about to consume the adversaries.…* [because God] said, Vengeance belongs to Me, I will repay, and again, *The Lord will judge His people*" (Heb 10:26, 30 HCSB). That judgment came on God's Mosaic-age people as Jesus had predicted in the Olivet Discourse.

Song: "They have dealt corruptly with him; *they are no longer his children* because they are blemished; they are a crooked and twisted generation." (Deut 32:5 ESV)

Jesus: "*Ye are of your father the devil*, and the lusts of your father ye will do." (John 8:44)

Peter: "And with many other words he bore witness and continued to exhort them, saying, 'Save yourselves from this crooked generation.'" (Acts 2:40 ESV; cp. Matt 17:17; Acts 2:40; Phil 2:14–15 ESV)

Note: Israel after the flesh rejected their Messiah. God officially ended his covenant with them when the temple fell; they are no longer his covenant children. God's messianic-age Spirit-born children are now "joint-heirs with Christ" (Rom 8:17).

Song: "Do ye thus requite the LORD, O foolish people and unwise? is not he thy father that hath bought thee? hath he not made thee, and established thee?" (Deut 32:6)

Peter: "But there were false prophets also among the people, even as there shall be false teachers among you, who privily shall bring in damnable heresies, even denying *the Lord that bought them*, and bring upon themselves swift destruction." (2 Pet 2:1)

Paul: "For *ye are bought with a price*: therefore glorify God in your body, and in your spirit, which are God's." (1 Cor 6:20; cp. 1 Cor 7:23; Eph 2:14)

Note: God bought Israel after the flesh in the Exodus. The false prophets in the "last days" of the Mosaic age denied him by "turning the grace of our God into lasciviousness" (Jude 4). Through Christ, God has bought, made, and established the antitypical Israel.

Song: "When the most High divided to the nations their inheritance, when he separated the sons of Adam, he set the bounds of the people according to the number of the children of Israel." (Deut 32:8)

Paul: "And hath made of one blood all nations of men for to dwell on all the face of the earth, and hath determined the times before appointed, and *the bounds of their habitation; That they should seek the Lord, if haply they might feel after him, and find him*, though he be not far from every one of us." (Acts 17:26–27)

Note: God set the bounds of Israel after the flesh in the land he gave them. The bounds of Israel after the Spirit extend to the entire world so that all nations might find God.

Song: "For the LORD'S portion is his people; Jacob is the lot of his inheritance." (Deut 32:9)
Paul: "Who gave himself for us, that he might redeem us from all iniquity, and purify unto himself a peculiar people, zealous of good works." (Tit 2:14)
Peter: "But ye are a chosen generation, a royal priesthood, an holy nation, a peculiar people; that ye should shew forth the praises of him who hath called you out of darkness into his marvellous light: which in time past were not a people, but are now the people of God: which had not obtained mercy, but now have obtained mercy." (1 Pet 2:9–10)
Note: The Lord's portion is his people. In the Old Covenant, he defined that people according to the flesh, but, in the New Covenant, according to the Spirit.

Song: "As an eagle stirreth up her nest, fluttereth over her young, spreadeth abroad her wings, taketh them, beareth them on her wings: so the LORD alone did lead him, and there was no strange god with him." (Deut 32:11–12)
Jesus: "For wheresoever the carcase is, there will the eagles be gathered together." (Matt 24:28); "And they answered and said unto him, Where, Lord? And he said unto them, Wheresoever the body is, thither will the eagles be gathered together." (Luke 17:37)
Note: God used positive eagle imagery to describe the start of the Mosaic age and negative eagle imagery to describe its end.

Song: "Of the Rock who begot you, you are unmindful, and have forgotten the God who fathered you." (Deut 32:18 NKJV)
Jesus: "Marvel not that I said unto thee, Ye [plural] *must be born again*." (John 3:7)

Peter: "Blessed be the God and Father of our Lord Jesus Christ, which according to his abundant mercy hath *begotten us again unto a lively hope by the resurrection of Jesus Christ* from the dead." (1 Pet 1:3)

Note: God gave birth to Israel after the flesh as a type; he gave birth to Israel after the Spirit as the antitype. Israel has been born again as a holy nation by the resurrection of Christ.

Song: "For fire has been kindled because of My anger and burns to the depths of Sheol; it devours the land and its produce, and scorches the foundations of the mountains." (Deut 32:22 HCSB)

Paul: "The Jews … both killed the Lord Jesus, and their own prophets, and have persecuted us; and they please not God, and are contrary to all men: forbidding us to speak to the Gentiles that they might be saved, to fill up their sins alway: *for the wrath is come upon them to the uttermost*" (1 Thess 2:14–16); "*In flaming fire taking vengeance on them* that know not God, and that obey not the gospel of our Lord Jesus Christ." (2 Thess 1:8)

Note: God's fiery wrath—in the form of Roman "scorched earth" tactics—would soon "devour the land" of Israel after Paul wrote these words. Everlasting destruction awaited those who were not covered by the blood of Christ.

Song: "For they are a nation void of counsel, neither is there any understanding in them." (Deut 32:28)

Paul: "But the natural man receiveth not the things of the Spirit of God: for they are foolishness unto him: neither can he know them, because they are spiritually discerned." (1 Cor 2:14)

Note: In Paul's thinking, the natural is first and the spiritual second (1 Cor 15:46). Israel after the flesh could not discern the spiritual things of the kingdom of heaven. This order is true for individuals, but also in a corporate sense: "Israel hath not obtained that which he seeketh for; but the election hath obtained it, and the rest were blinded" (Rom 11:7).

Song: "O that they were wise, that they understood this, that they would consider *their latter end!*" (Deut 32:29)

Jesus: "And when he was come near, he beheld the city, and wept over it, saying ... the days shall come upon thee, that thine enemies shall cast a trench about thee, and compass thee round, and keep thee in on every side, and shall lay thee even with the ground, and thy children within thee; and they shall not leave in thee one stone upon another; because thou knewest not the time of thy visitation." (Luke 19:41–44)

Note: The "latter end" of Israel after the flesh was destruction.

Song: "To me belongeth vengeance, and recompence; their foot shall slide in due time: for the day of their calamity is at hand, and the things that shall come upon them make haste. For the LORD shall judge his people, and repent himself for his servants, when he seeth that their power is gone, and there is none shut up, or left." (Deut 32:35–36)

Jesus: "For these be the days of vengeance, that all things which are written may be fulfilled." (Luke 21:22)

Paul: "For we know him that hath said, Vengeance belongeth unto me, I will recompense, saith the Lord. And again, The Lord shall judge his people." (Heb 10:30)

Peter: "And through covetousness shall they with feigned words make merchandise of you: whose judgment now of a long time lingereth not, and their damnation slumbereth not." (2 Pet 2:3)

Note: God's vengeance against his Mosaic-age people would come in Jesus' generation (Luke 21:32); the Son of Man would come in judgment very, very shortly (Heb 10:37).

Song: "If I sharpen My [lightning][2] sword, and My hand takes hold on justice, I will render vengeance on My adversaries, and I will repay those who hate Me." (Deut 32:41 NASB)

---

2 Marginal reading.

Jesus: "For as the lightning doth come forth from the east, and doth appear unto the west, so shall be also the presence of the Son of Man." (Matt 24:27 YLT)

Note: God's lightning sword struck Israel after the flesh in Jesus' generation (Matt 24:34); Jesus' presence (i.e. *parousia*) abides now with his churches.

Song: "Rejoice, O ye nations, with his people: for he will avenge the blood of his servants, and will render vengeance to his adversaries, and will be merciful unto his land, and to his people." (Deut 32:43)

Jesus: "Wherefore, behold, I send unto you prophets, and wise men, and scribes: and some of them ye shall kill and crucify; and some of them shall ye scourge in your synagogues, and persecute them from city to city: that upon you may come all the righteous blood shed upon the earth, from the blood of righteous Abel unto the blood of Zacharias son of Barachias, whom ye slew between the temple and the altar. Verily I say unto you, All these things shall come upon this generation." (Matt 23:34–36)

Jesus: "It cannot be that a prophet perish out of Jerusalem." (Luke 13:33)

Jesus: "And shall not God avenge his own elect, which cry day and night unto him, though he bear long with them? I tell you that he will avenge them speedily. Nevertheless when the Son of man cometh, shall he find faith [on the land; Gk. *epi tēs gēs*]?" (Luke 18:6–8)

The saints: "And they were crying with a great voice, saying, 'Till when, O Master, the Holy and the True, dost Thou not judge and take vengeance of our blood *from those dwelling upon the land* (Gk. *epi tēs gēs*) ?'" (Rev 6:10 YLT)

Jesus: "For these be the days of vengeance, that all things which are written may be fulfilled." (Luke 21:22)

Paul: "In the hope rejoicing; *in the tribulation enduring*; in the prayer persevering ... not avenging yourselves, beloved, but give place to the wrath, for it hath been written, '*Vengeance is Mine, I will recompense again*, saith the Lord.'" (Rom 12:19–20 YLT)

Note: The nations rejoice that God avenged the blood of his servants spilled by Israel after the flesh, for that was necessary to bring the blessings of the messianic age to them.

A Reference to the Song of Moses by Name

The Scriptures mention the Song of Moses by name in one other passage:

> And I saw another sign in heaven, great and marvellous, seven angels having the seven last plagues; for in them is filled up the wrath of God. And I saw as it were a sea of glass mingled with fire: and them that had gotten the victory over the beast, and over his image, and over his mark, and over the number of his name, stand on the sea of glass, having the harps of God. *And they sing the song of Moses* the servant of God, and the song of the Lamb, saying, Great and marvellous are thy works, Lord God Almighty; just and true are thy ways, thou King of saints. Who shall not fear thee, O Lord, and glorify thy name? for thou only art holy: for all nations shall come and worship before thee; for thy judgments are made manifest. (Rev 15:1–4)

Note: The apostles on the earth sang the Song of Moses in their generation; the saints in heaven were doing so, too. This suggests John wrote the Revelation before the temple's fall.

Conclusion

These passages fit well in the inmillennial prophetic model we have discovered. Jesus, the apostles, and the saints in heaven sang the Song of Moses in Israel's "latter days." This singing announced the wrath of God about to come on Israel after the flesh and prepared for the messianic age in which "all nations shall come and worship" (Rev 15:4) the true God.

APPENDIX F

1 Corinthians 15

The Gospel Foundation

[1] Moreover, brethren, I declare unto you the gospel which I preached unto you, which also ye have received, and wherein ye stand; [2] by which also ye are saved, if ye keep in memory what I preached unto you, unless ye have believed in vain. [3] For I delivered unto you first of all that which I also received, how that Christ died for our sins according to the scriptures; [4] and that he was buried, and that he rose again the third day according to the scriptures: [5] and that he was seen of Cephas, then of the twelve: [6] after that, he was seen of above five hundred brethren at once; of whom the greater part remain unto this present, but some are fallen asleep. [7] After that, he was seen of James; then of all the apostles. [8] And last of all he was seen of me also, as of one born out of due time. [9] For I am the least of the apostles, that am not meet to be called an apostle, because I persecuted the church of God. [10] But by the grace of God I am what I am: and his grace which *was bestowed*[1] upon me was not in vain; but I laboured more abundantly than they all: yet not I, but the grace of God which was with me. [11] Therefore whether *it were* I or they, so we preach, and so ye believed. (1 Cor 15:1–11)

The Resurrection of Christ

[12] Now if Christ be preached that he rose from the dead, how say some among you that there is no resurrection of the dead? [13] But if there be no resurrection of the dead, then is Christ not risen: [14] and if Christ be

---

1 The translators of the King James (Authorized) Version used italics to mark words not in the Greek manuscripts. All italics in this Appendix are in the original.

not risen, then *is* our preaching vain, and your faith *is* also vain. [15] Yea, and we are found false witnesses of God; because we have testified of God that he raised up Christ: whom he raised not up, if so be that the dead rise not. [16] For if the dead rise not, then is not Christ raised: [17] and if Christ be not raised, your faith *is* vain; ye are yet in your sins. [18] Then they also which are fallen asleep in Christ are perished. [19] If in this life only we have hope in Christ, we are of all men most miserable. (1 Cor 15:12–19)

The Reign of Christ

[20] But now is Christ risen from the dead, *and* become the firstfruits of them that slept. [21] For since by man *came* death, by man *came* also the resurrection of the dead. [22] For as in Adam all die, even so in Christ shall all be made alive. [23] But every man in his own order: Christ the firstfruits; afterward they that are Christ's at his coming.

[24] Then *cometh* the end, when he shall have delivered up the kingdom to God, even the Father; when he shall have put down all rule and all authority and power. [25] For he must reign, till he hath put all enemies under his feet. [26] The last enemy *that* shall be destroyed *is* death. [27] For he hath put all things under his feet. But when he saith all things are put under *him, it is* manifest that he is excepted, which did put all things under him. [28] And when all things shall be subdued unto him, then shall the Son also himself be subject unto him that put all things under him, that God may be all in all. [29] Else what shall they do which are baptized for the dead, if the dead rise not at all? why are they then baptized for the dead? [30] And why stand we in jeopardy every hour? [31] I protest by your rejoicing which I have in Christ Jesus our Lord, I die daily. [32] If after the manner of men I have fought with beasts at Ephesus, what advantageth it me, if the dead rise not? let us eat and drink; for to morrow we die. [33] Be not deceived: evil communications corrupt good manners. [34] Awake to righteousness, and sin not; for some have not the knowledge of God: I speak *this* to your shame. (1 Cor 15:20–34)

1 CORINTHIANS 15

The Resurrection of Christ's People

35 But some *man* will say, How are the dead raised up? and with what body do they come? 36 *Thou* fool, that which thou sowest is not quickened, except it die: 37 And that which thou sowest, thou sowest not that body that shall be, but bare grain, it may chance of wheat, or of some other *grain*: 38 But God giveth it a body as it hath pleased him, and to every seed his own body. 39 All flesh *is* not the same flesh: but *there is* one *kind of* flesh of men, another flesh of beasts, another of fishes, *and* another of birds. 40 *There are* also celestial bodies, and bodies terrestrial: but the glory of the celestial *is* one, and the *glory* of the terrestrial *is* another. 41 *There is* one glory of the sun, and another glory of the moon, and another glory of the stars: for *one* star differeth from *another* star in glory. 42 So also *is* the resurrection of the dead. It is sown in corruption; it is raised in incorruption: 43 it is sown in dishonour; it is raised in glory: it is sown in weakness; it is raised in power: 44 it is sown a natural body; it is raised a spiritual body.

There is a natural body, and there is a spiritual body. 45 And so it is written, The first man Adam was made a living soul; the last Adam *was made* a quickening spirit. 46 Howbeit that *was* not first which is spiritual, but that which is natural; and afterward that which is spiritual. 47 The first man *is* of the earth, earthy: the second man *is* the Lord from heaven. 48 As *is* the earthy, such *are* they also that are earthy: and as *is* the heavenly, such *are* they also that are heavenly. 49 And as we have borne the image of the earthy, we shall also bear the image of the heavenly. (1 Cor 15:35–49)

The Reign of Christ's People

50 Now this I say, brethren, that flesh and blood cannot inherit the kingdom of God; neither doth corruption inherit incorruption. 51 Behold, I shew you a mystery; We shall not all sleep, but we shall all be changed, 52 in a moment, in the twinkling of an eye, at the last trump: for the trumpet shall sound, and the dead shall be raised incorruptible, and we shall be changed. 53 For this corruptible must put on incorrup-

tion, and this mortal *must* put on immortality. ⁵⁴ So when this corruptible shall have put on incorruption, and this mortal shall have put on immortality, then shall be brought to pass the saying that is written,

> Death is swallowed up in victory.
> ⁵⁵ O death, where *is* thy sting?
> O grave, where *is* thy victory?

⁵⁶ The sting of death *is* sin; and the strength of sin *is* the law. ⁵⁷ But thanks *be* to God, which giveth us the victory through our Lord Jesus Christ. ⁵⁸ Therefore, my beloved brethren, be ye stedfast, unmoveable, always abounding in the work of the Lord, forasmuch as ye know that your labour is not in vain in the Lord. (1 Cor 15:50–58)

Bibliography

Adler, Mortimer J., and Charles Van Doren. *How to Read a Book: The Classic Guide to Intelligent Reading*. Revised ed. N.p.: Touchstone, 1972.
Alexander, Joseph Addison. *Commentary on the Prophecies of Isaiah*. Edited by John Eadie. 1875. Repr., Grand Rapids: Zondervan, 1953.
Alexander, Ralph H. "Ezekiel." Pages 735–996 in *Isaiah–Ezekiel*. Vol. 6 of *The Expositor's Bible Commentary*. Edited by Frank E. Gaebelein. Grand Rapids: Zondervan, 1986.
Alford, Henry. *The Epistle to the Hebrews, the Catholic Epistles, and the Revelation*. Vol. 2.2 of *The New Testament for English Readers*. London: Rivingtons, 1863.
———. *Alford's Greek Testament: An Exegetical and Critical Commentary*. 4 vols. Grand Rapids: Baker, 1980.
Archer, Gleason L., Jr. "Daniel." Pages 3–158 in *Daniel–Minor Prophets*. Vol. 7 of *The Expositor's Bible Commentary*. Edited by Frank E. Gaebelein. Grand Rapids: Zondervan, 1986.
Barbieri, Louis A., Jr. "Matthew." Pages 13–94 in vol. 2 of *The Bible Knowledge Commentary: An Exposition of the Scriptures*. Edited by J. F. Walvoord, and R. B. Zuck. Wheaton, IL: Victor, 1985.
Barker, Kenneth L. "Zechariah." Pages 593–698 in *Daniel–Minor Prophets*. Vol. 7 of *The Expositor's Bible Commentary: Daniel and the Minor Prophets*. Edited by Frank E. Gaebelein. Grand Rapids: Zondervan, 1985.
Beale, G. K. *The Book of Revelation: A Commentary on the Greek Text*. The New International Greek Testament Commentary. Grand Rapids: W. B. Eerdmans, 1999.
Beetham, Christopher A. *Echoes of Scripture in the Letter of Paul to the Colossians*. Leiden: Brill, 1980.
Benware, Paul N. *Understanding End Times Prophecy: A Comprehensive Approach*. Chicago: Moody, 2006.
Blomberg, Craig L. "Matthew." Pages 1–110 in *Commentary on the New Testament Use of the Old Testament*. Edited by G. K. Beale, and D. A. Carson. Grand Rapids: Baker Academic, 2007.
Blomberg, Craig L., and Sung Wook Chung. "Introduction." Pages xi–xix in *A Case for Historic Premillennialism: An Alternative to "Left Behind" Eschatology*. Edited by Craig L. Blomberg, and Sung Wook Chung. Grand Rapids: Baker Academic, 2009.

Brannan, Rick, Ken M. Penner, Israel Loken, Michael Aubrey, and Isaiah Hoogendyk, eds. *The Lexham English Septuagint*. Bellingham, WA: Lexham Press, 2012.

Braumann, Georg. "παρουσία." Pages 898–901 in vol. 2 of *The New International Dictionary of New Testament Theology*. Edited by Colin Brown. Grand Rapids: Zondervan, 1976.

Bray, John L. *Matthew 24 Fulfilled*. 5th ed. Powder Springs, GA: American Vision, 2008.

Broomall, Wick. "Type, Typology." in *Baker's Dictionary of Theology*. Edited by Everett F. Harrison, Geoffrey W. Bromiley, and Carl F. H. Henry. Grand Rapids: Baker, 1975.

Büchsel, Friedrich. "γενεά, κτλ." Pages 662–63 in vol. 1 of *Theological Dictionary of the New Testament*. Edited by Gerhard Kittel. Translated by Geoffrey W. Bromiley. Grand Rapids: Eerdmans, 1964–76.

Bullinger, Ethelbert W. *A Critical Lexicon and Concordance to the English and Greek New Testament*. London: Bagster, 1971.

———. *Figures of Speech Used in the Bible Explained and Illustrated*. Grand Rapids: Baker, 1968.

Campbell, James M. *The Presence*. New York: Eaton & Mains, 1911.

Carson, D. A. "Matthew." Pages 1–600 in *Matthew, Mark, Luke*. Vol. 8 of *The Expositor's Bible Commentary*. Edited by Frank E. Gaebelein. Grand Rapids: Zondervan, 1984.

Carson, D. A., Douglas J. Moo, and Leon Morris. *An Introduction to the New Testament*. Grand Rapids: Zondervan, 1992.

Churton, W. R. *The Uncanonical and Apocryphal Scriptures*. London: J. Whitaker, 1884.

Clarke, Adam. *The Old and New Testaments With a Commentary and Critical Notes*. 6 vols. Nashville: Abingdon, [1970?].

Covey, Stephen R. *Seven Habits of Highly Effective People: Restoring the Character Ethic*. 1st ed. New York: Simon & Schuster, 1989.

Cox, William E. *An Examination of Dispensationalism*. Phillipsburg, NJ: Presbyterian and Reformed, 1963.

———. *Amillennialism Today*. Phillipsburg, NJ: Presbyterian and Reformed, 1966.

Craigie, Peter C., Page H. Kelley, and Joel F. Drinkard Jr. *Jeremiah 1–25*. Word Biblical Commentary. Vol. 26. Dallas: Thomas Nelson, 1991.

Cremer, Hermann. *Biblico-Theological Lexicon of New Testament Greek.* Translated by William Urwick. 4th English ed. New York: Charles Scribner's Sons, 1895.

Danker, Frederick W., Walter Bauer, William F. Arndt, and F. Wilbur Gingrich, eds. *Greek-English Lexicon of the New Testament and Other Early Christian Literature.* 3rd ed. Chicago: University of Chicago Press, 2000.

Deissmann, Adolf. *Light From the Ancient East; the New Testament Illustrated By Recently Discovered Texts of the Graeco-Roman World.* Translated by Lionel R. M. Strachan. 4th ed. 1922. Repr., Grand Rapids: Baker, 1978.

DeMar, Gary. *Last Days Madness: Obsession of the Modern Church.* 4th ed. Atlanta: American Vision, 1999.

"The Forty Years in Biblical Typology." Todd Dennis. http://www.preteristarchive.com/Preterism/dennis-todd_p_40.html.

Dodd, C. H. *The Apostolic Preaching and Its Developments.* 2nd ed. New York: Harper & Brothers, 1954.

Elwell, Walter A., and Philip W. Comfort. *Tyndale Bible Dictionary.* Wheaton, IL: Tyndale House, 2001.

Fairbairn, Patrick. *Typology of Scripture.* 1900. Repr., Grand Rapids: Kregel, 1989.

Farquharson, James. *A New Illustration of the Latter Part of Daniel's Last Vision and Prophecy.* London: Smith, Elder, and Co., 1838.

Frame, John M. *Salvation Belongs to the Lord: An Introduction to Systematic Theology.* Phillipsburg, NJ: P&R, 2006.

France, R. T. *The Gospel of Matthew.* The New International Commentary on the New Testament. Edited by Ned B. Stonehouse, F. F. Bruce, and Gordon D. Fee. Grand Rapids: William B. Eerdmans, 2007.

Freed, Edwin D. *The New Testament: A Critical Introduction.* Belmont, CA: Wadsworth, 1986.

Friberg, T., B. Friberg, and N. F. Miller. *Analytical Lexicon of the Greek New Testament.* Grand Rapids: Baker, 2000.

Garrett, Duane A. *Proverbs, Ecclesiastes, Song of Songs.* Vol. 14 of *The New American Commentary.* Nashville: Broadman & Holman, 1993.

Gentry, Kenneth L., Jr. *He Shall Have Dominion: A Postmillennial Eschatology.* 2nd ed. Tyler, TX: Institute for Christian Economics, 1992.

———. *The Book of Revelation Made Easy.* 2nd ed. Powder Springs, GA: American Vision, 2010.

Gill, John. *An Exposition of the Old and New Testaments.* 9 vols. 1809–10. Repr., Paris, AR: The Baptist Standard Bearer, 1989.

Gingerich, Owen. *The Book Nobody Read: Chasing the Revolutions of Nicolaus Copernicus.* New York: Walker & Company, 2004.

Godet, Frederic Louis. *Commentary on First Corinthians.* 1889. Repr., Grand Rapids: Kregel, 1977.

Goldingay, John E. *Daniel.* Word Biblical Commentary. Vol. 30. Edited by David A. Hubbard. Dallas: Word, 1989.

Goodwin, Frank J. *A Harmony of the Life of St. Paul.* Grand Rapids: Baker, 1977.

Gouge, William. *Commentary on Hebrews.* 1866. Repr., Grand Rapids: Kregel, 1980.

Gould, Ezra P. *The Gospel According to St. Mark.* The International Critical Commentary. Edited by Alfred Plummer, and Samuel R. Driver. New York: Charles Scribner's Sons, 1896.

Gove, Philip Babcock, ed. *Webster's Third New International Dictionary of the English Language, Unabridged.* Springfield, MA: G. & C. Merriam Co., 1981.

Grenz, Stanley J. *The Millennial Maze: Sorting Out Evangelical Options.* Downers Grove, IL: IVP Academic, 2007.

Grogan, Geoffrey W. "Isaiah." Pages 1–354 in *Isaiah–Ezekiel.* Vol. 6 of *The Expositor's Bible Commentary.* Edited by Frank E. Gaebelein. Grand Rapids: Zondervan, 1986.

Gundry, Robert H. *The Church and the Tribulation.* Grand Rapids: Zondervan, 1973.

———. *Matthew: A Commentary on His Literary and Theological Art.* Grand Rapids: Eerdmans, 1982.

Hagner, Donald A. *Matthew 14–28.* Word Biblical Commentary. Vol. 33B. Edited by Bruce M. Metzger. Dallas: Word, 1998.

Hamilton, Floyd E. *The Basis of Millennial Faith.* Grand Rapids: Wm. B. Eerdmans, 1942.

Hart, John F. "Should Pretribulationists Reconsider the Rapture in Matthew 24:36–44?" *JGES* 20 (2007): 47–70.

Hawker, Robert. *The Poor Man's Concordance and Dictionary to the Sacred Scriptures.* London: Ebenezer Palmer, 1828.

Hawking, Stephen. *A Brief History of Time/The Universe in a Nutshell: Two Books in One.* New York: Bantam, 2007.

Hendriksen, William. *Exposition of the Gospel According to Matthew.* New Testament Commentary. Grand Rapids: Baker, 1973.

Hindson, Edward E. "Matthew." Pages 1867–965 in *KJV Bible Commentary*. Edited by Edward E. Hindson, and Woodrow Michael Kroll. Nashville: Thomas Nelson, 1994.

Hollett, Brock D. *Debunking Preterism: How Over-Realized Eschatology Misses the "Not Yet" of Bible Prophecy*. Kearney, NE: Morris Publishing, 2018.

Hulse, Erroll. "A Christianized World? The Post-Millennial Universal Reign of Christ." Paper presented at The Fourth International Baptist Conference. Toronto, 19 October 1988.

"IHEU Minimum Statement on Humanism." Humanists International, General Assembly. (1996): https://humanists.international/policy/iheu-minimum-statement-on-humanism/.

Ice, Thomas. "The Destructive View of Preterism." Paper presented at The 2nd Annual Meeting of the Conservative Theological Society. Ft. Worth, TX, 3 August 1999.

"Is 2012 Going to be the 'End of the World?'." http://mayas2012ingles.blogspot.com/2011/04/is-2012-going-to-be-end-of-world.html.

Jamieson, Robert, A. R. Fausset, and David Brown. *A Commentary, Critical and Explanatory, on the Old and New Testaments*. 2 vols. Hartford, CT: S. S. Scranton, 1871.

———. *A Commentary, Critical, Experimental and Practical on the Old and New Testaments*. 3 vols. n.d. Repr., Grand Rapids: Eerdmans, 1976.

Johnson, Sherman E. "The Gospel According to St. Matthew." Pages 229–626 in vol. 7 of *The Interpreter's Bible*. Edited by George Arthur Buttrick. Nashville: Abingdon, 1951.

Jones, Russell Bradley. *The Latter Days*. 1947. Repr., Grand Rapids: Baker, 1961.

Jordan, James B. *Through New Eyes: Developing a Biblical View of the World*. Brentwood, TN: Wolgemuth & Hyatt, 1988.

Josephus, Flavius. *The Works of Flavius Josephus*. Translated by William Whiston. 4 vols. Grand Rapids: Baker, 1974.

Kalland, Earl S. "Deuteronomy." Pages 1–235 in *Deuteronomy–2 Samuel*. Vol. 3 of *The Expositor's Bible Commentary*. Edited by Frank E. Gaebelein. Grand Rapids: Zondervan, 1992.

Karsh, Efraim. *Islamic Imperialism*. New Haven, CT: Yale University Press, 2006.

Keener, Craig S. *The Gospel of Matthew: A Socio-Rhetorical Commentary*. Grand Rapids: Eerdmans, 2009.

Kik, J. Marcellus. *An Eschatology of Victory*. Nutley, NJ: Presbyterian and Reformed, 1975.

King, Max R. *The Cross and the Parousia of Christ: The Two Dimensions of One Age-Changing Eschaton*. Warren, OH: Parkman Road Church of Christ, 1987.

Kittel, Gerhard. "εἰκών." Pages 381–97 in vol. 2 of *Theological Dictionary of the New Testament*. Edited by Gerhard Kittel. Translated by Geoffrey W. Bromiley. Grand Rapids: Eerdmans, 1964–76.

Kittel, Gerhard, Geoffrey W. Bromiley, and Gerhard Friedrich, eds. *Theological Dictionary of the New Testament*. 10 vols. Grand Rapids: Eerdmans, 1964–76.

Klein, William W., Craig L. Blomberg, and Robert L. Hubbard Jr. *Introduction to Biblical Interpretation*. Edited by Kermit A. Ecklebarger. Dallas: Word, 1993.

Köstenberger, Andreas J., and Peter Thomas O'Brien. *Salvation to the Ends of the Earth: A Biblical Theology of Mission*. Downers Grove, IL: InterVarsity, 2001.

Ladd, George Eldon. *A Commentary on the Revelation of John*. Grand Rapids: Eerdmans, 1974.

———. *Crucial Questions About the Kingdom of God*. Grand Rapids: Eerdmans, 1954.

———. *The Last Things: An Eschatology for Laymen*. Grand Rapids: Eerdmans, 1978.

———. "Historic Premillennialism." Pages 15–60 in *The Meaning of the Millennium: Four Views*. Edited by Robert G. Clouse. Downers Grove, IL: IVP Academic, 1996.

Lane, William L. *Hebrews 1–8*. Word Biblical Commentary. Vol. 47A. Edited by David Allen Hubbard, and Glenn W. Barker. Reissue ed. Dallas: Word, 1998.

Lee, Samuel. *Eschatology; or, the Scripture Doctrine of the Coming of the Lord, the Judgment, and the Resurrection*. Boston: J. E. Tilton, 1859.

———. *The Bible Regained and the God of the Bible Ours; or, the System of Religious Truth in Outline*. Boston: Lee and Shepard, 1874.

Liddell, Henry George, Robert Scott, Henry Stuart Jones, and Roderick McKenzie, eds. *A Greek-English Lexicon*. Oxford: Clarendon Press, 1996.

Liefeld, Walter L. "Luke." Pages 1–600 in *Matthew, Mark, Luke*. Vol. 8 of *The Expositor's Bible Commentary*. Edited by Frank E. Gaebelein. Grand Rapids: Zondervan, 1984.

Lightfoot, John. *A Commentary on the New Testament From the Talmud and Hebraica*. Edited by Robert Gandell. 4 vols. 1859. Repr., Peabody, MA: Hendrickson Publishers, 1997.

Louw, Johannes P., and Eugene Albert Nida. *Greek-English Lexicon of the New Testament: Based on Semantic Domains*. New York: United Bible Societies, 1996.

MacArthur, John. *The MacArthur Topical Bible: New King James Version*. Nashville: Word, 1999.

———. *The Second Coming: Signs of Christ's Return and the End of the Age*. Wheaton, IL: Crossway Books, 1999.

———. *1 & 2 Timothy: Encouragement for Church Leaders*. MacArthur Bible Studies. Nashville: W Publishing Group, 2001.

MacDonald, William. *Believer's Bible Commentary: Old and New Testaments*. Edited by Arthur Farstad. Nashville: Thomas Nelson, 1995.

Mangina, Joseph L. *Karl Barth: The Ecumenical Promise of His Theology*. Burlington, VT: Ashgate, 2004.

Mare, W. Harold. "1 Corinthians." Pages 173–298 in *Romans–Galatians*. Vol. 10 of *The Expositor's Bible Commentary*. Edited by Frank E. Gaebelein. Grand Rapids: Zondervan, 1976.

Mathison, Keith A. *Postmillennialism: An Eschatology of Hope*. Phillipsburg, NJ: P&R, 1999.

Mayhue, Richard L. "Jesus: A Preterist or a Futurist?" *TMSJ* 14/1 (Spring 2003): 9–22.

McDurmon, Joel. *Biblical Logic: In Theory & Practice*. Powder Springs, GA: American Vision, 2009.

Menn, Jonathan. *Biblical Eschatology*. Eugene, OR: Resource Publications, 2013.

Merrill, S. M. *The Second Coming of Christ Considered in Its Relation to the Millennium, the Resurrection, and the Judgment*. Cincinnati: Cranston & Stowe, 1879.

Meyer, Heinrich August Wilhelm. *Critical and Exegetical Hand-Book to the Gospels of Mark and Luke*. Edited by William P. Dickson. Translated by Robert Ernest Wallis, and Matthew A. Riddle. 6th ed. Winona Lake, IN: Alpha Publications, 1979.

"The Destruction of Heaven and Earth and the New Heaven and Earth Explained!" Daniel Morais. https://revelationrevolution.org/the-destruction-of-heaven-and-earth-and-the-new-heaven-and-earth-explained/#_ednref11.

Murray, George L. *Millennial Studies: A Search for Truth*. Grand Rapids: Baker, 1948.

Murray, Ian H. *The Puritan Hope: A Study in Revival and the Interpretation of Prophecy*. Carlisle, PA: The Banner of truth trust, 1975.

Oepke, Albrecht. "παρουσία, κτλ." Pages 858–71 in vol. 5 of *Theological Dictionary of the New Testament*. Edited by Gerhard Friedrich. Translated by Geoffrey W. Bromiley. Grand Rapids: Eerdmans, 1964–76.

Pentecost, J. Dwight. *Things to Come: A Study in Biblical Eschatology*. Grand Rapids: Zondervan, 1964.

Perrin, Nicholas. *Jesus the Temple*. Grand Rapids: Baker Academic, 2010.

Peters, George N. H. *The Theocratic Kingdom of Our Lord Jesus, the Christ, as Covenanted in the Old Testament and Presented in the New Testament*. 3 vols. 1884. Repr., Grand Rapids: Kregel, 1972.

Plevnik, Joseph. *Paul and the Parousia: An Exegetical and Theological Investigation*. Eugene, OR: Wipf & Stock, 2014.

Poole, Matthew. *A Commentary on the Holy Bible*. 3 vols. 1685. Repr., Carlisle, PA: The Banner of Truth Trust, 1962.

Ramm, Bernard. *Protestant Biblical Interpretation: A Textbook of Hermeneutics*. 3rd ed. Grand Rapids: Baker, 1970.

Ramsay, W. M. *The Letters to the Seven Churches of Asia and Their Place in the Plan of the Apocalypse*. 1904. Repr., Minneapolis: James Family, 1978.

Reymond, Robert L. *A New Systematic Theology of the Christian Faith*. Nashville: Thomas Nelson, 1998.

Riddlebarger, Kim. *A Case for Amillennialism: Understanding the End Times*. Grand Rapids: Baker, 2003.

Robertson, Archibald Thomas. *A Harmony of the Gospels for Students of the Life of Christ*. New York: Harper, 1922.

———. *Word Pictures in the New Testament*. 6 vols. Nashville: Broadman, 1930–33.

Robinson, John A. T. *Jesus and His Coming*. Philadelphia: Westminster Press, 1979.

———. *Redating the New Testament*. Eugene, OR: Wipf & Stock Pub, 2000.

Russell, Bertrand. *Why I Am Not a Christian: And Other Essays on Religion and Related Subjects*. Edited by Paul Edwards. New York: Simon & Schuster, 1957.

Russell, J. Stuart. *The Parousia: The New Testament Doctrine of Our Lord's Second Coming*. 1887. Repr., Grand Rapids: Baker, 1999.

Ryrie, Charles Caldwell. *The Basis of the Premillennial Faith*. Neptune, NJ: Loizeaux Bros., 1953.

———. *Basic Theology: A Popular Systematic Guide to Understanding Biblical Truth*. Chicago: Moody, 1999.

———. *Dispensationalism*. Chicago: Moody Publishers, 1995.

Saldarini, Anthony J. "Shekinah." Page 938 in *Harper's Bible Dictionary*. Edited by Paul J. Achtemeier. San Francisco: Harper & Row, 1985.

Schaff, Philip. *The Oldest Church Manual Called the Teaching of the Twelve Apostles*. 2nd ed. Edinburgh: T. & T. Clark, 1887.

———. *The Creeds of Christendom With a History and Critical Notes*. 3 vols. 1931. Repr., Grand Rapids: Baker, 1983.

Scherrer, Steven J. "Signs and Wonders in the Imperial Cult: A New Look At a Roman Religious Institution in the Light of Rev 13:13–15." *JBL* 103 (4) (Dec., 1984): 599–610.

Schneider, Johannes. "ἔρχομαι, κτλ." Pages 666–75 in vol. 2 of *Theological Dictionary of the New Testament*. Edited by Gerhard Kittel. Translated by Geoffrey W. Bromiley. Grand Rapids: Eerdmans, 1964–76.

Schreiner, Thomas R. *Spiritual Gifts: What They Are & Why They Matter*. Nashville: Broadman & Holman, 2018.

Scofield, C. I., ed. *The Scofield Reference Bible*. New York; London; Toronto; Melbourne; Bombay: Oxford University Press, 1917.

Scroggie, W. Graham. *The Unfolding Drama of Redemption: The Bible as a Whole*. Grand Rapids: Zondervan, 1976.

Smith, Ralph L. *Micah–Malachi*. Word Biblical Commentary. Vol. 32. Edited by David A. Hubbard. Dallas: Word, 1984.

Smith, William. *Smith's Bible Dictionary*. Nashville: Thomas Nelson, 1986.

Sproul, R. C. *The Last Days According to Jesus*. 3rd ed. Grand Rapids: Baker, 1998.

———. Introduction to *The Parousia: The New Testament Doctrine of Our Lord's Second Coming*, by J. Stuart Russell. 1887. Repr., Grand Rapids: Baker, 1999.

Stevens, Edward E. *What Happened in A.D. 70?* Bradford, PA: Kingdom Publications, 1997.

Storms, Sam. *Kingdom Come: The Amillennial Alternative*. Fearn, Scotland: Mentor, 2013.

Strimple, Robert B. "Hyper-Preterism on the Resurrection of the Body." Pages 287–352 in *When Shall These Things Be?: A Reformed Response to Hyper-Preterism*. Edited by Keith A. Mathison. Phillipsburg, NJ: P&R, 2004.

Stuart, Douglas. *Hosea–Jonah*. Word Biblical Commentary. Vol. 31. Dallas: Word, 2002.

Tacitus. *The Histories*. Edited by Betty Radice. Translated by Kenneth Wellesley. New York: Penguin Books, 1998.

Terry, Milton S. *Biblical Hermeneutics: A Treatise on the Interpretation of the Old and New Testaments*. Edited by George R. Crooks, and John F. Hurst. New York: Eaton & Mains, 1890.

———. *Biblical Apocalyptics: A Study of the Most Notable Revelations of God and of Christ*. 1898. Repr., Grand Rapids: Baker, 1988.

———. *Biblical Hermeneutics: A Treatise on the Interpretation of the Old and New Testaments*. 2nd ed. n.d. Repr., Grand Rapids: Academie Books, n.d.

Thayer, Joseph, and James Strong. *Thayer's Greek-English Lexicon of the New Testament: Coded With Strong's Concordance Numbers*. Milford, MI: Mott Media, 1982.

The Holy Bible: English Standard Version. Wheaton: Standard Bible Society, 2016.

Trench, Richard Chenevix. *Synonyms of the New Testament*. Grand Rapids: Eerdmans, 1953.

Vine, W. E. *Collected Writings of W. E. Vine*. 5 vols. Nashville: T. Nelson, 1996.

Vos, Geerhardus. *Biblical Theology, Old and New Testaments*. Grand Rapids: Wm. B. Eerdmans, 1948.

———. "Eschatology of the New Testament." Pages 979–93 in vol. 2 of *The International Standard Bible Encyclopaedia*. Edited by James Orr. Grand Rapids: Wm. B. Eerdmans, 1956.

———. *The Pauline Eschatology*. Phillipsburg, NJ: P&R, 1994.

Walker, Peter W. L. *Jesus and the Holy City: New Testament Perspectives on Jerusalem*. Grand Rapids/Cambridge: William B. Eerdmans, 1996.

Walvoord, John F. "Revelation." Pages 198–265 in vol. 2 of *The Bible Knowledge Commentary: An Exposition of the Scriptures*. Edited by J. F. Walvoord, and R. B. Zuck. Wheaton, IL: Victor, 1985.

Warren, Israel P. *The Parousia: A Critical Study of the Scripture Doctrines of Christ's Coming; His Reign as King; the Resurrection of the Dead; and the General Judgment.* Portland, ME: Hoyt, Fogg & Dunham, 1879.

———. *The Parousia: A Critical Study of the Scripture Doctrines of Christ's Coming; His Reign as King; the Resurrection of the Dead; and the General Judgment.* 2nd ed. Portland, ME: Hoyt, Fogg & Dunham, 1884.

Whitcomb, John C. "Millennial Sacrifices." Pages 226–28 in *The Popular Encyclopedia of Bible Prophecy.* Edited by Tim LaHaye, and Ed Hindson. Eugene, Oregon: Harvest House, 2004.

Whitney, Donald S. *Spiritual Disciplines for the Christian Life.* Rev. ed. Colorado Springs, CO: NavPress, 2014.

Wilson, Douglas. *Heaven Misplaced: Christ's Kingdom on Earth.* Moscow, ID: Canon Press, 2008.

Witherington, Ben, III. *The Jesus Quest: The Third Search for the Jew of Nazareth.* Downers Grove, IL: InterVarsity, 1995.

Wright, N. T. *The New Testament and the People of God.* Vol. 1 of *Christian Origins and the Question of God.* Minneapolis: Fortress Press, 1992.

———. *Jesus and the Victory of God.* Vol. 2 of *Christian Origins and the Question of God.* Minneapolis :Fortress Press, 1996.

———. *The Resurrection of the Son of God.* Vol. 3 of *Christian Origins and the Question of God.* Minneapolis: Fortress Press, 2003.

———. *Paul and the Faithfulness of God.* Vol. 4 of *Christian Origins and the Question of God.* Minneapolis :Fortress Press, 2013.

———. *The Day the Revolution Began: Reconsidering the Meaning of Jesus's Crucifixion.* San Francisco: HarperOne, 2016.

Wuest, Kenneth S. *The New Testament: An Expanded Translation.* Grand Rapids: Eerdmans, 1961.

Young, Robert. *The Holy Bible.* 3rd ed. Edinburgh: G. A. Young & Co., 1898.